YEARNING TO BREATHE FREE

YEARNING TO BREATHE FREE

Liberation Theologies in the United States

Edited by
Mar Peter-Raoul
Linda Rennie Forcey
and Robert Frederick Hunter, Jr.

ORBIS BOOKS

Maryknoll, New York 10545

The Catholic Foreign Mission Society of America (Maryknoll) recruits and trains people for overseas missionary service. Through Orbis Books, Maryknoll aims to foster the international dialogue that is essential to mission. The books published, however, reflect the opinions of their authors and are not meant to represent the official position of the society.

Published by Orbis Books, Maryknoll, NY 10545
Manufactured in the United States of America

Library of Congress Cataloging-in-Publication Data

Yearning to breathe free: Liberation theologies in the United
  States / edited by Mar Peter-Raoul, Linda Rennie Forcey, and Robert
  Frederick Hunter, Jr.
      p. cm.
    Includes bibliographical references.
    ISBN 0-88344-732-0
    1. Liberation theology. 2. Feminist theology. 3. Black theology.
  4. Church work with minorities—United States. 5. Church work with
  the poor—United States. 6. United States—Social conditions—1980—
  7. United States—Economic conditions—1981- 8. United States—
  Church history—20th century. 9. Sociology, Christian. I. Peter-
  Raoul, Mar. II. Forcey, Linda Rennie. III. Hunter, Robert
  Frederick.
  BT83.57.V55   1990
  230'.046—dc20   90-46164
                                                    CIP

Mar
In the midst of all the laughter and lament there are
Jody, Jamie, Jory-Pierre, Heather Summer, Tam
—constant, irreverent, close.

Linda
For my grandchildren
Brenden Patrick and Elizabeth,
and for all the wee ones of their
generation and those to come.

Bob
Always thinking of Carol,
my friend, colleague and wife.

Habakkuk 2:1–3

"Write the vision down, inscribe it on tablets to be easily read, since this vision is for its own time only: eager for its own fulfillment, it does not deceive; if it comes slowly, wait, for come it will, without fail."

Chief Seathl—Seattle

The Red Man's "religion is the traditions of our ancestors—the dreams of our old men, given them in solemn hours of night by the Great Spirit; and the visions of our sachems, and it is written in the hearts of our people."

Martin Luther King, Jr.

"We need the vision to see in this generation's ordeals the opportunities to transform both ourselves and society."

Anselm K. Min

"The praxis of transformation is the necessary condition for grasping reality precisely as a reality to be transformed."

Henri Nouwen

A community is "a gift born out of the common experience of the dark night of injustice."

James H. Cone

"Mutual participation in each other's communities will unquestionably deepen our dialogue."

Gustavo Gutiérrez

"The community now beginning to take shape will be a messianic community whose task is to offer a specific witness in the midst of human history."

Contents

PART IV
CONNECTING BEYOND

Acknowledgments

We wish to thank all the contributors to this volume. The seeds for this collection were first planted in 1984, with a conference at the State University of New York at Binghamton entitled "Liberation Theology: Marxist and Christian Perspectives," sponsored by the Division of Career and Interdisciplinary Studies in the School of Education and Human Development and funded by the New York Council for the Humanities. Among the contributors present at that conference were Orlando Costas, James H. Cone, and Dorothee Sölle, as well as we, the editors. In addition, we wish to express our deep appreciation to our families and to the following people who know full well the depth of their contribution—be it intellectual, spiritual, technical, or nurturant: George Yonemura, Otto Maduro, Luanne Schinzel, Máiréad Barrett, Niki Cukor, S. J. Luke-Cole, Ruy Costa, Jane Allen, Jean Barker Jeffers, John Kellogg, the research staff at the Broome County Library, Motlalepula Chabaku, Elizabeth Fox-Genevese, Rabbi Michael A. Robinson, Jill Kane, Albert White, Marie Soto, Richard Hugunine, Ann Pierce, Jean Leonard, Barbara Tierno, Ted Rector, Michael Malloy, and our editors, John Eagleson, Hank Schlau, Catherine Costello, Eve Drogin, Robert Ellsberg, and our final editor Susan Perry who suggested the title.

Introduction

LINDA RENNIE FORCEY

Quite a few readers even today will ask: What has liberation theology to do with the United States? Until several years ago our own answer would have been rather vague. At most we, the editors of this volume, associated the term *liberation theology* with a struggling movement of uncertain promise among Latin American Catholics — a movement whose aim was to somehow direct the moral force of religion against the widespread social, economic, and political despotism of their region. Neither the movement's theology nor its promise of liberation had much, we thought, to do with us. A great deal that we have learned since, including how wrong were our perspectives, is contained in the collection of materials presented here. These articles open a spiritual world of promise for the oppressed in North America.

This book emerged from what turned out to be a two-year dialogue among ourselves and others who were thinking about and "doing" liberation theology — a dialogue that forced us to reexamine our self-inscribed labels, our private understandings of national, racial, sexual, ethnic, and class identities. The dialogue also forced us to sharpen our definitions of social justice and the meaning of praxis in our own lives in the United States, our pedagogical practices and beliefs as educators, and ultimately our visions for a better world.

Our intention in focusing on the liberation theologies of the United States is not to break our connections with all those throughout the world who are engaging in the praxis of liberation. On the contrary, we have been ever mindful of the Latin American and global contexts of liberation theology; they reverberate throughout the discourse between North American liberation theologians — particularly those of black or Hispanic backgrounds — and theologians of the Third World.

Liberation theology emerged from the efforts of Latin American bishops at the 1968 Medellín Conference to create a fresh theological approach to reflection and praxis, or committed involvement. This new approach, as articulated by Peruvian priest Gustavo Gutiérrez, entailed "a radical questioning of the prevailing social order." The implications of the new approach were clearly political. Gutiérrez writes:

1

Opting for the poor, exploited classes and the Latin American pro-
letariat; seeing politics as a dimension that embraces all of human
life, entails conflict, and demands a scientific line of reasoning; and
rediscovering evangelical poverty as fellowship with the poor and a
protest against their poverty—lead us to a wholly different way of
perceiving ourselves as human beings and Christians. ... Only by
getting beyond a society divided into classes, only by establishing a
form of political power designed to serve the vast majority of our
people, and only by eliminating private ownership of the wealth created by human labor will we be able to lay foundations for a more
just society.[1]

Out of Latin America's theological reflections and experiences have
emerged radically different perspectives resulting in deeply divided Catholic and Protestant churches. The new message is that the poor and
oppressed need not passively accept their fate while awaiting heavenly
peace in the next world. Rather, it is God's will that the poor and oppressed
be empowered to change the course of their lives and of history by uniting
for social, political, and economic change.

We welcome the way people everywhere are learning the important texts
of Latin American liberation theologians. Yet, we are mindful of the fact
that there are "Third World" pockets in the United States too; that there
is poverty in the United States as well as in Latin America; that during the
past decade we have witnessed a growing gap between the rich and the
poor; that a seemingly permanent underclass has taken hold; that, more
than two decades after the Civil Rights movement, racism remains firmly
embedded in the culture. If we are to listen, as we must, to the voices of
the victims, we must hear those of vision among the victims nearest us.

We are also mindful that so many in the United States are still unaware
of the voices of liberation struggling to be heard on the reservations and
in the ghettos; that few realize black liberation theology rose independently
of, though concurrently with, Latin American liberation theology. Today
important theologies are emerging from among Asian Americans, Native
Americans, and from Jews, Hispanics, and other marginated groups in the
United States.

The creators of these "new" theologies are interpreting the history and
experience of their people not in terms of God's existence and mercy, but
more compellingly with such blunt questions as: How is God with us in our
struggle for freedom? What does the gospel of liberation mean to those
working for peace? What does it mean to women who, among all victims,
are doubly oppressed? All the writers in this volume have seen injustice in
their communities, and they passionately challenge us to become more
aware and engaged.

Our book is divided into four parts: "Connections," "Communities,"
"Praxis," and "Connecting Beyond." Because much of North American

liberation theology is indebted to global theological reflection, Part 1 begins with Mar Peter-Raoul's overview of liberation theology and its implications for the United States, "South Bronx to South Africa: Prayer, Praxis, Song." In the second essay in Part 1, Orlando Costas, a professor of missiology and Hispanic studies before his death, draws parallels among Latin American, Hispanic, and black theologies of liberation in the United States. For Costas these theologies represent the protest of the oppressed against injustice. As a theologian, he had a vision for Hispanic theology that took seriously the realities of both its Latin roots and its North American experiences. Costas sought to awaken in the North American community an Hispanic identity to challenge stereotypes and bring forth a new Hispanic church to reinterpret the faith.

With Peter-Raoul's overview of liberation theology and Costas's interconnecting essay, the stage is set for Part 2, "Communities." In taking up the theologies that emerge from these communities, all our contributors find their central themes in vision, praxis, and community. The writers believe that vision comes from within a community and that meaningful theological reflection cannot be primarily abstract or academic. Its relevance comes from praxis, from its ability to challenge and liberate the community from which it arises.

The writers in this group also agree that faith is not just an upward looking to God; rather, it implies a fundamentally horizontal relationship with God and with all others. Praxis is part of faith. Praxis is action — action that arises from reflection. The contributors echo the biblical words in James, that "faith without works is dead." Intellectual assent is not the sole test of faith. Faith can find concrete reality in the experience of an oppressed community.

The first of our contributors in this section is James Cone, a professor of theology. Cone traces the history of black theology from the Civil Rights movement of the 1960s and forcefully shows how it challenges dominant white definitions of social justice according to the gospel. He argues that black theology offers the black church and society-at-large a vision for a world free of the excesses of both monopoly capitalism and authoritarian state socialism, a world that moves beyond classism, racism, and sexism to one where there can be black unity, dignity, and love of self. This is a vision for a new social order based upon justice for all, the latter dream now meaningfully including all the oppressed of the world.

A theology of liberation specifically affirming the struggle of African-American women is emerging. As Delores S. Williams describes in Chapter 4, many women have appropriated novelist Alice Walker's concept of "womanist" to affirm themselves as African Americans while simultaneously owning their connection with feminism and with the African-American community of both men and women. The traditions of black women become valuable resources for bringing women's social, religious, and cultural experience into the discourse of theology, ethics, and biblical and religious studies. A womanist theology will give authoritative status to black women's moral wisdom, and a theological language rich in female imagery, metaphor, and story.

Vine Deloria, Jr., a lawyer and theologian from the Sioux tribe, interjects an empathetic, yet cautiously skeptical, dimension to Cone's description of liberation theology's vision for a better world. In order to assess the impact of liberation theology's spiritual energy upon the American Indian community, he begins by delineating four segments of this community: the Indians who accept the premises of materialistic capitalism and "insist upon salvation through intercourse with transnational corporations and commodities markets"; the practicing Christians affiliated with "missions" because they have not had sufficient income to be self-supporting in the manner of prosperous non-Indian parishes; the Indians who practice old traditional ways; and, finally, those who have experienced traditional tribal religions to some degree and feel they have been commissioned to bring these religions to the aid and assistance of the non-Indian by traveling "the conference and psychological workshops circuit."

Deloria finds it is with this last segment that the importance of the American Indian contribution to a vision for liberation theology can be found. These "new Indian missionaries/entrepreneurs" have a vision with both positive and negative attributes. It is, Deloria argues, a vision of "a unified and experiencing humanity"; it emphasizes the living nature of the universe; and it provides a positive sense of community and companionship. He cautions the reader, however, arguing that this spiritual expansion can become but another North American fad, creating "networks" for the often spiritually or emotionally needy rather than genuine communities. The challenge for liberation theology from this American Indian perspective lies in its responsibility to energize and inspire people to free their communities from oppression while nourishing their spiritual and emotional lives.

The statement of the Catholic bishops of the Appalachian region responds to the poverty embedded in their beautiful area. Jobs are scarce, human services for the poor are minimal, safety standards for the workers are inadequate. The driving force behind the oppression of the region, they argue, is "maximization of profits." Too many people are forced to accept abysmal conditions or lose their jobs. The bishops see the call of the liberating church as the call of Jesus: "To bring good news to the poor" (Luke 4:18). They call for the church to involve itself in the spiritual life of the people, in the potential cooperative power of the people, and in a reverent use of the land's resources.

Kosuke Koyama, a professor of ecumenics and world Christianity, begins his essay with a definition of liberation theology as "ethical walking and theological beholding," which he has taken from Micah and John in the Bible. To "do justice and to walk humbly" are wedded with "behold[ing] the lamb of God." By this Koyama means that doing justice and looking to

God go hand in hand. Such a combination prevents self-righteousness while engendering humility. Koyama questions the thrust of North American individualism by setting it in the context of the Asian concept of *karman*. He cautions materially successful Asian Americans to take care not, by fantasies of cultural superiority, to develop racist attitudes toward others, from which they themselves have suffered enough in past times.

The final piece in this part is Ada María Isasi-Díaz's *"Mujeristas: A Name of Our Own."* *Mujeristas* is the name the author chooses for Hispanic women (*mujeres*) who are struggling to liberate themselves while being faithful to the task of peace, justice, and liberation.

Because liberation theology has meaning only insofar as it is actively and passionately committed to helping the poor gain greater participation in their churches and their society, the third part focuses on praxis. Here are voices of people sharing their stories, experiences, and reflections on the meaning of their faith from the standpoint of their commitment. They represent the poor, the oppressed, the refugees, the imprisoned, as well as pastors, political activists, and others committed to liberating change.

Part 4, "Connecting Beyond," begins once more to move us outward. Elisabeth Schüssler Fiorenza, a professor of New Testament studies, lays the groundwork for an expression of women's experience with God that is free of androcentric theology and a patriarchal church. Her developing feminist theology, while not conceived for women alone, insists on the reconceptualization of intellectual frameworks in such a way as to truly become inclusive of women as subjects of human scholarship and experience.

A Jewish theology of liberation is articulated by Marc H. Ellis, Director of the Institute for Justice and Peace at the Maryknoll School of Theology. This new Jewish theology, for Ellis, must be grounded in more than the overwhelming experience of suffering and anguish of the victims of the Holocaust. It must be grounded in recognition of the Palestinian uprising, the essential dynamic of solidarity, and the importance of self-criticism of abuses of power. Ellis argues that the key to a Jewish theology of liberation entails the "deabsolutizing" of the state of Israel, the differentiation of the Holocaust and the contemporary Jewish situation, and recovery of the history of solidarity within the Jewish tradition. The challenge for Jews is to remember, to survive and seek empowerment, but also to resist the temptation to build empires, to manipulate, control, and dominate others, so that "we can become what we are called to be."

Dorothee Sölle—a German-born, internationally known theologian, peace activist, and poet who teaches at Union Theological Seminary in New York—movingly poses the question members of her generation asked their parents: How could it have been that good, intelligent people stood by while their government killed six million Jewish people? Her fear is that our children will be asking us what we were doing when preparations were being made for a nuclear holocaust. Sölle challenges us to consider the necessary steps for a theology of peace—a peace based not on militarism (the *Pax Romana*) but on justice (the *Pax Christi*).

As Robert Frederick Hunter, Jr., notes in the conclusion, all of these theologies when taken together are concerned with the meaning of the gospel of liberation in the context of an oppressed people and with the responses and reflection of the people themselves to both their oppression and to the task of liberation. With these expressions of liberation a challenge is laid at the doorstep of an affluent United States. It comes from the marginalized communities who cry with anguish as they challenge us to dare to imagine a church committed to social change and a society committed to justice and human community.

We realize that there are still many other cries in our country not heard here—from the homeless, the unemployed, the handicapped, the children, women, old people, and many other helpless or abused human beings. We have heard, too, the rising and anguished voices of those who are gay and lesbian. We offer this collection, however, as a partial step in the direction of awareness and theological reflection on the realities of life in the United States. Both editors and contributors have tried to listen more compassionately and to sound a call for all to become more committed to the cries for liberation.

Our book, as we see it finally, is an attempt to share stories both in relationship to each other and within the context of peoples everywhere in the world committed to the praxis of liberation. Theologian Robert McAfee Brown writes in *Theology in a New Key*: "I now have to see my story and indeed the whole American story in relation to the *black story* ... , to confront the clash between my story and the *Native American* story, and internalize that what had previously been the noble story of the white man's expansion of the West was in reality the ignoble story of the white man's expulsion and near extinction of the red man (and woman and child), using techniques perfected by God-fearing Christians in the Massachusetts Bay Colony. My American story has to be retold in the light of the *international* story. . . ."[2]

Our book, then, is an attempt to give voice to the theological vision of those who are telling their stories and trying to sing the Lord's song in this complex, disparate, troubled land of ours.

Part I

Connections

1

Lines

GUSTAVO GUTIÉRREZ

Without "songs" to God
without celebration
of God's liberating love
there is no Christian life.

South Bronx to South Africa:
Prayer, Praxis, Song

MAR PETER-RAOUL

Hardly new to the resisters of our lifetime . . . [is] that noble "third world" that has invaded our own with its sublime evangel of liberation. . . . A Jesus witnessed to in art and music and poetry and dance, the noble testimonies and testaments of the tortured. . . . — Daniel Berrigan, S.J.[1]

During the late 1960s and early 1970s, the liberating themes of scripture together with the meaning of these themes within the struggle of oppressed people for liberation were brought into theological focus—both in Latin America and among African Americans in the United States. Today, this theological perspective, known as the theology of liberation, has become a global phenomenon.

Within a world context of religious and ideological pluralism, the distinctive characteristic of this perspective is its effort to seek for God in the suffering and struggle of the poor. It is a theology from the underside, from among the "anonymous," the "powerless," and the "nonpersons." It is found not in the center of economic, ecclesial, or academic power, but at the edge, at the periphery. At the site of the "excluded," this theology enters into the struggle for liberation, a struggle rooted in prayer, in praxis, and in song.

In this essay, I offer: (1) an introduction to liberation theology through an explication of its spirituality, an incarnational spirituality of prayer, praxis, song; (2) selected sketches of liberation theologies in the global context; and (3) a sense of the context and call of liberation theologies in the United States—from the South Bronx to the Texas border.

LIBERATION THEOLOGY: A SPIRITUALITY OF PRAYER, PRAXIS, SONG

For liberation theology, spirituality is an encounter with God, an encounter which calls a people to follow Jesus in the midst of human history, a history ravished with rope, burnings, rape. For example, black liberation theology, from its very beginnings, has listened deeply to black history and

10

experience, experience found in the songs, stories, prayers, sermons, and slave narratives of black people. For liberation theology's radical spirituality, one incarnated into concrete historical existence, prayer rises out of anguished experience, praxis is committed to liberation, and songs to God are celebrations of hope.

A source and continuing inspiration for this incarnated spirituality are found in the New Testament in Mary's canticle, a prayer which is praise, message, and manifesto. This canticle is sung in response to the historical "fulfilment of what was spoken to her from the Lord" (Luke 1:45). Mary sings both of what has happened to her as the Lord's "handmaiden," and of the expectation of those of "low degree" — an expectation that God will deliver them from "the mighty." She sings:

> My soul magnifies the Lord,
> and my spirit rejoices in God my Savior,
> for God has regarded the low estate of God's hand-
>   maiden. . . .
> God has shown strength with God's arm,
> God has scattered the proud in the imagination of
>   their hearts,
> God has put down the mighty from their thrones,
> and exalted those of low degree;
> God has filled the hungry with good things,
> and the rich have been sent empty away
>   [Luke 1:46–53].

In Mary's song, the multiple modes of a radical spirituality — prayer, praise, expecting deliverance, preferring those of "low degree," perceiving the Lord as liberator in concrete historical situations — are interrelated and all part of this perspective from the periphery.

Through the prism of the poor, this perspective yields the recognition that the spiritual essence of a people's encounter with God includes both the expectation that God will establish justice on the earth and the requirement that God's people join this work of liberation. Oft-quoted is Isaiah 58:6–7, a passage in which God says to God's chosen Israel:

> Is not this what I require of you as a fast:
> to loose the fetters of injustice, to untie the knots of
>   the yoke
> . . . sharing food, taking in the homeless. . . .

For liberation theology, a highly significant context for this task of justice is the small Christian community. Within the broader, worldwide context of contemporary aspirations toward freedom, small groups of socially marginalized Christians have been meeting together, first in Latin America and increasingly throughout the world, in basic Christian communities. With a concrete spirituality of prayer, reflection, committed action, and song, these small groups of "forgotten ones" consider together both scripture and the social situation of their lives. Phillip Berryman describes these basic Christian communities as "small, lay-led groups of people, primarily poor, who combine consciousness, Bible study, worship, mutual help, and (often) political action in defense of their rights."[2]

Within this context of small Christian communities, poor Christians move toward critical consciousness — that is, they become increasingly aware of the true nature of the injustice to which they are subject, of God's will for their liberation from this injustice, and of themselves as agents together with God for bringing about this liberation. With increased consciousness, the faith-discussions in these communities challenge deeply rooted fatalistic concepts and often lead to a collective commitment to change.

As this commitment leads to concrete action, it is accompanied by consideration of the implications of this action in the light of biblical faith. There is a continuing interchange between action — organizing for land rights and clean water, forming cooperatives, etc. — and reflection on the faith-meaning of these actions. Each informs the other. Scripture itself takes on new meanings in light of a people's active participation in the task of liberation, and this task, seen within the context of prophetic cries for justice, becomes a response to biblical injunctions. In the language of liberation theology, this interchange between action and biblical reflection is known as "praxis." Praxis is at the core of an incarnational spirituality. It is *in* the concrete historical situation that God *acts*, and God's people in continuing action and reflection understand themselves as agents, together with God, of their own liberation and the liberation of the world.

The exodus event, the formative event of Jewish history, provides a central paradigm for this praxis of basic Christian communities. That God chose to be on the side of powerless, enslaved Israel, leading that nation, under Moses, from Egypt to liberation, matters today to a people's faith. It informs their active participation in the work of God's realm.

The Christ event of the New Testament extends the experience of exodus to the whole world. In Jesus, God is revealed as the liberator not only of Israel, but of all humankind. At the inauguration of his mission, Jesus announces in the synagogue at Nazareth:

> The Spirit of the Lord is upon me,
> because God has anointed me to preach good news
>   to the poor.
> God has sent me to proclaim release to the captives
> and recovering of sight to the blind,
> to set at liberty those who are oppressed,
> to proclaim the acceptable year of the Lord
>   [Luke 4:18–19].

In its essence, the liberation offered by God through Jesus is understood as liberation from the fundamental fracturing of human existence, a fracturing from the beginnings of history of the relationship between God and humankind and between human beings themselves. A liberative spirituality is a God-centered struggle against this brokenness, the very root of which is known as sin. It is a struggle against all the dark powers of pride, selfishness, greed, and empire — out of which all kinds of oppression arise.

In aspiring to human connectedness and committed to overcoming the injustice rife in the world, a liberative spirituality takes seriously Jesus' admonition to feed the hungry, clothe the destitute, and visit those in prison, believing this is the way to incarnate the love which is of the essence of the gospel. Not content, however, simply to dispense charity — for charity is never sufficient to feed all the hungry — this theology asks: What are the *root* causes of poverty?

In order to answer this question, social analysis is important. This analysis becomes part of a faith community's reflection. It is part of the praxis — the continuous circle of action and reflection — of a liberative spirituality. Because it is believed that people are made poor — they are not poor by accident — liberationists ask: What are the forces, cultural, religious, social, ideological, that structure and sustain this poverty? With critical structural analysis, including among others a Marxist analysis, a faith community attempts to answer this question, animated by the hope of a new society where no one starves, is illiterate, or is forced to live in inhuman conditions.

Increasingly, structural analysis has been given serious attention by North American liberation theologians, especially by progressive blacks and Hispanics who have moved from an exclusively racial analysis to one more inclusive of culture and class. Throughout the Third World, including the "Third World" in the United States, liberationists recognize that "to *do* justice" requires an understanding of the underlying causes of injustice. In his book *Religion and Social Conflicts*, Otto Maduro writes, "It is not enough to be solidly committed to a struggle in order for it to have a successful outcome. No, all this is insufficient. We have to come to *know* — to know how and why things have come to this pass in the church and in society. We have to learn what changes are possible."[3]

Thus, from Mary's song to social analysis, liberation theology seeks God among the poor. Relating the liberating themes of scripture to the striving, singing, and sorrow of a people, this theology encounters God in unexpected places — in the anguished prayer of those "outside," in the history and hope of those who struggle, in the heroism of those who keep fidelity in the midst of loss, in reflective analysis and action, in the signs of the times (the events and aspirations of our time which call for response), in slave songs and sermons, in celebrations of the faithful. Concrete historical experience is the site of the radical spirituality of liberation theology; the world itself is the terrain for an encounter with God, an encounter recognized and incarnated in prayer, praxis, song.

SELECTED SKETCHES OF LIBERATION THEOLOGIES
IN THE GLOBAL CONTEXT

Latin American Theology

Priests and religious murdered, as well as an untold number of lay people. Liberation theology has risen in Latin America as a spiritual response to brutal repression, repression often provoked by Sisters and priests taking the side of the poor. Meeting in Medellín, Colombia, in 1968, Latin American bishops, in following the directives of Vatican II, reflected together on the "signs of the times." Interpreting for their own apostolate God's biblical concern for the oppressed, they affirmed for the Latin American church a "preferential option for the poor." Since that time, many Christians have begun to read and interpret scripture from "the underside of history." With a radically changed perspective, theological concern has shifted from the European theologians' concern for the "nonbeliever" to the present "option" for the "nonperson." The poor have become "subjects," and are gradually realizing that they are participants in the process of liberation. This process of liberation is even seen as an obligation for the Christian life. The Peruvian doyen of liberation theology, Gustavo Gutiérrez writes, "Liberation is an obligatory and privileged *locus* for Christian life and reflection."[4] He continues, "In this participation will be heard nuances of the word of God which are imperceptible in other existential situations and without which there can be no authentic and fruitful faithfulness to the Lord."[5]

The hope inspiring this participation is for the radical transformation of social, economic, and political structures—a process of transformation necessary for the creation of a new humanity. Enacted in a context of oppression and hope, the process becomes, according to Brazilian theologian Leonardo Boff, "a dialectical relationship between suffering and liberation, between the cross and resurrection."[6] It is also a dialectical relationship between history and eschatology, between the present praxis of liberation and the expectation of God's coming realm. Gutiérrez writes, "The process of liberation will not have conquered the very roots of oppression . . . without the coming of the kingdom, which is above all a gift."[7]

A truly liberating love moving dialectically toward this gift of God's realm seeks not only the liberation of the oppressed, but also the liberation of the oppressor from his or her selfishness, greed, and ambition. Gutiérrez writes that it is not a question of not having enemies, but of "not excluding them from our love." It is love of enemies that challenges the whole system and becomes subversive. This concern to love one's enemies is particularly compelling in the Latin American context of summary executions, systems of torture, death squads.

To achieve this love for one's enemies requires an uncommon spirituality. For Gutiérrez, it is a spirituality that regards "the unique and absolute relationship with God as the horizon of every human action. . . . [It] is to place oneself, from the outset, in a wider and more profound context."[8]

Expressing the struggle toward this liberating love, Salvadoran poet Claribel Alegrias writes in her poem "Creed":

> I don't know if I believe
> in the forgiveness of all sin
> but, yes, I believe in the resurrection
> of the death squads
> of the oppressed . . .
> in the power of the people

African Theology

Africans are profoundly religious; they characteristically perceive the cosmic dimension in all of life, and in counterdistinction to Western individualism, are wholly communal. For Africans, the "basic structure of the human person is a network of interpersonal and cosmic relations."[9] Their sense of community embraces even the dead and unborn and is integrally connected with the land. Through the land they are in some way mystically bound to the dead.

With their soul deeply split by colonialism, Africans find a liberative theology marked by a quest for inculturation—that is, by a process of rediscovering and reclaiming their traditional roots and participating in the creation of a new, integrated form of society. Discovering ancient meanings in their popular narratives, sayings, riddles, songs, dances, and prayers, African theologians are seeking a new relationship between the gospel and their traditional cultures. Especially central for this quest is the hallowed tradition of rites and myths.

The key concept within the rites and myths of African belief is the life-force—"the force which permeates total reality and in which human beings share."[10] In this holistic vision of reality, religion is the binding force.

For African theology, the salvation of the person is bound to the salvation of the universe. In his incarnation, Christ is seen as assuming the totality of both the cosmos and the human. There is a "unity and continuity between the destiny of the human person and the destiny of the cosmos."[11]

The determinative moment in this destiny for African humanity is found in the conflict between life and death. All African art, music, rites, and dance celebrate the prevailing of the life-force over death. In this pervasive religious vision, the whole of African culture is a cosmic liturgy.

Today, the life-force is calling Africa to liberation from the tyranny that has in various forms gripped black African humanity. The Kenyan poet Ngugi wa Theong'o writes:

The trumpet of the masses has been blown
Let's preach to all our friends
The trumpet of the masses has been blown
We change to new songs
For the revolution is near.

South African Theology

In a *New York Times* article (October 13, 1987), a cast member of the musical drama *Sarafina!*, which played in New York City, conveyed something of the horror of being a subjugated people in South Africa under apartheid. "My father was coming home from the movies," he related. "The security police stopped the car. He showed them the papers. But they were drunk. They beat him to his knees. Then they tore off his pants and set the dogs on him. The dogs dragged him around for two hours."

Apartheid—minority white rule, legal, structured racism—is the context out of which South African liberation theology proclaims the gospel of liberation. With an emphasis on biblical proclamation, this black theology, in theologian Allan Boesak's words, is "a rebirth, a re-creation, a renewal, a reevaluation of our self."[12] South African black theology is a vigorous affirmation of blackness and an unconditional rejection of the apartheid system. Rejecting incremental reform, this liberation theology seeks a radical restructuring of the South African reality. Archbishop Desmond Tutu says, "We don't want our chains made comfortable, we want them removed." Removing the chains of apartheid, however, is costly. It means "imprisonments, bannings, arrests without trial . . . exile. . . . "[13]

In South Africa where an inferior education is mandated for black students, where many black domestics are forced to raise other people's children while separated from their own, where black miners are allowed to travel the long distance home only once a year, where piteously low wages are paid the "fortunate" ones who find work, and where there is violent repression of protest, black liberation theology is forbidden reading. It is considered the "theological arm of black power and a means of propaganda for a revolutionary Marxist ideology."[14]

Nevertheless, black theologians continue to move toward liberation. Through a series of meetings beginning in Soweto in 1985, more than one hundred lay and professional theologians participated in writing *The Kairos Document*—*kairos* meaning "moment of truth." Identified as "a theological comment on the political crisis in South Africa today," this document critiques the reigning "State Theology," which "canonises the will of the powerful," as well as the alienating "Church Theology," which tries to restrict religion to an apolitical "spiritual" realm, and articulates in their place a "Prophetic Theology," one calling for a "bold and incisive response" to the apartheid regime.[15]

Within this struggle for freedom and emphasizing the reclamation of community, black theology listens seriously to the cries and anguish—as well as the joy—expressed in the people's spontaneous songs, popular theater, and prayers. With so much black life broken, imprisoned, and blood-stained, the recovery of community is not easy. It is on the far side of struggle and courage. But it is a community toward which black South Africa moves, as intimated in the African proverb,

> A person is a person only because of others
> and in behalf of others.

Asian Theology

Asian liberation theology is an effort to discover the "Asian face of Christ." In Korea, in particular, minjung theology recognizes Christ in "the little people." In the Asian context of structural inequalities, of divergent religious and cultural traditions, and of authoritarian governments which arrest, torture, and detain those who challenge the debilitating lot of most of the people, a liberative Asian theology is a praxis-centered commitment to "passion, compassion, and contemplation."

In *Asia's Struggle for Full Humanity*, a book she edited, Virginia Fabella cautions Christian Asian theologians to take seriously the religious experience and Asian culture "which have given to countless millions the meaning, unity, wisdom, and strength of life as well as inspiration for their struggles for full humanity."[16] In her book *Compassionate and Free: An Asian Woman's Theology*, Marianne Katoppo asks, "Is it heresy to say that the Spirit sings to us in the *Bhaghavad Gita, the Song of God*, or dances for us in Lord Shiva's dance, or speaks to us in the words of the Enlightened One?"[17]

Asian folk culture, rising from the lives of the people and "expressed in story, song, symbol, mask-dances, and drama," is considered more valuable for finding the liberating moment to be lived and practiced than is much of dogmatic Christian theology. Finding this liberating element is central to a dialogue between Asian Christians and those who practice other Asian religions. Asian liberation theology seeks to discover the transformative moment in the respective traditions—e.g., in Buddhism, the affirmation of a communal mutuality, and in Hinduism, the image of Arthanareesvara, a male/female deity which models a nondualistic, noncompetitive way of being and thinking.

An Asian liberation theology attempts to hold this interreligious dialogue in creative tension with critical social analysis and action. Critical social analysis is in turn held in tension with a deep introspection characteristic of Asian people. Perhaps most characteristic of Asian thinking is the ability to hold the union of opposites in the mind. Expressing something of this tension within an image of the resurrection, a Korean poet writes from prison:

> And this sound of the brass trumpets
> tells of the long battle between withering
> and the force bursting again into bloom. . . .

Feminist Theology

Feminist theology has today significantly, if not definitively, informed almost all major religious traditions in the United States. It is also finding expression cross-culturally within all forms of liberation theology, in particular in the newly emerging black "womanist" theology and the *mujerista* theology of Hispanic women.

In every liberationist context, women as well as a few men have begun seriously to study scripture from a feminist perspective and also to study society with this new perception. With a cutting critique of patriarchy, feminist theologians are challenging the structures of male-centered cultures as well as patriarchal interpretations of scripture which have made both the social context and the institutional church instruments of oppression.

Feminists are also finding long overlooked images of who God is. They are finding a God who weeps over her children, draws them to her breast, and gives birth — "the God who brought you to birth" (Deut. 32:18). Feminist theologian Luanne Schinzel explores Jesus' question to Peter as "Who do women say I am?"

Women are also saying that language is where theology begins. Conscienticized to inclusive language, they are finding many hymns, papal documents, and theological treatises oppressive with their use of the exclusive "he," "his," and "mankind."

And women are finding God within themselves. As a kind of primal divinity, this "God within" emerges into recognition as women share their experience with one another, and in Judith Plaskow's words, "hear each other into speech."

For women, a new consciousness is being forged; it is characterized by a theological valuing of personal experience, an affirmation of self, a global concern, and a new understanding, informed by a clear analysis, of the religio-societal causes of women's oppression for millennia. This new way of being includes a sense of bonding with all the world's "wimmin" and a concern for all human beings who are living dehumanized lives. In her book *Human Liberation in a Feminist Perspective: A Theology*, Letty Russell writes, "We have only just begun the search for human liberation in a feminist perspective. No one knows what it would be like 'if they gave a revolution and everybody won.'"[18]

For this "human revolution" to happen, women are empowering themselves and each other for change. With circles of prayer and celebrations, women are creating new symbols for a just, peaceful, and connected world. One feminist antinuclear activist writes,

I am a woman
whistling new music
   at Seneca
   at Greenham Common. . . .

SOUTH BRONX TO THE TEXAS BORDER: THE CONTEXT AND CALL OF LIBERATION THEOLOGY IN THE UNITED STATES

Locus Imperium

The United States is the site of multiple worlds, worlds contrasting and contradictory. With a middle class losing hold, there exist, with an increasing separation and an almost obscene disparity between them, worlds of the rich and worlds of the poor. Many of the worlds of wealth are given to the corporate climb, competition against all comers (whatever the enterprise), the comforts of the "American way of life" — that is, consumerism, the exigencies of empire, defense of "strategic interests" through vast military power (not to mention expense), and the imperial project, which involves making the world safe for democracy (American style). For theologian Robert McAfee Brown, "The god of the American way of life," is the "god who blesses free enterprise, a rising GNP, napalm when necessary, and a life of luxury for us at the cost of misery for others; a god who finally becomes indistinguishable from ourselves. . . . Such a god," Brown concludes, ". . . is an idol."[19] It seems that idolatry is alive and well in the United States.

While some interpreters of this free-for-all enterprise declare that we are living at a time of wide-open possibility, that opportunities abound (which may be quite true for those at the centers of power), others, inhabiting the world of city shelters and sweatshops, give evidence, as one commentator puts it, that "we are terminally ill." Using the image of a "metropolis" for the modern technocracy that is affluent America, Ched Myers in his political study of the gospel of Mark writes that the policies and ideologies sustaining this system "have resulted in a 'fortress America' " with the cornerstones of this fortress being both triage economics and nuclear militarism.[20] Myers continues, "We understand the present crisis of empire to have everything to do with the ordering of power, the distribution of wealth, and the global plague of militarism."[21] In this technocratic "metropolis," worlds of privilege and worlds at the periphery exist in stark contrast.

Illustrating this disparity, columnist Robert Maynard, formerly a New Yorker, has described an experience during a recent visit to Manhattan. Following an elegant dinner, Maynard was accosted on the street by a figure hunched over and wearing a filthy blanket and tattered clothes. Rasping at Maynard, the man demanded money. After relating the story later to a business executive friend, Maynard was told, "This is not the New York you grew up in. This is a city now of the filthy rich and the desperately poor." Whatever heroic (or, more likely, halfhearted) efforts, the damage has already been done. Maynard concludes, "The city has become two starkly different cities, one of awesome wealth and the other of abject poverty," and those "who are homeless are increasingly bold and aggressive toward those they assume to be affluent."[22] In a *New York Times* article, "How Despair Is Engulfing a Generation in New York," the story is told of sixteen-year-old James Voorhees of 114th Street in Harlem, who is holding his family together in a neighborhood that has all but collapsed. Commenting, the author writes, "The day-to-day deprivation and misery of the thousands of children in poor neighborhoods has prompted only scattered outrage and little action."[23]

Extreme conditions of deprivation, however, are found not only on the streets and in the tenements of New York City but throughout the country, on reservations, in barrios, in the projects of Chicago and Detroit. In an article entitled "What It's Like To Be in Hell," attorney Adam Walinsky writes about children being raised in the Henry Horner Homes Project in Chicago. Walinsky describes the recruiting of eight-year-olds by gangs, mothers trying to shelter their younger children with nowhere else to go, friends seen "shot and bleeding to death on the street." In the context of Detroit where the child mortality rate rivals that of a Third World country, Bishop Thomas Gumbleton remarks with anguish that we live in the richest nation in the world and cannot find it in our hearts to make the radical change needed so that so many of our citizens would not have to live degrading lives.

Further, in the heartland of this country, the story of family farms lost under staggering debt is not pretty. Nor is the lot of many young Native Americans seriously afflicted with alcoholism and harboring few hopes for the future. In Appalachia, legendary disregard by mining companies of both the environment and the welfare of the miners continues. And all across the land, crack-cocaine in the streets, murder, institutional brutality, ethnic violence, and an almost exponentially increasing prison population impact the character of U.S. existence.

Also impacting the character of who we are as a people is the official—and unofficial—treatment of perhaps the most outcast in the American context—the refugee, the uprooted. Unable to return home and rarely embraced by this country, those here in exile, legally or illegally—from El Salvador, Guatemala, Iran, Turkey, black South Africa, Laos, Cambodia—find the words imprinted on the Statue of Liberty, "Give me your tired, your poor, your huddled masses yearning to breathe free," estranged from our national consciousness—and from present immigration policy. Through national news media, this I.N.S. policy has recently been made visible to the American public. We have viewed the Texas border in Brownsville where thousands of illegal aliens, many fleeing brutal conditions and death, have been detained and "processed," with only a very few granted asylum.

For author Carlos Fuentes, the Texas border is not a border but a scar. Says Bill Moyer in his special "On Both Sides of the Rio Grande," "The two worlds meet on this border and merge. . . . There is nowhere where the Third World so dramatically joins the First. . . . In Brownsville one finds the poorer of the poor." Of those crossing over, someone has said, "They have a world of hurt on them." This hurt joins America's own poor, huddled masses yearning to breathe free.

So it is in the *locus imperium*. The metropolis includes its own "Third World." In an article entitled "America's Third World," the writers begin, "Although we are loathe to admit it, there are increasing pockets of 'Third World' society here in America." The text continues, " . . . slowly but surely, the frightening reality of a seemingly permanent, even expanding underclass has begun taking hold in the United States. . . . Whether urban or rural, these enclaves of the American poor harbor a growing and increasingly permanent underclass of people that today appears to be way beyond the pale of any meaningful social reform."[24]

Partial Analysis of This Locus Imperium

There is not space here for a full answer to the question of why there is a "Third World" in the United States, but at least a few lines of response might be drawn. The first is offered by Richard Shaull in *Heralds of a New Reformation: The Poor of North and South America*. Outlining different tracks of possibility for the relatively affluent white and the poorer dark-skinned Hispanic, Shaull writes:

> While living in the South Bronx I had daily contact with young men who had come from Puerto Rico to New York with the expectation that they too could have a share of those things promised by the propaganda of our consumer society. They wanted the same things I or anyone else wants, and they assumed they could get them by following the same track: getting an education, finding a job with the promise of upward mobility, relying on credit and loans. The only problem was that the system that worked for me did not work for them. They never were able to get onto the right track. The school system did not lead them, as it had me, to a college degree. Most of them could find no regular work, let alone jobs with opportunities for advancement. When they depended on credit and loans to get a few things they badly needed, they ended up becoming victims.[25]

Another line of the analysis deals with institutional injustice. In his *Making Peace in the Global Village*, Brown writes,

> If we are concerned about violence in the United States, we must direct our attention to injustice — to the violence of the status quo, to

the structural and institutional violence through which America abuses so many of its citizens. . . . We need constant reminders that violence occurs not only when a person is mugged, raped, or shot, but also when minority people are denied job opportunities, when blacks are harrassed by the police, when Chicano workers are denied collective bargaining rights, when women are given unequal pay, when homosexuals are denied jobs, and when the impoverished are given inferior schooling. Such injustices destroy people and, as such, are acts of violence.[26]

Ched Myers draws out a third line of analysis. He writes, "The present arrangement of world power is not a reward for hard work, or a happy accident, or the white man's burden, or a divine vocation. The first awakening is that our prosperity is based upon a system of robbery and domination."[27] He continues, "We need . . . to 'decode' the various cultural texts thrown at us in the politics of everyday life. . . . Behind police torture rooms, the trade in military hardware, the rape of women, IMF economic blackmail, death squads, elite world price-fixing, or ICBMs, stand ideological systems that justify, sanitize, and reproduce murder in the hearts of ordinary persons.'"[28]

Call to Liberation

So it is across America, from the South Bronx to the Sioux Nation to the Texas border—in contrast to worlds of plenty exist sites of the Third World. In a common context of collapse, Third World communities in the United States are casualties of the "metropolis."

And yet, with all the pain, there is something else. At these very sites, a stubborn vision is holding forth. Persisting through the rubble is a spiritual response to conditions of ruin. Both in these Third World communities and among citizens of, in Dorothee Sölle's words, "pharaoh's household," a call to the struggle for liberation is being sounded. As a theological reflection in the midst of this struggle, liberation theologies are emerging from among African Americans, Mexican Americans, Puerto Ricans, prison inmates, Native Americans, Asian Americans, Appalachians, women of color, and from among those of privilege who are choosing to take sides with the refugee, the homeless, the abused. Although distinctive in their theological reflection, these Third World communities share a radical incarnational spirituality. God is encountered on the hard terrain of the struggle. And for many of us, says Ched Myers, it is a "painful encounter with our imperial selves." This encounter with God turns us toward our neighbor, not only to bind up our neighbor's wounds, but to admit—and repent—our complicity in the wounding. We are called to repent the structures that benefit those "inside" but which diminish the life-chances of those "outside"—the disenfranchised who are duped and seduced by the "American dream."

Committed to the transformation of these structures through the praxis of liberation, Third World theologies in the United States call us to live out the biblical mandate for justice and to incarnate this justice into the social order. They also call us to confront and challenge the powers of the metropolis, powers which run the marketplace, the police, the surveillance of peace patriots. ... Says Myers, we need to "confront the human faces and voices of real victims for whom the imperial truth is clear."[29]

Today, within the United States, those attempting to respond to this difficult call are encountering the enormous cost of response. Those of the sanctuary movement, peace movement, and Free South Africa movement are experiencing for themselves the powers of the *locus imperium*. More than a few are serving prison sentences for their resistance. The losses are heavy, unromantic, and many feel broken. Yet, this radical praxis, rooted in a persistent vision of liberation, endures. Myers writes, "It is a terrible realization that despite experiences of miscarriage, collapse, debacle, defeat, and despair, there is still no more compelling alternative to the corruption of the age than radical discipleship."[30]

Incarnating this spirituality into the precincts of the *locus imperium* calls also for a new singing of Mary's song, a song summoning the defeated to hope in the God who "puts down the mighty from their thrones / and exalts those of low degree." Ritually kneeling at the Pentagon, fasting and praying across from the White House for and with the homeless, and candlelight vigils outside of prisons are part of this new singing. Public liturgy is moving, in part, from stained glass sanctuaries to the sanctuaries of the "gods of metal," to the "barbed-wired sacred sites of weapons factories. ... "[31] As the site of worship is extended to picket lines and nonviolent actions, one remembers that black theology began in the Civil Rights movement with resisters singing, clapping, and praying in the black church, and then moving from there into the streets, kneeling at sites of oppression.

The call to liberation evoked in these liturgies of liberation is a call to a subversive hope, a call to rally from the hard losses of the struggle. For sanctuary communities in the Southwest, Mary's song, heard anew in the Mexican-American festival of Our Lady of Guadalupe, takes on full meaning as the powers of state array themselves against the undocumented. From San Antonio, Texas, out of the context of deportations and despair, Virgilio Elizondo says of the Our Lady of Guadalupe celebration: "Fiestas can be used as rallying moments that ... nourish the movements of liberation. ... They are the moments of life that enable us to survive, to come together, to rally, and to begin anew."[32]

CONCLUSION: SOUTH BRONX TO SOUTH AFRICA

The global village is amove everywhere with the call to liberation. Recognizing that God's Spirit has pitched God's tent among those on the outside, liberation theology finds God within this movement, at the reaches, down at the edges of the world, at the periphery. In the poetry and prayers of the people, in their hard acts of struggle, in their artwork, foot-work, and raps, in the telling of their stories, the Spirit of liberation is breaking through. From Chinatown to Taiwan, from the United States to El Salvador, a vision of justice is being evoked in the very midst of, in Daniel Berrigan's words, "the iron course of injustice." In one Third World community after another, the call to a spirituality of liberation is being sounded. It is a call to encounter God in the prayer, the praxis, and the singing of a people. It is a call that recognizes that among the poor—from the South Bronx to black South Africa—God is here. And here. And here.

2

"On the Death of Archbishop Oscar Romero and the First Anniversary of Three Mile Island"

SHEILA COLLINS

A bishop is dead
at the altar.   a single bullet.
      expert.
screams in the chapel.
the heart of the people pierced.
   the hands, the feet.

Is it again expedient
that one man should die for the people?

"Get up and walk!"
  he had said, "Do not be afraid,
yet do not have revenge in your heart."
"You are the salt of the earth;
      if the salt loses its savor . . . "

A bishop is dead
at the altar.

and we send telegrams

sit safe in America where death
to the middle class comes slowly
and stealthily
in small doses the NRC declares
pose absolutely no hazard to health

except

that animals in Middletown are stillborn
grass won't grow
and strange skin rashes appear

and we send telegrams.

A bishop is dead
at the altar. His . . . words:

"Soldiers, the law of God is higher
than the laws of men.

IN THE NAME OF GOD,
STOP THIS REPRESSION!"

Twelve peasants were shot
as they sat in a Bible study class
reading aloud the gospels.
A fire sweeps through the streets
of San Salvador: "General Strike!"

"EL PUEBLO UNIDO JAMAS SERA
VENCIDO!"

There will be no strike benefits
the union leaders are all dead.
No savings to fall back on;
in a country of day laborers
mothers will leave their portion
for the young
praying it won't go rancid
in the stifling heat.

A sure martyrdom
defines the battle, focuses vision

and we send telegrams
sing hymns
and pray for the dead.

"Get up and walk!" he said,
but our limbs are drugged:

"National Security"

"Two Sides to Every Question"

"Being Experts, They Must Know"

and we send telegrams
estimating costs

of conversion.

Liberation Theologies in the Americas: Common Journeys and Mutual Challenges

ORLANDO E. COSTAS

The rise of liberation theologies in the Americas during the last decades reflects a growing movement among Christians against oppression and injustice. Liberation theologies advocate engagement in a process of emancipation and justice for a new social order. These theologies seek to articulate the meaning of the Christian faith from the perspective of the powerless in society and the voiceless in the church. They speak of sin as a personal reality and as a social factor. They understand salvation comprehensively, as forgiveness and healing, spiritual reconciliation and social transformation. Their special concern for the social dimensions of the faith, particularly in relation to such issues as class, race, and sex, have made them one of the most controversial and gravely misunderstood movements in the Americas.

In North America, for example, some have branded liberation theology as nothing more than old social gospel theology. Liberation theology is, however, so different from social gospel theology that we do a disservice to both when we confuse them with one another.

The social gospel movement flourished in the United States during the latter part of the nineteenth century and the first decades of the twentieth (ca. 1870 to 1920). Like liberation theology it emphasized the personal and social dimensions of sin and salvation. It advocated the redemption of society, which would lead to a social order undergirded by the prophetic principles of love and justice and an ethic of the kingdom of God. But unlike liberation theology, the social gospel movement assumed a Christendom framework (i.e., the vision of a Christian society upheld by Christian principles and values with the church as its manager). Thus social gospel theologians called for the redemption of society through the Christianization of its structures. Furthermore, the theology of the social gospel movement was informed by a romantic view of society and an optimistic concept of history. It assumed that with good individual actions and intentions society could change and that the kingdom of God would be gradually established upon the earth. Liberation theology, on the other hand, particularly in Latin

America, not only questions the premises of a Christendom model of society, but is informed by a much deeper and more critical understanding of society and a more dialectical view of history and the kingdom of God.

There are also those who much too quickly and uncritically associate liberation theology, especially in Latin America, with violence and Marxist-Leninist revolutionary change. *Time* magazine, for instance, has stated that "among its extreme proponents, liberation theology has been used as an apologia for revolutionary upheaval in the Third World that strives to link the imperatives of Christian charity with the dictates of Marxist class struggle."[1] It is true that liberation theology in Latin America shares the same context and reflects on similar issues as Marxist thought, but its source of inspiration and motivation is rather different. It is an undeniable fact that liberation theology is the most formidable Christian response to the Marxist critique of religion. Indeed, it has demonstrated that religion does not have to be an opium; it can be a force for positive revolutionary change. Liberation theology has not been afraid to interact critically with Marxist thought, questioning, for instance, the absolutism of orthodox Marxist-Leninism and revealing its anachronism in non-European, nonindustrialized societies. This is no different from what other Christian theologies do with other philosophical and social currents of thought. Liberation theology is not as philosophically and ideologically naive as some of its uninformed critics purport it to be! Therefore, it should not be confused with Marxism.

Liberation theologies are neither refried versions of the social gospel nor mere religious components of revolutionary movements. They are rather critical reflections on the praxis of the faith from within a context of oppression and engagement in the process of liberation. This has been called a *theopraxis* — i.e., a reflection on the transforming activity of faith in the living God who has been revealed in the stories of Israel and Jesus as the God of the poor, the powerless, and the oppressed; this God is committed to the liberation of the poor and to bringing into being a new order of life, justice, and well-being (i.e., peace).

In this essay, I propose to survey the contexts, methods, and goals of three liberation theologies in the Americas, namely, Latin American theology, African-American theology, and Hispanic-American theology, with an emphasis on the latter, which is the perspective I represent. My purpose is to demonstrate their common journeys and pinpoint some of their mutual challenges.

LATIN AMERICAN LIBERATION THEOLOGY

Latin American liberation theology is without question one of the better-known liberation theologies in the world. Indeed its influence throughout the world has led some to characterize it as the most representative model of liberation theology. This is not to suggest, however, that Latin American liberation theology is a homogeneous model. On the contrary, it is as diverse as the lands and cultures and peoples that make up the countries south of the Rio Bravo. Nevertheless, given their variety and diversity we can identify certain common characteristics that make it possible to speak of liberation theologies in Latin America as a single model.

Context

There is first the socio-historical reality of Latin America: a situation of poverty, powerlessness, and oppression, of institutional violence, social marginalization, and economic exploitation. This is such an obvious reality that I need not say too much about it. Whether in economics, politics, or socio-cultural relations, Latin America is an oppressed, powerless, and impoverished continent. The struggle against this situation can be dated as far back as the sixteenth century when Bartolomé de Las Casas, a Dominican missionary-theologian, bishop of Chiapas (Mexico), eloquently, vigorously, and passionately defended the rights of the Indians to exist and be treated as human beings. Las Casas was one of several prophetic bishops in the sixteenth century who became spokespersons for the spiritual, social, and political rights of the aboriginal communities. We can further witness the struggle for liberation in the African slaves who rebelled in multiple ways (most notably in North America, the Caribbean, and Brazil), questioning and challenging the oppressive powers of Europe through song and dance, religious practices and military uprisings. We see the intuitions of liberation theology emerging out of Father Hidalgo y Casilla's call to the Indians of his parish in Dolores, Mexico, on September 16, 1810, to rise against their Spanish rulers under the banner of the Virgin of Guadalupe, thereby initiating the wars for independence and laying the ground work for what in the twentieth century has been described as "the irruption of the poor." Their cry for a free, just, and peaceful society is the outstanding fact of our time.

The situation in Latin America is also one of post-Christendom. By Christendom I do not mean the sum total of Christians, as is often thought in North America. Rather, as I have already noted, Christendom is a society built upon supposedly Christian values and principles with the church as manager or spiritual mentor. In history there have been various forms of Christendom, including that of the East with its hub in Constantinople, that of the West headed by Rome, and those of North America, South Africa, and Australasia. In Latin America, there has been a dependent form of Iberian Christendom, different from those of Europe and North America.

Since the 1930s the house of Christendom has been slowly coming apart notwithstanding church efforts to the contrary. We have thus witnessed a most unusual process of de-Christianization. Whereas the majority of the population is baptized, church attendance is relatively low. In past decades the Roman Catholic church argued that Latin America was already evangelized. More recently, however, it has had to recognize that Latin America is still a continent of mission and that large sectors of its population have yet to be evangelized (or at least re-evangelized), as was dramatically demonstrated by the third General Conference of Latin American Bishops, held at Puebla, Mexico, in 1979.

This de-Christianization has questioned the role of the church as an institution in society, especially with reference to the social, economic, and political problems that Latin America faces. It is obvious that the church has neither the moral strength nor the technical know-how to deal with problems of poverty, land, housing, and a more equitable social organization. In places where the church has attempted in recent decades to deal with these problems, as in Chile, Venezuela, and Costa Rica, it has failed. The people know too well that for too long the church has operated under a coalition of state, army, and church. The Protestant churches and mission boards have offered no better alternatives, for they too have often acted as allies of liberal capitalistic governments. Protestants have a history of alliances with the economic vested interests of North America and Europe and have neither the moral strength to propose alternatives nor any technical know-how to do so.

Christendom in Latin America has been slowly breaking apart. This does not mean, however, that there are no religious interests anymore. On the contrary, Latin America is today, as never before, a continent of religious effervescence. The one phenomenon which many Latin American observers will agree on as a sign of ecclesial and faith renewal is the basic ecclesial communities that have sprung up in practically every country. These communities do not fit any one mode. Many are in close link with the pastoral and hierarchical structures of the church. They are part of the ongoing life and mission of the parishes. Others are more para-parochial and even para-ecclesiastical. Most are Catholic, but some are ecumenical. The important thing about these communities is that they are made up of Christians from the grassroots of the church, affirming their faith in connection with the issues of the "bases" of the respective societies of which they are part and parcel. Such issues as the struggles for justice, liberation, and peace, which are fundamentally related to the core and heart of the faith, become the focus of their Bible study, worship, and witness.

It is out of this context that Latin American liberation theology emerges. It is a theological reflection rooted, on the one hand, in social and historical reality, and, on the other, in the ecclesial awakening of the grassroots.

Method

Latin American liberation theologians hold that theirs is not so much a new theology as a new way of doing theology. They work with a dialectical-critical method. Three action verbs have been used to describe this method: *see, hear,* and *do.*

To *see* is to have a direct confrontation with or a critical immersion in the situation of the poor and the oppressed. Before you can reflect upon the world you must *see* what the world is all about. This calls for the use of the social sciences. The social sciences, however, are not value free. Many years ago Karl Barth suggested that the theologian should study both the Bible and the newspaper. That was before some theologians got smart and asked, *which* newspaper? And from which side are we going to look at the scriptures? Here is where Marxism has become a helpful tool to the Latin American liberation theologians, for it has enabled them to see reality, not from a supposedly neutral perspective, but rather from the position of the poor, the powerless, and the oppressed.

Liberation theology has developed a new theological discourse from a new setting. This social location has facilitated the *hearing* of the word of God anew. Christian theology is fundamentally concerned with the interpretation of the word of God, i.e., with revelation as we understand it in both the traditions of Israel and the church, and especially in the story of Jesus the Christ, and his continuing presence in the world through the Spirit and the witness of the church. Thanks to their social location, Latin American liberation theologians have been able to detect the presence of the poor through the pages of the Holy Scripture. Thus they have asked why have the poor been so absent from the work of biblical scholars? How is it that the scriptures, which tell the stories of faith of the poor, oppressed, and humble people, of former slaves and their descendants, have been often utilized to repress the cry of the poor, to neutralize the struggle for liberation, and to minimize God's explicit commitment to justice and peace?

When you have honestly faced such a question, argue many Latin American theologians, you can only become suspicious of the way many classical and contemporary biblical scholars have interpreted the scriptures. Indeed, you also begin to question the way that historians have dealt with the Christian tradition and systematic theologians have articulated Christian doctrines. In the same process, you begin to discern a horizon of hope. New possibilities begin to appear. You become evermore aware of the kingdom of God as a radically different order of life from the world order we have allowed to be established in the name of God, in the name of Christianity, in the name of the church. You begin to hear the word anew — as a word of liberation and hope announcing the coming of God's kingdom and the possibility of anticipating its fruits in history: freedom, justice, and well-being. Then you realize that it is possible to rearrange the structures of society, to build a more just, freer, and more peaceful planetary space. In other words, you gain a new understanding of the Christian faith.

And then comes the *doing*. You discover that the mission that has been entrusted to the church is not merely personal but social, not simply inner directed but prophetic—a mission geared toward the transformation of history and therefore of the institutional church as a constituent part of history. This understanding produces a new mission theory and strategy, beyond Christendom. In Christendom-oriented missiologies, the manipulation and control of people on behalf of the ecclesiastical institution are not only tolerated but justified. In a missiology beyond Christendom, mission is seen in the perspective of incarnation, service, and liberating suffering. Mission becomes a place of service and commitment to the needy, of suffering and hope for a new world. A Pentecostal pastor in Cuba has put this understanding of mission in a beautiful gospel song:

> Sent by the Lord am I
> My hands are ready now
> to help construct a just
> and peaceful loving world.
>
> The angels cannot change
> a world of hurt and pain
> into a world of love,
> of justice, and of peace.
> The task is mine to do,
> make it reality.
> Oh help me God obey,
> help me to do your will.

Goals

What are the goals of this way of doing theology? First, to lead Christians to *experience* their faith from the underside of history — i.e., from the situation of those who have become the victims ("the sinned-against," a Chinese friend of mine calls them) rather than the shapers of history — and to *discover* the situation of the victims as a privileged Christian place.

Second, Latin American liberation theology aims to help Christians interpret and understand their faith in light of the situation of the poor and oppressed. The latter are not added factors in the Christian faith. Rather they are subjects of the Christian discourse. If we want to know what the Christian faith is about, we have to interpret it in the "key" of the poor and oppressed.

Third, liberation theology in Latin America seeks to empower Christians to communicate their faith from the underside, to give them new categories, new ways of articulating or bearing witness to the faith, and to be able to do that, not in cheap and empty words, but in the liberating power of the gospel. In other words, this theology seeks to enable them to understand what the Apostle Paul said to the Corinthian church: "The kingdom of God is not talk but power" — i.e., liberating power (1 Cor. 4:20).

Finally, liberation theology in Latin America seeks to lead Christians to become a factor in the transformation of their social reality in the light of their faith, to understand that they have been called by God to be world-transforming agents. After all, everything we can say about the Christian faith is inevitably linked to the fundamental category of transformation. Just as Christians have been transformed into new creations (2 Cor. 5:17) and are then called to be continually transformed by the renewal of their minds (Rom. 12:2), so they are to be instruments of God in the transformation of the world (Rom. 12:2). Liberation theologians in Latin America want to see Christians take this mandate seriously and become a transforming presence in the struggle for justice and peace.

AFRICAN-AMERICAN THEOLOGY

African-American theology is the earliest form of liberation theology in North America. It began about the same time as Latin American liberation theology. James Cone's book *Black Power and Black Theology* was published in 1969, the same year that Rubem Alves's *A Theology of Human Hope* (the first formal articulation of Latin American liberation theology) was released. Thus in some ways the beginnings of black theology and Latin American theology parallel each other. Their focus and background are different, however.

Context

The context of black theology is the experience of slavery and institutional racism in the United States. This experience involves the awareness that in the United States oppression follows the color line, and that integration leads only to assimilation and hence perpetual domination by whites. Black theology is an affirmation of black American culture and values as having their own legitimacy in the face of the racist experience of the United States. It involves a rediscovery of black religious experience as the matrix of an indigenous theology. The sources of black liberation theology are to be found, therefore, in the black religious experience in North America, which has its own history.

Method

I describe the method of black theology as involving "no" but "yes." I will use four key words here: *challenge, hear, see,* and *articulate.* The first step in black theology is to *challenge* the dominant theology for its white bias. Blackness is affirmed as a key theological category. This means that hearing the story as told by the black community is of utmost importance. "The story" is the account of suffering and freedom of the black community as well as of biblical faith. This story is told through the spirituals and the blues, through the black preacher and the unique black church worship experience. Once you are able to hear the story from the black community, you are able to *see* eschatologically. That is, you are able to see the promised future as manifested in the dream of freedom and the vision of justice that have always been with the suffering black community in North America. More than that, seeing involves both being able to grasp the promised future and appropriating that future in political action. It is not enough to long for the land beyond the Jordan. The task is now to appropriate it, to bring the land beyond the Jordan to the here and now.

This is followed by an *articulation* of the truth of the faith from within the suffering and liberating experience of the black community, an articulation that is validated in the praxis of the black church. Black theology follows the experience of the community, the struggle of black people, and interprets its theological significance in the light of scripture and the trajectory of the Christian faith. The legitimacy of black theology is established by whether or not black people can see themselves, their struggle for justice and liberation, and their experience of faith represented in it. It is further justified when such experiences—after having been informed and tested by scripture and tradition—are formulated coherently *for* the community.

Goals

Black theology has at least four identifiable goals. The first is to unmask the ideological captivity of dominant white theology. This has made necessary the construction of an opposite theological edifice fundmentally different from traditional dominant racist theologies in North America.

Second, black theology is geared to the theological articulation of the religious experience of the black church and the demonstration of its correspondence with bibical faith. Such a task has demanded of black scholars historical, biblical, and systematic research and writing.

Third, black theology has sought to demonstrate that the truth of the gospel can be affirmed only from the perspective of the oppressed—which in the United States means especially nonwhite minorities. Black theology is a call to repentance of the dominant sectors of society. This means that black theology has to be ethical, prophetic, and even evangelistic.

A fourth goal of black theology is the mobilization of the black church for a greater militancy in the quest for freedom. Thus it has set up participation in freedom as a fundamental test of a valid Christian theology. Indeed, this fourth goal represents the heart and soul of the faith of the black church, as expressed in the following spiritual:

> Oh, Freedom! Oh, Freedom!
> Oh, Freedom, over me!
> An' befo' I'd be a slave,
> I'll be buried in my grave,
> An' go home to my Lord an' be free.

HISPANIC-AMERICAN THEOLOGY

Hispanic-American theology is one of the latest expressions of the liberation discourses in North America. There are several factors that explain why Hispanic-American theology has been so late in developing. The fact that Hispanics have had to live and work in the shadow of Latin American theology, on the one hand, and North American theologies (black and white), on the other, is not without significance. Moreover, there is a sense in which Hispanic Americans have been deprived of a vernacular language. If to do theology is to reflect critically on the faith and articulate coherently and contextually its meaning in the language of a particular community, how can Hispanics have been able to do so when so many have lacked a proper grasp of either Spanish or English? It has taken many years before a handful of Hispanic theologians have acquired the courage, the heart, and the energy to begin to reflect out loud on the faith in light of their socio-cultural reality through their broken English and tarnished Spanish. As with the other two theologies considered, so in the case of Hispanic-American theology, we will look at its context, method, and goals.

Context

The context of Hispanic-American theology has been shaped by the experience of conquest, colonialism, migration, and biculturalism. The historical consciousness of conquest is mediated especially by the two leading Hispanic communities in North America—the Mexican and the Puerto Rican. The reality of colonialism has been experienced, especially, in the Southwest and Puerto Rico. The Treaty of Guadalupe-Hidalgo (1848) was but the formalization of a progressive conquest by the United States of half the territory of Mexico, to which many U.S. citizens had been welcomed and which others had penetrated illegally. It is ironic that the descendants of the country that opened its doors to "Anglos" and lost a significant portion of its territory are designated today by U.S. immigration authorities as "illegal aliens." The Treaty of Guadalupe-Hidalgo may have created a political border but could not impose a cultural one. Mexican families live today on both sides of the Rio Bravo. They have a historical and cultural claim to the Southwest. This region belongs as much to them as it does to Anglo-Americans.

As to Puerto Rico: It is an occupied island. You call it what you may—a federal territory, a commonwealth, a "free-associated state," or any other euphemism. The fact remains that Puerto Rico became part of the United States as "war booty" from the Spanish-American War (1898). This makes it plainly and simply a "colony." Puerto Rican people have not had a chance to decide their own future, notwithstanding the so-called plebiscite of 1952. A colonized people cannot decide their political future if they are living under colonial rule.

This colonial reality extends to the Caribbean and Central America. Even though these regions are made up of supposedly independent nations, they are really neo-colonies because of the regional domination by the United States. Thus, for example, Honduras has had to give up its territorial integrity to accommodate the several thousand U.S. troops stationed near the Nicaraguan border. Costa Rica is being forced to give up the most precious value of its people (their peaceful character and nonaligned tradition) in order to play the role assigned to it by the United States. El Salvador is involved in a terrible guerrilla war which neither side can ever expect to win. Grenada was invaded by the United States in a flagrant violation of the charter of the Organization of American States. Guatemala is living the agony of suffering and death on account of political and economic corruption and a state of institutionalized repressive and subversive armed violence.

The painful experience of migration — external and internal — has further shaped the context of Hispanic-American theology. With the exception of the descendants of the early settlers of St. Augustine and Tampa, Florida, and the Southwest, Hispanics are either immigrants or their offspring. They bear in their collective memory the pain of becoming uprooted from their loved ones and cultures, adopting to a new environment and struggling through social and economic hardship. They have come as political refugees, immigrants in search of a better way of life, or migrant workers. Most recently the Hispanic community has experienced a tremendous influx from Mexico, Central America, and the Caribbean. The new immigrants have taken up jobs few seem to want in factories, on farms, and in restaurants. Not being able to get adequate documentation, they have been at the mercy of the immigration department or their employers. Indeed, they have become a new army of cheap labor, without benefits or rights, unable to anticipate what tomorrow might bring, eligible for arrest and deportation at any moment. They cannot trust anybody — not even other (whether documented residents or U.S. born) Hispanics. The system has been so excruciating for the new immigrants that it has created a split in the Hispanic community. Thus, the experience of migration has been not only the result of an economic and political situation back home — a situation in which the United States has not been a passive observer — but also a divisive cultural and political factor in the Hispanic community.

A fourth piece in the Hispanic contextual mosaic is the phenomenon of biculturalism. Hispanic Americans are the offspring of a double process of *mestizaje* (from mestizo, "hybrid," a racial and cultural mixture). This process has encompassed the triple encounter between European (Iberian), Native American, and African peoples, which is the direct result of the Spanish/Portuguese conquest and civilization and which gave birth to the Latin American peoples. It has also involved the encounter between the Anglo-American civilization and the civilization of Latin America, an encounter which since 1848 has been giving way to a new Hispanic-American community. This double *mestizaje* is the result of the military, cultural, and religious invasions and conquests that have characterized the history of Hispanics in North America. Each has produced multiple variants. In the case of the first, it produced the multiple national and regional cultures of the Latin American mosaic; in the case of the second, the emerging regional and subcultural varieties to be found in Hispanic communities throughout the United States. Consequently, Mexican American and Central American groups have the imprint of the Spanish-Indian confrontation out of which emerged the Mexican and Mesoamerican peoples, whereas Puerto Ricans and other Hispanics from the Eastern Caribbean reflect the Native American-Spanish-African confrontation.

Hispanic Americans belong to two worlds and yet they are not bona fide members of either. They must communicate in two languages without having full ownership of either one. Virgilio Elizondo's description of a mestizo group, which he applies just to the Mexican American, is, nevertheless, descriptive of all Hispanics.

> A *mestizo* group represents a particularly serious threat to its parent cultures. The *mestizo* does not fit conveniently into the analysis categories used by either parent group. The *mestizo* may understand them far better than they understand him or her. To be an insider-outsider, as is the *mestizo*, is to have closeness to and distance from both parent cultures. A *mestizo* people can see and appreciate characteristics in its parent cultures that they see neither in themselves nor in each other. It is threatening to be in the presence of someone who knows us better than we know ourselves.[2]

Given this reality, Hispanic Americans have to struggle against the temptation of assimilation or isolation in order not to be a threat to their parent cultures. Either alternative will be detrimental to their collective future and their prophetic role in the Americas. One of the most important challenges before Hispanic-American liberation theology is that of enabling Hispanics to discover their promise for the common good of the Americas, a promise which ultimately lies in the recovery of their bicultural identity. The future of Hispanics in the Americas lies neither in assimilation nor isolation, but rather in the recovery and affirmation of their double identity.

Method

This is why Hispanic-American theology works with an historico-cultural method. Three steps characterize this approach.

The first is to *remember* the rich cultural heritage of the Hispanic peoples in the Americas and the events that have led the various Hispanic groups in North America to their present situation. This pilgrimage backwards is necessary in order to move forward. Without the recovery of their historical and cultural roots, Hispanics will not be able to transcend their alienated consciousness introjected by the dominant sectors of North American society through many years of conquest and domination. Indeed, the pilgrimage to the past is essential not only to overcome all the stereotypical images and inferior status Hispanics have been led to believe about themselves, but especially to recover the liberating potential of their religio-cultural heritage. Whether Catholic or Protestant the Hispanic religious past is filled with powerful symbols of resistance, survival, and hope. Unfortunately, the social and theological significance of these symbols has often been blurred, distorted, or minimized by non-Hispanic interpeters. One of the first tasks of a liberating Hispanic-American theology is to read anew, from within, and restore the "subversive" and "liberating" memory of Hispanics in North America.

The second step is to correlate the past with the present: the Hispanic reality in North America with that of Latin America and the Caribbean, and indeed with the entire Third World; the experience of "outsiders" (Hispanics) with the reality of "insiders" (North Americans); and finally, the personal and social existence of Hispanics with the triune God whose eternal son has been revealed in Jesus, whose Spirit makes him present in the struggles of Hispanic history and culture. This Spirit has been sent by the Father in the name of the Son to set the world free, to reconcile it with God and thus bring glory to the one who was, who is, and who will always be.

To correlate "now and then" is to explore the historical linkage between the present reality of Hispanics and their cultural and religious tradition. Hispanic Protestants must come to terms with their Catholic cultural background. Indeed, they must confront the fact that Anglo-Saxon Protestantism has, by and large, denied them theological access to their cultural heritage and values. Catholics, on the other hand, must be aware of the *chiroscuro* past of Iberian-Catholic Christianity in the Americas — its oppressive and alienating role. Moreover, as Hispanic Catholics in North America they must confront the fact that European Catholic theology and practice have been repressive forces against the Hispanic-American Catholic church. Hispanic-American liberation theology passes, thus, through a process of emancipation from other cultural traditions *within* the North American church.

The correlation of "here and there" involves a comparative reflection on the relation between the situation in Latin America and that in the United States. Since being Hispanic implies being linked historically and culturally with the Iberian-American world, it is not possible to be and act as an Hispanic American without understanding the Latin American cultural experience and social reality. Being a Neorican (U.S.-born Puerto Rican) is, to be sure, different from being an islander, but it is not possible to claim a Puerto Rican identity without understanding what the island is culturally all about and appreciating its contemporary struggles. (Likewise, it is not possible for Puerto Rican islanders to claim a twentieth century patriotic identity without understanding the Puerto Rican diaspora in the U.S. mainland.) By the same token, being a Chicano (U.S.-born Mexican) is different from being a Mexican, but it is not possible to be a true Chicano without coming to terms with Mexico. Likewise, a twentieth-century Mexican identity must deal with the *larger* Mexican reality, including the two hundred plus aboriginal groups spread throughout the republic and the Mexican-related groups throughout the United States.

The correlation of the experience of "outsiders" and "insiders" involves a confrontation with the reality of a minority community in a dominant society; this community is aware of its alien status and yet free to be itself and contribute to the well-being of all. This implies a fundamental challenge to the notion of Anglo-white supremacy expressed historically in the ideologies of "manifest destiny" and "the melting pot." Over against the traditional Anglo view that one can maintain one's ethnicity and speak other languages besides English so long as it is not done publicly, Hispanic-American theology insists on the *public* value of a culturally heterogeneous society, the proven social benefits of a bilingual society, and the cultural impoverishment of monolingualism. Moreover, Hispanic-American theology demands a space in North American culture and society not only to learn and teach the language and traditions of the Hispanic peoples and reflect on the faith from within its historico-cultural heritage, but also to make a socio-theological contribution to North American society. To do so is to demand to be taken seriously and not be simply tokens to be used for political gains every four years or as an attractive new market to be exploited with promotional gimmicks. Though Hispanics stand "outside the gate" of mainstream North American society, Hispanic-American theology enables them to stand tall and be seen! Though they speak with a "broken accent," they are empowered to speak the truth loud and clear and make their cry for justice be heard in the centers of power.

The correlation of the personal and social existence of Hispanics with the revelation of the triune God enables theology to plumb the depth of faith implicit in the Hispanic experience. Indeed it is not possible to understand the Hispanic struggle for liberation apart from the faith of a people in

> ... the God of all names, ...
> who makes all people of
> tenderness and ... dust ... ,
> the Father, who makes
> all flesh, the black and
> the white, red in the blood.
>
> ... the Son, Jesus our brother,
> who was born dark, of the race of Abraham.
>
> ... the Holy Spirit, banner and song.
> ... the true God who loved us first without divisions. ...
> The Three who are one only God.[3]

God has never been a stranger for the Hispanic community, as God was not unknown to their forebears. For Hispanics are a Spirit-conscious people deeply aware of the presence of the almighty in their history. This awareness, however, is not so much rooted in reason or nature as in the story of Jesus. It is through Christ that Hispanics have made the link between Yahweh and the supreme deity of their forebears. The spirit that binds the Hispanic tradition is none other than the Spirit of Christ. Thus Christology lies at the center of Hispanic-American theology. To explore the relationship between Hispanic reality and faith it is necessary in the first place to ask: Who is Jesus Christ for Hispanics? This is vividly demonstrated in a "Canon of Puerto Rican Nostalgia," by Antonio M. Stevens Arroyo[4]:

> When our forefathers sinned
> and lost the beauty of Eden,
> you did not abandon us,
> but promised a new Adam [*Gen. 3:15; Rom. 5:12ff.*],
>   Christ your only Son.
>
> Rich as he was, he made himself poor for our sake
> in order to make us rich
> by means of his poverty. . . .
>
> In the fullness of time,
> with a happiness beyond reason [*"Lamento Borin-
>   cano" by Rafael Hernándéz*],
> Christ the savior set out from the mountains of Gal-
>   ilee. Traveling by the footpaths of the countryside,
> he brought the tidings of good news to the City of
>   Man.
> Scorned for his humble birth [*Isa. 53:2ff.; Matt. 26:73;
>   Heb. 46:16–25*],
> slighted for his parables and manner of speech,
> he was rejected by this world's wisdom
> as a *jíbaro*[5] in a city of heartlessness.
> But he bore his sufferings without violence,
> offering his life as a ransom for many. . . .
>
> Remember the faithful
> who walked through the valley of darkness on their
>   way to you;
> those who earned their bread by the sweat of their
>   brows,
> those who toiled in the heat of the tropical sun
> and who fell in their youth like cane under the
>   *machete*

And do not forget those who offered their life's blood
in patient pursuit of a freedom
which still remains your promise to us. . . .

But we recall that you summoned Abraham from his
    homeland,
that you led Moses in the Exodus,
and John the Baptist in the desert.
As Christ hung on the cross between earth and sky,
we are crucified in a Limbo,
belonging neither here nor there
because you have given us the lot of serving you
as a solitary spirit in great expectation [*"Ultima
    Actio," by José De Diego*].

O that our plea would be your praise!
Because we do not see the *fiamboyán*[6]
in this gray jungle of steel and cement,
we seek you with a faith more pure.
Because we do not hear the song of the *coquí*[7]
above the din of people in the streets,
we bless you with proven faithfulness.
Because we do not dance in the *barrio* or *batey*,[8]
we paint a mechanized world
the color of an eternal smile.

Exiles twice-over from the Promised Land,
we speak to you with the stubborn badgering, *la
    peleíta monga*,[9] of a child
until we can glorify you with straightforwardness.

¡*Ay Bendito*,[10] Lord!
We will never be able to praise you as you deserve.
But if our prayer is united with Christ's,
we will have a song for thanking you.

Through him,
with him, in him,
Almighty Father,
in the unity of the Holy Spirit,
all glory and honor is yours,
forever and ever. Amen [ibid.].

In this prayer we see the connection between Christ and the Hispanic
community. He is viewed as the promised son of God who became a Gal-

ilean *jíbaro* and lived the Hispanic experience of poverty and ignorance, of being "slighted for his . . . manner of speech," of rejection, loneliness, exile, suffering, and death—all of these leading "to the Almighty Father, in the unity of the Holy Spirit."

The correlation between reality and faith is thus achieved Christologically. Yet, as the prayer demonstrates, Christology opens the way for a much larger connecting link (between God and humanity) and a more concrete expression of faith (the Hispanic church).

The third and concluding step in Hispanic-American theology is the *articulation* of the insights derived from the process of correlation. Inevitably this involves a theological account of the spiritual journey of the Hispanic community as lived and expressed in the various Hispanic churches. It implies a new and more Hispanically oriented reading of the scriptures and Christian history. It assumes an Hispanic interpretation of traditional Christian doctrines. Above all, it presupposes the formulation of a new missiology inspired in the festive spirit of the Hispanic community, informed by the joyous character of the gospel, and focused on the God who wills life for the whole earth.

Goals

From the foregoing, the goals of Hispanic theology become readily apparent: first, to awaken a new Hispanic identity and bridge its various expressions; second, to challenge Hispanic stereotypes in the Americas and overcome stigmatization; third, to enable the Hispanic church to hear God's word in the periphery of North American life so as to reinterpret the faith from an Hispanic perspective; and, fourth, to help bring forth a new Hispanic church engaged in the struggle for a more humane, free, just, and peaceful society and a new person in the United States and the Americas.

It is a fact that Hispanic theology as a formal discourse is still in an embryonic stage. What has been described as such is as much an interpretation of several anthologies, articles, and monographs as an agenda for the immediate future.

The three theologies considered in this essay have much in common and mutually challenge one another. They share the following common convictions about the Christian faith:

1. The God of Jesus, Israel, and the church is the God of the poor, the powerless and the oppressed.

2. The Christ of God is Jesus of Nazareth, the liberator.

3. Salvation is liberation from personal and collective sin and death, for justice, community, and well-being.

4. To believe in God is to do God's will; to know God is to do justice.

5. The church is the company of Jesus, the community of the poor, the people of God.

Liberation theologies in the Americas not only share common journeys and convictions but also have mutual challenges. Latin American liberation theology brings forth the economic and political reality of oppression. It challenges African-American theology to see underneath the reality of racism and economic conflict (which is a struggle of social classes). It challenges Hispanic-American theology to sharpen its double identity and be aware of the danger of assimilation or cooptation by the dominant Anglo sectors of society.

African-American theology brings forth the racist reality of oppression in the Americas. It challenges Latin American theology to see the "white hand" behind Latin American church history and theology. It confronts Hispanic-American theology with the role of race in the history of oppression and with the role of those who have oppressed blackness in the Americas.

As for Hispanic-American theology, it brings forth the racial-class reality behind oppressive structures in the Americas. It challenges Latin American and black theology to see the culturo-linguistic dimensions of oppression, the complementary nature of their respective discourses, and the need to move beyond one-sided social analyses and theological formulations. The struggle for liberation is far more complex than what any perspective can encompass.

PART II

COMMUNITIES

3

"At the Lincoln Monument in Washington, August 28, 1963" (excerpts)

MARGARET WALKER

Write this word upon your hearts
And mark this message on the doors of your houses
See that you do not forget
How this day the Lord has set our faces toward Freedom
Teach these words to your children
And see that they do not forget them.
Recite them in your going out and your coming in
And speak them in the silence of the night.
Remember the covenant we have made together
Here in the eyes of our Liberator. . . .

Black Theology: Where We Have Been and a Vision for Where We Are Going

JAMES H. CONE

The concept of black theology refers to a theological movement that emerged among North American black people during the second half of the 1960s. The origin of black theology has three contexts: (1) the Civil Rights movement of the 1950s and 1960s, largely associated with Dr. Martin Luther King, Jr.; (2) the publication of Joseph Washington's book *Black Religion*[1] in 1964; and (3) the rise of the black power movement strongly influenced by Malcolm X's philosophy of black nationalism. These three contexts are largely responsible for the formation of black theology as it was articulated by myself and others. However, when people ask me about the influence upon my theological perspective I usually say something about my father and mother and what it meant for a black person to grow up in Bearden, Arkansas, during the 1940s and 1950s.[2] Two things happened to me in Bearden that helped to shape my theological perspective: I encountered the harsh realities of white injustice that was inflicted daily upon the black community; and I was given a faith that sustained my personhood and dignity in spite of white people's brutality.

The person most responsible for my deep resentment against oppression was my father. My father prided himself in being able to outthink white people, to beat them at their own game. His sixth-grade education was no measure of his quick, substantial intelligence. That was why he managed to avoid much of the dehumanizing climate of the black-white social arrangements. For example, he refused to work at the sawmills and other factories in and around Bearden because he contended that a black person could not keep his or her dignity and also work for white people. My father always called my mother "Mrs. Cone" while in the presence of whites. It was his way of forcing whites to address her with dignity and not by her first name. In such situations, most whites resisted by ignoring her or by asking for her first name, which was never given. My father would not permit any white person to address my mother as "girl" or himself as "boy." Any white person who used these derogatory terms in the presence of my father had to be prepared for an apology or a fight.

Growing up with my father and observing his dealings with whites and blacks had a profound effect upon my perspective on the world. He gave me the conviction that survival for black people requires constant struggle, and that no black person should ever expect justice from whites. "How could they treat us justly when they do not regard us as people?" he often asked rhetorically.

Although my father seldom earned more than a thousand dollars per year, he refused to allow white politicians during election time to place their signs on any of his property, for allowing them to do so would have suggested that he supported their candidacies. When asked about it he would reply, "Don't let anybody buy your integrity, especially white people. Tell them that it is not for sale. Do what you do because it is right and not because of the money involved. And never let yourself be put in a position where you are dependent on your enemies in order to survive. For God will make a way out of no way, and he will make your enemies your footstool."

In the context of the Macedonia African Methodist Episcopal church, resistance to white injustice was joined with faith in God's righteousness. My mother was one of the pillars of the Macedonia church, and a firm believer in God's justice. The spirituality that my mother embodied was typical of black Christians in Bearden, especially those in the Macedonia church. It was not until my graduate school days that I heard many professors and students use the black church as a prime example of the truth of the Marxist critique of religion—that it is the opiate of the people. The force of the logic seemed to fit perfectly the white churches in Bearden but did not appear to apply to the true essence of black religion as I had encountered it. I do not ever remember any black church person in Bearden using religion to cover up oppression or as an escape from the harsh realities of life. Religion was rather the source of identity and survival on the one hand and the source of empowerment in the struggle for freedom on the other.

As the source of identity and survival, the faith of the church was that factor which sustained the people when everything else failed. God was that reality to which people turned for identity and worth because the existing social, political, and economic structures said they were nobody.

The value structures in society were completely reversed in the church. The last became the first in that the janitor became the chairman of the Steward Board and the maid became president of Stewardess Board Number One. Everybody became somebody, and there were no second-class people in the Macedonia church. Furthermore, during my childhood, every fight for justice and civil rights was initiated and led by the church. The leader was usually the minister or some other self-employed black person. Because there were very few black people who were not dependent upon white people for a livelihood, the burden of the leadership fell upon the preacher, whose salary was paid by his congregation. Seeing so many courageous ministers leading the struggle for justice in the name of the gospel and also seeing the support of the church people undoubtedly had much to do with why I chose the ministry as my vocation, and why I chose liberation as the central theme of my perspective in black theology.

Let's look at the first context for the development of black theology — the Civil Rights movement and Martin Luther King, Jr.

All persons involved in the rise of black theology were also involved in the Civil Rights movement, and they participated in the protest demonstrations led by King. It is important to know that, unlike most contemporary theological movements in Europe and North America, black theology's origin was not in the seminary or university. In fact, most of the early interpreters of black theology did not have advanced academic degrees. Black theology came into being in the context of black people's struggle for racial justice, which was instituted in the church but chiefly identified with such protest organizations as the Southern Christian Leadership Conference (SCLC), the National Conference of Black Churchmen (NCBC), the Inter-Religion Foundation for Community Organization (IFCO), and many black caucuses in white denominations.

From the beginning, black theology was understood by its creators as a Christian theological reflection upon the black struggles for justice and liberation. This was defined largely in the light and thought of Martin Luther King, Jr., when he and other black church people began to relate the gospel to the struggle for justice in American society. The great majority of white theologians denied any relationship between the struggle of black people for justice and the gospel. They claimed that politics and religion did not mix. Liberal white Christians, with few exceptions, remained silent on the theme of justice; or worse, they advocated a form of gradualism that denounced boycotts, sit-ins, and freedom rides. Therefore, contrary to popular opinion, Martin Luther King was not well received by the white American church establishment when he inaugurated the Civil Rights movement with the Montgomery bus boycott in 1955.

Because black people received no support from white churches or their theologians, we had to search deeply into our own history in order to find theological bases for our prior political commitment to set black people free.

We found support in people like Richard Allen, the founder of the African Methodist Episcopal (AME) church. We found support in Henry Howland Garnet, a nineteenth-century Presbyterian preacher who urged slaves to resist slavery; in Nat Turner, a slave and Baptist preacher who led an insurrection that resulted in the death of sixty whites; in Henry Turner, an AME bishop who claimed that God was a Negro; and in many others. When we investigated our religious history, we were reminded that our struggle for political justice did not begin in the 1950s or 60s, but had roots stretching back for many years. It was also encouraging to find out that black people's struggle for political justice in North America has always been located in their churches. Black Christians have always known that the God of Moses and Jesus did not create them to be slaves or second-class citizens to whites in North America. This conviction is found throughout the black church experience — whether we consider (1) the independent churches such as the AME, the African Methodist Episcopal Zion church (AMEZ), and the Baptist churches; (2) the so-called invisible institutions among the slaves in the South which merged with the independent churches after the Civil War; or (3) the black people in white organizations. Thus in order to make a theological witness of this religious knowledge, black preachers and civil rights activists of the 1960s developed a black theology that rejected racism and affirmed the black struggle for liberation as consistent with the gospel of Jesus.

The second context for the development of black theology was Joseph Washington's book *Black Religion*. When black preachers and activist Christians began to search for the radical side of their black church history, they also began to ask about the distinctive religious and theological contribution of black people. It was generally assumed by most whites, and unfortunately, by many blacks as well, that black people's culture had no unique contribution to make to Christianity in particular and to humanity in general. Indeed, white liberal Christians understood integration to mean assimilation and that meant blacks rejecting their own culture and adopting European cultural values. The assumption behind the white definition of integration was a belief that African cultural values were completely destroyed during the time of slavery. Therefore, if blacks were to develop cultural knowledge of themselves, it was claimed that they had to find it in identification with white American values.

Joseph Washington wrote his book in the context of this dominant theme which was emphasized in black-white relations in America during the 1960s. Contrary to this dominant view, Washington contended that there were a unique black culture and a distinctive black religion that could be placed alongside Protestantism, Catholicism, and secularism. "Black religion," he said, "is not identical with white Protestantism or any other expression of Euro-American Christianity." Washington, however, was not pleased with the continued existence of black religion, and he placed the blame squarely upon white Christians. He contended that black religion exists only because black people have been excluded from the genuine Christianity of white churches. Further, Washington felt that because blacks were excluded from the faith of white churches, black churches were not genuine Christian churches. And if there are no genuine black Christian churches there can be no genuine black Christian theology. Blacks have only folk religion and folk theology. Washington expressed it this way: "Negro congregations are not churches but religious societies — Religion can choose to worship God as it so pleases. But a church without a theology, the interpretation of the will of God for the faithful, is a contradiction in terms."[3]

Joseph Washington's book was received with enthusiasm in the white community, but it was strongly denounced in the black church community. In fact black theology was created in part to refute Washington's thesis. Black preachers wanted to correct two misconceptions: (1) that black religion was not Christian and therefore had no Christian theology, and (2) that the Christian gospel had nothing to do with the struggle for justice in society.

The third context for black theology was the black power movement. After the march on Washington in August, 1963, the integration theme in the black community began to lose ground to the black national philosophy of Malcolm X. The riots in the ghettos of the U.S. cities were shocking evidence that many blacks agreed with Malcolm's contention that America was not a dream but a nightmare. However, it was not until the summer of 1966, after Malcolm's assassination, that the term *black power* began to be used. The occasion was the continuation of the James Meredith march against fear in Mississippi. This was a march continued by King, Stokely Carmichael, Floyd McKissick, and other civil rights activists after James Meredith was shot during the first part of the march. Stokely Carmichael seized this occasion to sound the black power slogan, and it was heard loud and clear throughout the United States. The rise of black power had a profound effect upon the appearance of black theology. When Carmichael and other black activists separated themselves from King's absolute commitment to nonviolence by proclaiming black power, white church people called upon their black brothers and sisters in the gospel to denounce the black power slogan as un-Christian. But to the surprise of white Christians, black ministers refused to follow the advice. Instead black ministers wrote a black power statement which was published in the *New York Times* on July 31, 1966. The publication of this statement may be regarded as the beginning of the conscious development of a black theology by black ministers. It was in these three contexts—the Civil Rights movement, the publication of Washington's book, and the black power movement—that black theology emerged.

However, it is important not only to proclaim black theology, but to give it theological substance. Many white Christians and almost all white theologians dismiss black theology as nothing but rhetoric. Since white theologians control the seminaries and the university departments of religion, they try to make black people feel that only Europeans (and persons who think like them) can define theology. In order to challenge the white monopoly on the definition of theology, many young black scholars realized that they had to carry the fight to the seminaries and the universities where theology was being written and taught. The first book on black theology was written by me in 1969; it was entitled *Black Theology and Black Power*.[4] The central thesis of the book was the identification of the liberating elements in black power with the Christian gospel. One year later (1970) I authored a second book, *A Black Theology of Liberation*.[5] This book made liberation the organizational center of my theological perspective. I wrote, "Christian theology is a theology of liberation; it is a rational study of the being of God in the world, in the light of an existential situation of an oppressed community struggling for freedom, relating the forces of liberation to the essence of the Gospel which is Jesus Christ."

After my works appeared, other black theologians joined me, supporting my theological project, but also challenging what they regarded as my theological excesses. For example J. Deotis Roberts published a book in 1971 which supported my emphasis on liberation, but which claimed that I overlooked reconciliation as central to the gospel and to black-white relations.[6] A similar position was advocated by Major Jones in his book *Black Awareness: A Theology of Hope*, published in 1971.[7] Other black theologians claimed that I was too dependent on white theology and thus was not sufficiently aware of the African origins of black religion. This position was taken by Cecil Cone in his book *Identity Crises in Black Theology* (published in 1975).[8] This same criticism is found in Gayraud Wilmore's book, *Black Religion and Black Radicalism* (1983).[9]

Even though my perspective on black theology was and continues to be challenged by other black scholars, these scholars support my claim that liberation is the central core of the gospel as found in the scriptures and in the religious history of black Americans. For black theologians the political meaning of liberation was best illustrated in the exodus. And its future meaning (its eschatological meaning) was found in the life, death, and resurrection of Jesus. Nat Turner's slave insurrection and Harriet Tubman's liberation of an estimated three hundred slaves were interpreted to be analogous to the exodus. The slave songs (often called negro spirituals) and the sermons and prayers express the eschatological character of liberation found in the resurrection of Jesus.

Because many black male theologians were reluctant to take up the subject of sexism and others were openly hostile toward it, a black feminist theology has emerged as an open challenge to the patriarchal nature of the current perspectives of black theology. The writings of Jacquelyn Grant and Pauli Murray are examples of this new emerging theology. While the proponents of feminist theology accept the liberation theme of black theology, they reject the narrow limitations of that theme to racism—as if sexism were not an important problem in the black community. Because of the urgency of the problem of sexism, black women have begun to insist on doing theology out of their own experience. Black feminist theology is both a challenge to the sexist orientation of black male theology and a deepening of the struggle against racism.

The challenge for black theology to appreciate a larger definition of liberation also comes from contact with other forms of liberation theology in Africa, Latin America, and Asia. Black theology in South Africa, of course, is a natural ally. Black and Latin American theologies became partners in their identification of the gospel with the liberation of the poor—

although black theology has emphasized racism while Latin American theology has emphasized classism. A similar partnership has taken place with African and Asian theologians regarding the importance of culture in the definition of theology.

In this dialogue with Third World theologians, the striking difference between the theologies of the poor and the theologies of the rich became very clear to us. Dialogue has helped us to move beyond our critique which had been confined to North American racism. African, Asian, and Latin American theologians have enlarged our vision by challenging us to do theology from a global perspective of oppression. These Third World theologians urged us to analyze racism in relation to international capitalism, imperialism, colonialism, world poverty, classism, and sexism.

For the first time black theologians began to consider socialism as an alternative to capitalism. We began to see the connection between the black ghettos in the United States and the poverty in Africa, Asia, and Latin America; between the rise in unemployment among blacks (and other poor people) in the United States and exploitation of Third World peoples; between the racist practices of white churches in North America and Europe and their missionaries in the Third World. These discoveries deeply affected our political and theological vision. And we began to see clearly that we could not do theology in isolation from the struggle of our brothers and sisters in the Third World. As oppressors have banded themselves together in order to keep the poor of the world in poverty, so the world's poor must enter into political and theological solidarity if they expect to create a movement of liberation that is capable of breaking the chains of oppression.

Early in the dialogue, black and Third World theologians realized the importance of building a common movement of liberation. Although we experienced several differences among ourselves, our mutual commitment to do theology in solidarity with the poor held us together. We had too much in common to allow our differences to separate us. Furthermore, it became increasingly apparent that our differences were largely due to a difference in our contexts and to our mutual internalization of the lies that our oppressors had told us about each other. And after over a decade of dialogue within the Ecumenical Association of Third World Theologians, our differences have diminished considerably and our similarities have increased to the extent that we are now engaged in the exciting task of attempting to create a Third World theology of liberation that we all can support.

When asked how we do theology, black and Third World theologians agree that theology is not the first act of the religious community, but rather the second. Although our Latin American brothers and sisters were the first to explicitly use the Marxist concept of praxis (reflective political action), it was already present in all our theologies, and now has been reaffirmed. So the first act, before theologizing, is both a religio-cultural and political commitment on behalf of the poor and powerless people of our world.

Our cultural identity and political commitment are worth more than a thousand textbooks of theology. That is why we do not talk about theology as the first order of business in our association. Rather, our first concern is with the quality of commitment that each of us had made and will make for those about whom and with whom we claim to do theology. We contend that we know what people believe by what they do, and not by what they say in their creeds, conference statements, and theological textbooks. Therefore, praxis comes before theology in any formal sense.

Our reason for making theology arises out of our experiences in the ghettos, the villages, and the churches of the poor in our countries. We do not believe that it is necessary for our people to remain poor. Something must be done about their misery.

Because the starting point of our theologies is defined by a prior affirmation of and political commitment to be in solidarity with the poor, our theologies bear the names that reflect our affirmations and commitments. We call our theologies black, African, Hispanic-American, Asian, red, Latin American, minjung, black-feminist, and a host of other names that sound strange to people whose theological knowledge has been confined to European and white North American theologies. The identities of our theologies are determined by the human and the divine dimensions of reality to which we are attempting to bear witness.

We do not begin our theology with a reflection on divine revelation as if the God of our faith is separate from the suffering of our people. We do not believe that revelation is a deposit of fixed doctrines or an objective word of God that is then applied to the human situation. On the contrary, we contend that there is no truth outside of, or beyond, the concrete historical events in which our peoples are engaged. Truth, therefore, is found in the histories, the cultures, and in the religions of our peoples.

Our focus on social and religio-cultural analysis separates our theology, our theological enterprise, from the abstract theologies of Europe and North America. It also illuminates the reason why praxis, in contrast to orthodoxy (correct doctrine), has become for many of us the criterion for doing theology. Although black and Third World theologians have been accused of reducing theology to ideology by European and North American critics, we contend that the criticism is misplaced. It camouflages the human character of all theologies, particularly the fact that our critics are already doing theology from the perspective of the rich and powerful. Unlike our critics, we do not claim to be neutral in our theology. The enormity of the suffering of our people demands that we choose *for* their liberation and *against* the structures of oppression. We cannot let the people who support the structures of oppression define theology for us. Black theologians identify with the way in which Malcolm X expressed it: "Don't let anybody who's oppressing us ever lay down the ground rules. Don't go by their game, don't play by their rules. Let them know that this is a new game and we've got some new rules."[10]

The dominant theologians in Europe and North America want to retain the current theological rules because they made those rules. And their rules will help keep the world like it is: whites dominating blacks, men dominating women, and the rich nations keeping the poor nations dependent. But we are living in a new world situation and this new situation requires a new way of doing theology. Again I like the way Malcolm X expressed it:

> The time we are living in . . . and . . . are facing now is not an era where one who is oppressed is looking toward the oppressor to give him some system or form of logic or reason. What is logical to the oppressor isn't logical to the oppressed, and what is reason to the oppressor isn't reason to the oppressed. The black people in this country are beginning to realize that what sounds reasonable to those who exploit us doesn't sound reasonable to us. There just has to be a new system of reason and logic devised by us who are on the bottom, if we want some results in this struggle that is called the "Negro Revolution."[11]

In the Ecumenical Association of Third World Theologians, black and Third World theologians have been attempting to develop a new way of making theology. In contrast to the dominant theologies of Europe and North America that are largely defined by their responses to the European Enlightenment and the problem of the unbeliever that arose from it, our theological enterprise focuses on Europe's and North America's invasion of the continents of Asia, Africa, and Latin America, inaugurating the slave trade, colonization, and neocolonialism.

Our primary theological question, therefore, is not how we can believe in God in view of modern Western confidence in science, reason, and technology, a confidence which seems to exclude the necessity of faith. Rather, our primary theological question and problem arise from the encounter with God in the experience and misery of the poor. How can we speak about Jesus' death on the cross without first speaking about the death of poor people? How can the poor of our country achieve worth as human beings in a world that has attempted to destroy our cultures and our religions?

The chief issue of our theologies is the problem of the nonperson, the poor person. That is why our partners in the universities are not the philosophers, metaphysicians, and other socially disinterested intellectuals. Rather we are interested in talking with social scientists and political activists who are concerned about and engulfed in the struggle for the liberation of the poor.

Black and Third World theologians' concerns about the oppressed person forced us to establish links with the communities of the poor. In the ecclesial church-life of these communities we have seen something more than a routine gathering of like-minded people. In their worship-life is revealed a knowledge of themselves that cannot be destroyed by the structures that oppress them. The liberating character of their spirituality can be seen in the way that their faith in God evolves out of their cultural and political aspirations. It can be observed in the basic communities of Latin America, the black and Hispanic churches of North America, the indigenous churches and traditional religions of Africa, and in the religious life of Asia. In their worship, the God of grace and of judgment meets poor people and transforms them from nobodies to somebodies and bestows upon them the power and the courage to struggle for justice and peace.

Worship, therefore, is not primarily an expression of the individual's private relationship to God. Rather it is a community happening—an eschatological invasion of God into the gathered community of victims, empowering them with the "divine Spirit from on high" to "keep on keeping on" even though the odds might be against them. In the collective presence of the poor at worship, God re-creates them as the liberated community who must now bring freedom to the oppressed of the land. Black and Third World theologies are being created out of the poor people's church and religious life as these poor people seek to interpret the God encountered in their religio-cultural and political struggle to overcome European and U.S. domination. Where do we go from here? The spirituality of black churches, creatively expressed in worship, and the black theology emerging from it have been taken to many parts of the globe, strengthening the determination of the oppressed "to keep their faith in the God of justice," whose righteousness is always found in the liberation of the oppressed.

In black religion, faith in the God of justice and the human struggle to implement it belong together and cannot be separated without both of them losing their authenticity. The faith of African Americans is deeply embedded in our African and slave past. It has sustained our identity amid wretched circumstances, extending our spiritual and political vision far beyond the alternatives provided by whites who enslaved us.

Since 1955 the misery of the poor has increased to massive proportions in a world of plenty for a few. Do not the widening gap between the rich and the poor and the real possibility of nuclear annihilation mean that we need to reevaluate our definition of freedom and the methods we have used to work for it? Is not a deeper analysis of our struggle required if we expect to achieve liberation for the poor and survival for all? When I evaluate the historical development of black churches and the Civil Rights movement, as well as the theological and political reflection connected with them, I think we blacks have a right to say that they have brought us "a mighty long way." But I am not sure that they will be able to take us much farther if they do not lead to radical changes in our analysis of black freedom and the methods we have used in our attempts to implement it.

We need a vision of freedom that includes the whole of the inhabited earth and not just black North America, a vision enabling us to analyze the causes of world poverty and sickness, monopoly capitalism and antidemocratic socialism, opium in Christianity and other religions among the oppressed, racism and sexism, and the irresolute will to eliminate these evils. We must analyze these complex and deeply rooted evils in such a manner that the black struggle and faith can be seen expressing solidarity with the struggle and faiths of others who are fighting for the liberation of the wretched of the earth.

Although I do not believe that blacks will achieve full freedom through the election process, I do want to emphasize that political action is a necessary step toward freedom. Unless the masses assume responsibility by voting, they will not be able to affect the political process. The freedom of our children and of others in the world is dependent upon our political engagement in the struggles for justice. To be a Christian is to love one's neighbor, and that means making a political commitment to make the world a habitable place for one's neighbor. Christians are called not only to pray for justice, but to become actively involved in establishing it.

Black churches have a special responsibility for the world because we claim that Christ died to redeem it. When others give up in despair, feeling overwhelmed by the enormity of the evil that engulfs us, black churches continue to preach hope, because "when a people has no vision, it perishes."

Yet how can we sing "Glory Hallelujah" when our people's blood is flowing in the streets and prisons of this nation? What do we blacks have to shout about when our families are being broken and crushed by political, social, and economic forces so complex that most of us do not know what to do to resist them? This is the paradox that makes faith necessary if we are to survive the oppression, and analysis necessary if we are to overcome it. To pray for justice without analyzing the causes of injustice is to turn religion into an opium of the people. The time has come for the black church to take a critical look at its vision with the intent of radically changing its priorities. We need to dream about radically new possibilities for the future or our people will perish, not only of racism and capitalism, but also of our own neglect and illusions.

The vision of a new social order should not be taken from any one person. The vision should be the result of a group of committed persons whose love for freedom is deep and broad enough to embrace and consider many viewpoints. This would include a cross section of the total black community, including community grassroots activists and scholars, scientists and politicians, artists and lawyers, teachers and preachers, men and women, youth and senior citizens, Christians and non-Christians. The chief requirement should be commitment to the freedom of all. The initiative for the new vision and the creation of a team to help should come from the black church. The financial resources for the program must come from the black community. No oppressed people has ever had its freedom given as a gift or financed by its oppressor. Freedom must be taken, and it involves risk, struggle, and a commitment to stand against those who deny it. I should like to make a few suggestions regarding some elements in the new vision of freedom.

1. The new vision will need to include an emphasis on black unity through an affirmation of the value of black history and culture. Whatever vision of the new black future is created, it must be derived from and include at its center black love of self—it must include the history and culture of an African people in white America.

2. After black unity has been achieved, the new vision will need to include the best in the integrationist tradition as articulated by Martin Luther King, Jr., in his dream of the "beloved community." Freedom will come only through the building of a society that respects the humanity of all, including whites.

3. The vision of the new social order must be antisexist. Half the members of the team must be women with diverse dimensions of a feminist consciousness. A truly liberated social order cannot have men dominating women.

4. The new social order should be democratic and socialist, including a Marxist critique of monopoly capitalism. The socialist vision must be democratic, protective of individual liberties, and must involve all persons in the community in its creation.

5. The new black perspective must be a global vision that includes the struggles of the poor in the Third World. There will be no freedom for anybody until all are set free.

6. Any new vision of a just social order must affirm the best in black religion and embrace the creative elements in the poor who are struggling for freedom throughout the globe.

The life and thought of Martin Luther King, Jr., and Malcolm X are the best examples in the black community of the creative role that religion can play in the transformation of society. They combined their religious vision with their political commitment, but they refused to allow either their politics or their faith to separate them from other persons struggling for justice even though those persons held different views.

The creation of a just social order must be grounded in the hopes that have been engendered by the poor as they have emerged from their encounter with God in their fight for freedom. Thus, the prereflective visions of the poor as defined by their political struggles and as celebrated in their religious life must be taken seriously.

Although I am a Christian theologian, I contend that a just social order must be accountable to not one but many religious visions. If we are going to create a society that is responsive to the humanity of all, then we must not view one religious faith as absolute. Ultimate reality, to which all things are subject, is too mysterious to be exclusively limited to one people's view of God. Any creation of a just social order must take into account that God has been known and experienced in many different ways. Because we have an imperfect grasp of divine reality, we must not regard our limited vision as absolute. Today such a view must be firmly rejected. God's truth comes in many colors and is revealed in many cultures, histories, and unexpected places. Because, however, I am a Christian whose theological and political perspective has been defined by the black church tradition, my view of a just social order cannot be understood apart from my faith in God's liberating presence in Jesus. The importance of God and Jesus for black Christians is best explained when we consider the preponderance of suffering in black life and blacks' attempts to affirm their humanity in spite of it. We have survived slave ships, auction blocks, and chronic unemployment because the God of faith has bestowed upon us an identity that cannot be destroyed by white oppressors. No matter what trials and tribulations blacks encounter, we refuse to let despair define our humanity. We simply believe that "God can make a way out of no way." The eschatological hope in black faith is born of struggle here and now because black Christians refuse to allow oppressors to define who we are.

4

"I Am a Black Woman" (excerpt)

MARI EVANS

I am a black woman
the music of my song
some sweet arpeggio of tears
is written in a minor key
and I
can be heard humming in the night
can be heard
                humming
in the night.

Womanist Theology:
Black Women's Voices

DELORES S. WILLIAMS

Daughter: Mama, why are we brown, pink, and yellow, and our cousins are white, beige, and black?
Mother: Well, you know the colored race is just like a flower garden, with every color flower represented.

Daughter: Mama, I'm walking to Canada and I'm taking you and a bunch of slaves with me.
Mother: It wouldn't be the first time.

In these two conversational exchanges, Pulitzer Prize-winning novelist Alice Walker begins to show us what she means by the concept "womanist." The concept is presented in Walker's *In Search of Our Mother's Gardens*, and many women in church and society have appropriated it as a way of affirming themselves as *black* while simultaneously owning their connection with feminism and with the African-American community, male and female. The concept of womanist allows women to claim their roots in black history, religion, and culture.

What then is a womanist? Her origins are in the black folk expression "You acting womanish," meaning, according to Walker, "wanting to know more and in greater depth than is good for one . . . outrageous, audacious, courageous and willful behavior." A womanist is also "responsible, in charge, serious." She can walk to Canada and take others with her. She loves, she is committed, she is a universalist by temperament.

Her universality includes loving men and women, sexually or nonsexually. She loves music, dance, the Spirit, food and roundness, struggle, and she loves herself. "Regardless."

Walker insists that a womanist is also "committed to survival and wholeness of entire people, male and female." She is no separatist, "except for health." A womanist is a black feminist or a feminist of color. Or as Walker says, "Womanist is to feminist as purple to lavender."

Womanist theology, a vision in its infancy, is emerging among African-

62

American Christian women. Ultimately many sources—biblical, theological, ecclesiastical, social, anthropological, and economic—will inform the development of this theology, as will material from other religious traditions. As a contribution to this process, I will demonstrate how Walker's concept of womanist provides some significant clues for the work of womanist theologians. I will then focus on method and God-content in womanist theology. This contribution belongs to the work of prolegomena—prefatory remarks, introductory observations intended to be suggestive and not conclusive.

CODES AND CONTENTS

In her definition, Walker provides significant clues for the development of womanist theology. Her concept contains what black feminist scholar Bell Hooks in *Feminist Theory from Margin to Center* identifies as cultural codes. These are words, beliefs, and behavioral patterns of a people that must be deciphered before meaningful communication can happen cross-culturally. Walker's codes are female-centered and they point beyond themselves to conditions, events, meanings, and values that have crystallized in the African-American community *around women's activity* and formed traditions.

A paramount example is mother-daughter advice. Black mothers have passed on wisdom for survival—in the white world, in the black community, and with men—for as long as anyone can remember. Female slave narratives, folk tales, and some contemporary black poetry and prose reflect this tradition. Some of it is collected in "Old Sister's Advice to Her Daughters," in *The Book of Negro Folklore*, edited by Langston Hughes and Arna Bontemps.

Walker's allusion to skin color points to a historic tradition of tension between black women over the matter of some black men's preference for light-skinned women. Her reference to black women's love of food and roundness points to customs of female care in the black community (including the church) associated with hospitality and nurture.

These cultural codes and their corresponding traditions are valuable resources for indicating and validating the kind of data upon which womanist theologians can reflect as they bring black women's social, religious, and cultural experience into the discourse of theology, ethics, and biblical and religious studies. Female slave narratives, imaginative literature by black women, autobiographies, the work by black women in academic disciplines, and the testimonies of black church women will be authoritative sources for womanist theologians.

Walker situates her understanding of a womanist in the context of non-bourgeois black folk culture. The literature of this culture has traditionally reflected more egalitarian relations between men and women, much less rigidity in male-female roles, and more respect for female intelligence and ingenuity than is found in bourgeois culture.

The black folk are poor. Less individualistic than those who are better off, they have, for generations, practiced various forms of economic sharing. For example, immediately after emancipation, mutual aid societies pooled the resources of black folk to help pay for funerals and other daily expenses. *The Book of Negro Folklore* describes the practice of rent parties, which flourished during the depression. The black folk stress togetherness and a closer connection with nature. They respect knowledge gained through lived experience monitored by elders who differ profoundly in social class and worldview from the teachers and education encountered in American academic institutions. Walker's choice of context suggests that womanist theology can establish its lines of continuity in the black community with nonbourgeois traditions less sexist than the black power and black nationalist traditions.

In this folk context, some of the black female-centered cultural codes in Walker's definition (e.g., "Mama, I'm walking to Canada and I'm taking you and a bunch of slaves with me") point to folk heroines like Harriet Tubman, whose liberation activity earned her the name "Moses" of her people. This allusion to Tubman directs womanist memory to a liberation tradition in black history in which women took the lead, acting as catalysts for the community's revolutionary action and for social change. Retrieving this often hidden or diminished female tradition of catalytic action is an important task for womanist theologians and ethicists. Their research may well reveal that female models of authority have been absolutely essential for every struggle in the black community and for building and maintaining the community's institutions.

FREEDOM FIGHTERS

The womanist theologians must search for the voices, actions, opinions, experience, and faith of women whose names sometimes slip into the male-centered rendering of black history, but whose actual stories remain remote. This search can lead to such little-known freedom fighters as Milla Granson, whose courageous work on a Mississippi plantation broadens our knowledge of the variety of strategies black people have used to obtain freedom. According to scholar Sylvia Dannett, in *Profiles in Negro Womanhood*:

Milla Granson, a slave, conducted a midnight school for several years. She had been taught to read and write by her former master in Kentucky ... and in her little school hundreds of slaves benefited from her learning. ... After laboring all day for their master, the slaves would creep stealthily to Milla's "schoolroom" (a little cabin in a back alley). ... The doors and windows ... had to be kept tightly sealed to avoid discovery. Each class was composed of twelve pupils and when Milla had brought them up to the extent of her ability, she "graduated" them and took in a dozen more. Through this means she graduated hundreds of slaves. Many of whom she taught to write a legible hand [forged] their own passes and set out for Canada.

Women like Tubman and Granson used subtle and silent strategies to liberate themselves and large numbers of black people. By uncovering as much as possible about such female liberation, the womanist begins to understand the relation of black history to the contemporary folk expression: "If Rosa Parks had not sat down, Martin King would not have stood up."

While she celebrates and *emphasizes* black women's culture and way of being in the world, Walker simultaneously affirms black women's historic connection with men through love and through shared struggle for survival and for a productive quality of life (e.g., "wholeness"). This suggests that two of the principal concerns of womanist theology should be survival and the building and maintenance of community. The goal of this community-building is, of course, to establish a positive quality of life — economic, spiritual, educational — for black women, men, and children. Walker's understanding of a womanist as "not a separatist" ("except for health"), however, reminds the Christian womanist theologian that her concern for the building and maintenance of community must *ultimately* extend to the entire Christian community and beyond that to the larger human community.

Yet womanist consciousness is also informed by women's determination to love themselves. "Regardless." This translates into an admonition to black women to avoid the self-destruction of bearing a disproportionately large burden in the work of building and maintaining community. Walker suggests that women can avoid this trap by connecting with women's communities concerned about women's rights and well-being. Her identification of a womanist as also a feminist joins black women with their feminist heritage extending back into the nineteenth century in the work of black feminists like Sojourner Truth, Frances W. Harper, and Mary Church Terrell.

In making the feminist-womanist connection, however, Walker proceeds with great caution. While affirming an organic relationship between womanists and feminists, she also declares a deep shade of difference between them ("Womanist is to feminist as purple to lavender"). This gives womanist scholars the freedom to explore the particularities of black women's history and culture without being guided by what white feminists have already identified as women's issues.

But womanist consciousness directs black women away from the negative divisions prohibiting community-building among women. The womanist loves other women sexually and nonsexually. Therefore, respect for sexual preferences is one of the marks of womanist community. According to Walker, homophobia has no place. Nor does "colorism" (i.e., "yella" and half-white black people valued more in the black world than black-skinned people), which often separates black women from each other. Rather, Walker's womanist claim is that color variety is the substance of universality. Color, like birth and death, is common to all people. Like the navel, it is a badge of humanity connecting people with people. Two other distinctions are prohibited in Walker's womanist thinking. Class hierarchy does not dwell among women who "love struggle, love the Folks ... are committed to the survival and wholeness of an entire people." Nor do women compete for male attention when they "appreciate and prefer female culture ... [and] value ... women's emotional flexibility ... and women's strength."

The intimations about community provided by Walker's definition suggest no genuine community-building is possible when men are excluded (except when women's health is at stake). Neither can it occur when black women's self-love, culture, and love for each other are not affirmed and are not considered vital for the community's self-understanding. And it is thwarted if black women are expected to bear "the lion's share" of the work and to sacrifice their well-being for the good of the group.

Yet, for the womanist, mothering and nurturing are vitally important. Walker's womanist reality begins with mothers relating to their children and is characterized by black women (not necessarily bearers of children) nurturing great numbers of black people in the liberation struggle (e.g., Harriet Tubman). Womanist emphasis upon the value of mothering and nurturing is consistent with the testimony of many black women. The poet Carolyn Rogers speaks of her mother as the great black bridge that brought her over. Walker dedicates her novel *The Third Life of Grange Copeland* to her mother "who made a way out of no way." As a child in the black church, I heard women (and men) give thanks to God for their mothers "who stayed behind and pulled the wagon over the long haul."

It seems, then, that the clues about community from Walker's definition of a womanist suggest that the mothering and nurturing dimension of African-American history can provide resources for shaping criteria to measure the quality of justice in the community. These criteria could be used to assure female-male equity in the presentation of the community's models of authority. They could also gauge the community's division of labor with regard to survival tasks necessary for building and maintaining community.

WOMANIST THEOLOGY AND METHOD

Womanist theology is already beginning to define the categories and methods needed to develop along lines consistent with the sources of that theology. Christian womanist theological methodology needs to be informed by at least four elements: (1) a multidialogical intent, (2) a liturgical intent, (3) a didactic intent, and (4) a commitment both to reasons *and* to the validity of female imagery and metaphorical language in the construction of theological statements.

A multidialogical intent will allow Christian womanist theologians to advocate and participate in dialogue and action with *many* diverse social, political, and religious communities concerned about human survival and a productive quality of life for the oppressed. The genocide of cultures and peoples (which has often been instigated and accomplished by Western white Christian groups or governments) and the nuclear threat of omnicide mandate womanist participation in such dialogue/action. But in this dialogue/action the womanist should also keep her speech and action focused upon the slow genocide of poor black women, children, and men by exploitative systems denying them productive jobs, education, health care, and living space. Multidialogical activity may, like a jazz symphony, communicate some of its most important messages in what the harmony-driven conventional ear hears as discord, as disruption of the harmony in both the black American and white American social, political, and religious status quo.

If womanist theological method is informed by a liturgical intent, then womanist theology will be relevant to (and will reflect) the thought, worship, and action of the black church. But a liturgical intent will also allow womanist theology to challenge the thought/worship/action of the black church with the discordant and prophetic messages emerging from womanist participation in multidialogics. This means that womanist theology will consciously impact *critically* upon the foundations of liturgy, challenging the church to use justice principles to select the sources that will shape the content of liturgy. The question must be asked: How does this source portray blackness/darkness, women, and economic justice for nonruling-class people? A negative portrayal will demand omission of the source or its radical reformation by the black church. The Bible, a major source in black church liturgy, must also be subjected to the scrutiny of justice principles.

A didactic intent in womanist theological method assigns a teaching function to theology. Womanist theology should teach Christians new insights about moral life based on ethics supporting justice for women, survival, and a productive quality of life for poor women, children, and men. This means that the womanist theologian must give authoritative status to black folk wisdom (e.g., Brer Rabbit literature) and to black women's moral wisdom (expressed in their literature) when she responds to the question, How ought the Christian to live in the world? Certainly tensions may exist between the moral teachings derived from these sources and the moral teachings about obedience, love, and humility that have usually buttressed presuppositions about living the Christian life. Nevertheless, womanist theology, in its didactic intent, must teach the church the different ways God reveals prophetic word and action for Christian living.

These intents, informing theological method, can yield a theological language whose foundation depends as much upon its imagistic content as upon reason. The language can be rich in female imagery, metaphor, and story. For the black church, this kind of theological language may be quite useful, since the language of the black religious experience abounds in images and metaphors. Clifton Johnson's collection of black conversion experiences, *God Struck Me Dead*, illustrates this point.

The appropriateness of womanist theological language will ultimately reside in its ability to bring black women's history, culture, and religious experience into the interpretive circle of Christian theology and into the liturgical life of the church. Womanist theological language must, in this sense, be an instrument for social and theological change in church and society.

WHO DO YOU SAY GOD IS?

Regardless of one's hopes about intentionality and womanist theological method, questions must be raised about the God-content of the theology. Walker's mention of the black womanist's love of the Spirit is a true reflection of the great respect African-American women have always shown for the presence and work of the Spirit. In the black church, women (and men) often judge the effectiveness of the worship service not on the scholarly content of the sermon or on the ritual or on orderly process. Rather, worship has been effective if "the Spirit was high," i.e., if the Spirit was actively and obviously present in a balanced blend of prayer, cadenced word (the sermon), and syncopated music ministering to the pain of the people.

The importance of this emphasis upon the Spirit is that it allows Christian womanist theologians, in their use of the Bible, to identify and reflect upon those biblical stories in which poor, oppressed women had a special encounter with divine emissaries of God, like the Spirit. In the Hebrew Testament, Hagar's story is most illustrative and relevant to African-American women's experience of bondage, of African heritage, of encounter with God/emissary in the midst of fierce survival struggles. Kate Cannon, among a number of black female preachers and ethicists, urges black Christian women to regard themselves as Hagar's sisters.

In relation to the Christian Testament, the Christian womanist theologian can refocus the salvation story so that it emphasizes the beginning of revelation with the Spirit mounting Mary, a woman of the poor: "the Holy Spirit shall come upon thee, and the power of the Highest shall overshadow thee ... " (Luke 1:35). Such an interpretation of revelation has roots in the nineteenth century black abolitionist and feminist Sojourner Truth. Posing an important question and response, she refuted a white preacher's claim that women could not have rights equal to men's because Christ was not a woman. Truth asked, "Whar did your Christ come from? ... From God and a woman! Man had nothin' to do wid Him!" This suggests that womanist theology could eventually speak of God in a well-developed theology of the Spirit. The sources for this theology are many. Harriet Tubman often "went into the Spirit" before her liberation missions and claimed her strength for liberation activity came from this way of meeting God. Womanist theology has grounds for shaping a theology of the Spirit informed by black women's political action.

Christian womanist responses to the question, Who do you say God is? will be influenced by these many sources. Walker's way of connecting womanists with the Spirit is only one clue. The integrity of black church women's faith, their love of Jesus, their commitment to life, love, family, and politics will also yield vital clues. And other theological voices (black liberationist, feminist, Islamic, Asian, Hispanic, African, Jewish, and Western-white-male-traditional) will provide insights relevant for the construction of the God-content of womanist theology.

Each womanist theologian will add her own special accent to the understandings of God emerging from womanist theology. But if one needs a final image to describe women coming together to shape the enterprise, Bess B. Johnson in *God's Fierce Whimsy* offers an appropriate one. Describing the difference between the play of male and female children in the black community where she developed, Johnson says:

> The boys in the neighborhood had this game with rope . . . tug-o'-war . . . till finally some side would jerk the rope away from the others, who'd fall down. . . . Girls . . . weren't allowed to play with them in this tug-o'-war; so we figured out how to make our own rope — out of . . . little dandelions. You just keep adding them, one to another, and you can go on and on. . . . Anybody, even the boys, could join us. . . . The whole purpose of our game was to create this dandelion chain — that was it. And we'd keep going, creating till our mamas called us home.

Like Johnson's dandelion chain, womanist theological vision will grow as black women come together and connect piece with piece. Between the process of creating and the sense of calling, womanist theology will one day present itself in full array, reflecting the Divine Spirit that connects us all.

5

"A Totem Dance as Seen by Raven"

ARONIAWENRATE/PETER BLUE CLOUD

(for Ranoies)

Slowly and gently
    foot to foot balanced
and awkward in beauty
    the child dances
And grandfather taps,
    delicately taps
the drum and his voice is very, very low,
    and a song is a promise
    given a people
in the ancient days of tomorrow

And grandmother's stiff
    and swollen fingers
weave cedar and fern and spruce
    and occasionally
    in a far away closeness
her eyes seek the dancing child.

Vision and Community:
A Native-American Voice

VINE DELORIA, JR.

In the last decade liberation theology has moved considerably beyond its original Christian moorings to become an important perspective in addressing the problems of human societies. Even as social, economic, and political institutions tighten their grip on the lives of people and military adventurism runs rampant, there is an identifiable current of spiritual energy flowing through the events and attitudes of our times. Ecological concerns, peace protests, the movement back to small communities, shamanism, interreligious dialogues, and the widespread perception of the common humanity of our diverse peoples are but elements of an emerging vision of wholeness that promises to deliver us from the particularities of history and to present us with a truly planetary view of our common destiny.

In discussing the impact of liberation theology on the American Indian community, it is necessary to see the four segments of this community in its contemporary expression. There are, unfortunately, a good many American Indians who have accepted, without criticism, the premises of materialistic capitalism and who, in spite of the best efforts of the elders and traditional leaders, insist upon salvation through intercourse with transnational corporations and commodities markets. Although they do not constitute a majority in any Indian tribe, these people are favored by the federal government and their demands are accepted as the valid yearnings of the American Indian community for economic freedom. Their basic activity, the exploitation of the reservation's natural and human resources as a means of generating capital for projects, is anathema to the majority of Indians, and consequently every project they undertake is bitterly and sometimes violently opposed by the majority of the people. Unless and until these Indians forsake the enticements of materialistic capitalism, the horn-of-plenty of the consumer society, ultimate American Indian liberation will be a long time coming.

American Indians have been converted, devoted, and practicing Christians for many generations. A good estimate of the number of Indian Christians is difficult to make because of the great and persistent fluidity of the

Indian population. Indians living in the urban areas may not attend church regularly or participate in the various outreach programs established by the major Christian denominations. But most certainly these people return to their old reservation churches for the important holidays and look upon themselves as members of century-old missions and parishes. These Indians are more directly related in a fundamental kind of liberation theology. For most of this century Indian churches and chapels have been classified as missions because they have not had sufficient income to be self-supporting in the same manner as prosperous non-Indian parishes. Mission, however, connotes a status in which the immediate human environment is hostile to the church or overwhelmingly lethargic. Indian missions are theologically sound; they represent generations of faithful church attendance; and it galls Indian Christians considerably to be seen as unchurched and needing conversion simply because they lack large parish budgets.

In the last decade Indian clergy and dedicated and active laypeople have made great strides in overcoming this image which has been unfairly thrust upon them by bookkeeping church bureaucrats. New programs for clergy recruitment and retention have been initiated and the Native American Theological Association, although now financially depleted, has worked to create additional opportunities for Indians in Christian seminaries. Charles Cook Theological School—once a Bible-based coloring-book program of enhancement for the native religious leaders who were presumed to be serving at the convenience of the white missionary—has expanded its programs and added sophisticated theological content to its activities. It now serves as a focal point for intellectual adventures of Native Americans wishing to reach beyond the traditional confines of the institutional church programs and engage in dialogue with other people dealing with pressing social, political, and religious issues.

Liberation, for this group of American Indians, is a desperate effort to gain sufficient footholds within the institutional church so that (1) Indian program budgets will not be destroyed in the annual reshuffling that the major Protestant denominations seem to enjoy, and (2) the heritage of American Indians in the spiritual realm will be respected and understood by non-Indian Christians. For these people, freedom and liberation must be seen based in respect. They have no plans for moving outside the institutional ecclesiastical framework and don't seem to understand that liberation from the clutches of non-Indian ecclesiastical bureaucrats inevitably requires them to withdraw from the major denominations and create a Native American Christian church in which both administrative policies and theological content reflect the Indian traditions and experiences.

An equally devoted group of American Indians practice the old ways, and their numbers are probably roughly similar to those of the committed Indian Christians. The twentieth century has seen a massive erosion of traditional tribal religions because of substantial outmigration from the reservation communities and the extensive importation of the electronic media in the form of telephones, radios, television, and videocassette recorders. With outmigration, kinship responsibilities have declined precipitously as missing relatives make it necessary for people to substitute other relatives in roles and functions which they would not otherwise undertake. The electronic entertainment media have become surrogate parents and grandparents and consequently it has become increasingly difficult to pass down the oral traditions of the tribe to the proper people and in the properly respectful context.

In many ways the practice of traditional religion today is somewhat akin to the practice of Christianity, being available to meet life crises and to provide the colorful context for social events, but not dominating the day-to-day life of the people in the communities. In the summertime today many reservations are in a state of constant flux as competing medicine men sponsor their own Sun Dances or Sweat Lodges or Sings. Concern for the continuing well-being of the community or tribe is thus expressed in a situation in which the participants withdraw from the community rather than represent it, thus individualizing a religious tradition that had its most powerful influence in its ability to synthesize diverse feelings, beliefs, and practices.

This segment of the Indian community is showing amazing strength in some obscure places in the United States and is attracting the younger people. The chief characteristic of this strength is the voluntary withdrawal from tribal politics, educational programs, and secular activities and the effort to live on a subsistence basis away from the confusion and disorder that mark the modern agency settlements. Rigorous traditionalism, therefore, is a threat not simply to organized Christian efforts to extend the influence of reservation churches but to the programmatic schemes of the materialistic capitalist Indians who see the reservation primarily as a resource to be exploited. Unfortunately many of the people who have been adopting this mode of life have already been through years of alcoholism, unemployment, and sometimes crime of various kinds. There is a real question, therefore, whether the old traditionalism has a message for young people embarked on the road of personal and professional dissolution or whether it can serve only as a spiritual rescue mission for people who have no other place to turn.

The last identifiable group of Indians, considerably smaller in number than any of the groups already discussed, are those people who have experienced traditional tribal religion to some degree, who have significant knowledge of and experiences with the white people's world, and who now insist that they have been commissioned to bring the tribal religions to the aid and assistance of the non-Indian. As a rule these people live and work far from their own reservations where they would be severely chastised by people for commercialization of tribal rituals. They form a reasonably close network of people who travel the conference and psychological workshop circuit performing for whoever is willing and able to pay the sometimes exorbitant entrance fees.

This group is very interesting. Some of the practitioners are unquestionably fraudulent and their message can be found in any of the popular books on Indian religion such as *Black Elk Speaks* or *Book of the Hopi*. To a white populace yearning for some kind of religious experience it is enough that they speak kindly and administer a message of universal fellowship during a friendly ceremonial occasion. Few people have any extensive knowledge of the ways of any tribal religion and so the ceremonies used by these practitioners, which would be instantly discredited within the reservation context, are taken as real expressions of religious piety by their followers. But it cannot be denied that on many occasions what these people have done has helped the people they have served. There is sufficient evidence that some kind of religious energy is present in these modernized versions of tribal ritual so that the movement cannot be discredited on the basis of its commercialism alone.

It is in the objective vision possessed by this last group of Indians that the importance of the American Indian contribution to liberation theology can be found. Obviously the materialistic capitalists possess only the idea of accumulating wealth and power, and their view—for it can hardly be called a vision—of reality is hardly an improvement on the speculations of English political and economic thinkers of the eighteenth century. Indian Christians also lack a unifying vision; basically they attempt to fit themselves into a two-thousand-year-old paradigm of salvation which has little relevance to the longstanding tribal traditions. The purist reservation traditions are bound in the same way, using the old images and visions as a framework within which present realities can be judged. While there is considerably more power and familiarity in these old visions, nevertheless there is very little in them that addresses the modern social and physical context in which people live. And so we are left with the vision of the new Indian missionaries/entrepreneurs, partly by default, partly by the emphasis on outreach.

The new vision is not without its faults and, like other things of the Spirit, is hardly predictable. But an examination of its positive aspects is necessary before its negative attributes can be considered. First, within this context the vision is one of a unified and *experiencing* humanity. We must emphasize the element of experience because the philosophical message of the Indians who participate in the workshop network is as much a demand for new ceremonial and ritual participation as it is an explanation of the basis for the experiences. So the justification for sharing some of the tribal ceremonies and philosophies is that these beliefs and practices have a universal applicability and the practitioners have a divine commission to share them.

The positive second dimension is the emphasis placed upon the living nature of the universe. This belief is solidly tribal in origin but has been given an added value because it is now being connected to the beliefs of other traditions and to the findings of modern science. In this respect the modern shamanism teaches its adherents to develop once again an understanding of the animals and to cultivate relationships with them. Primarily this is now accomplished by a variation of Jungian active imagination, but within the Indian context. People who would otherwise have a reverence for birds and other animals, except for their lack of familiarity with the natural world, come to see that in the most profound sense humankind cannot live alone. Not only do humans need a companion and community but they also need the fellowship, help, and sense of community of all living things. Surprisingly this idea is strikingly powerful when it is experienced in ceremonies and made concrete in people's lives.

The third point of positive stature in the Indian missionary thrust is a corollary of the second point but must be stressed in this context because it carries with it a call to action that makes it a unique experience in itself. Companionship, in the religious sense, is stressed by these outgoing religious representatives so that people following their directions find themselves dealing with higher and/or different spiritual personalities in both a healing and personal-vocational sense. In the old traditional way of handling these experiences there was an alliance between the Vision Quest participants and higher spiritual personalities, but this kind of alliance was generally restricted to those who had successfully endured the ordeal and for whom the spirits had shown pity. The experiences of people today are not nearly as powerful as they were in the old days, but they are more precisely tuned to the needs of average persons. It helps them deal with the many minor personal vocational and ethical choices which, taken together, make up the consistency of human social life. It is almost as if the spiritual energies inherent in the American Indian tribal universe were deliberately expanding, losing some of the potency they enjoyed in the restricted traditional context, but in turn providing spiritual guidance for an increasingly numerous group of people.

In contrast to these positive aspects of the modern effort to extend the influence and practice of traditional tribal religions into the non-Indian world, there are a number of negative things that can be identified and which, unless they are corrected, can abort this kind of spiritual expansion and reduce it to simply another American fad, a fate which too many spiritual and artistic energies suffer in our society. Most important in this respect is that these experiences, while helpful to most people attending the workshops and conferences, are not held in or responsible to any identifiable community. A network is not a community — it is simply an elongated set of connections held together by common interests or experiences. A network can easily become a set of highly charged spiritual dominoes unless it finds a center, becomes sedentary and indigenous, and begins to exert a constant influence on a group of people whose lives and actions are thereby changed for the better. Here we need not so much institutionalization as we need to find a means of stabilizing religious experiences within a definite geographical context so that as people accumulate spiritual insights and powers, they can have a community in which these powers can be manifested. Community is essential because visions are meant for communities, not for individuals although it is the special individual who, on behalf of the community, undertakes to receive divine instructions for the community.

The second danger is that as people gain in spiritual understanding they run the danger of misusing what they have received in the constant effort to spread the word of the realities they have experienced. Many of the Indian practitioners who tread the workshop network today are very close to falling into this trap. Surveying the progress and accomplishments of the ten most popular and respected of the Indians who work the non-Indian social networks will show that there is virtually no individual spiritual progress. The feats which they are able to accomplish are basically those gifts which first enabled them to gain a measure of respect and a following in the non-Indian world. Thus while there is progress in bringing the substance of tribal religious experiences to non-Indians, the workshops, Sun Dances, and Sweat Lodges are becoming something akin to the Christian Mass. These presentations on the non-Indian circuit are not only repetitious but lack potential to probe spiritual realities at any increasing depth of experience or understanding.

The traditional religious revelation of the tribes was very people-specific. That is to say, tribes held their religious secrets very firmly to themselves because the nature of the original revelation required the people to follow certain paths, to act in certain ways, and to fulfill a specific covenant with higher powers. Unlike Jews and Christians, who have interpreted their religious mission in terms of absolute divine commissions to oppose other religious traditions, regardless of value or content, the tribal-specific revelations did not spawn religious intolerance. Rather the Indians rigorously followed the universal admonition to remove the mote from their own eyes before they arrogated to themselves the power to correct their neighbors' practices and beliefs. There is not one single instance of wars or conflicts between or among American Indian tribes, or between Indians and non-Indians, which had as its basis the differences in religious practices or beliefs.

Given this tradition, there is a real concern among the reservation traditionals of the impact and meaning of spreading the tribal teachings to anyone who has a spiritual or emotional need. The belief has always been that the Great Spirit and/or the higher spirits are also watching others and they will provide the proper religious insights and knowledge to others. Therefore it behooves Indians to obey the teachings of their own traditions and hold them close. If they were meant for other people, the other people would have them. Such thinking has prevented most tribes from engaging in religious imperialism, and the humility underlying this attitude is admirable. But what happens today when individuals of the various tribes spend their time on the lecture-workshop-conference circuit indiscriminately instructing non-Indians and non-tribal members in a variety of beliefs, some giving simple homilies and others offering deep and profound truths? Will not this kind of behavior, which in traditional terms is utmost sacrilege, ultimately call down the wrath of the spirits on the tribe? These concerns are real and pressing for many American Indians and there is no easy or certain answer to them.

The present situation of American Indians speaks directly to the context in which liberation theology is being done. It is not difficult to trace the paths which liberation theology must inevitably tread, and consequently an intersection between other people and American Indians can easily be discerned sometime in the future. Liberation theology first and foremost seeks to help human beings overthrow or deflect the tremendous oppression that is visited upon us by our own institutions which, in the name of a variety of false deities, have taken control of our lives and emotions. For the first two groups of American Indians there is no question that liberation theology has an immediate and profound message. The sabbath is made for human beings; human beings are not made for the sabbath: and so it is with all of our institutions. To the degree that oppression exists because of ill-informed or ill-intentioned use of human social, religious, and economic structures, to that degree people must act to take control of their lives. Institutions must be responsible to people and people must take responsibility to eliminate institutions and replace them with the free-flowing and spontaneous positive energy of love that flows from deep within themselves.

As liberation theology energizes and inspires people to become what they are intended to be, the task will be shifting from the need to escape from oppressive institutions and situations to the responsibility to free oneself from oppressive doctrines and beliefs and the corresponding practices which keep them in the forefront of our spiritual and emotional lives. Eventually liberation theology must engage in a massive critique of itself and its historico-theological context and inheritance. Here, as the issues become sharper and more profound, liberation theology will encounter traditional American Indian religions and their practitioners, first the modern Indian missionaries of the workshop network and then at last the few remaining traditionals on the reservations. Liberation theology must not only confront these representatives of American Indian religion but it must have a message for them which transcends their experiences and practice *and* makes sense of the Indian tradition in a more universal and comprehensive manner.

At this point of interaction liberation theology must dig deep into the Christian-Judeo tradition and bring forward whatever insights into the nature of reality it may have to present to the traditional Indians. It is not difficult to see that the cupboard is exceedingly bare at this level and that liberation theology must, perhaps inevitably, depart from its historico-theological moorings and deal with important philosophical questions. Is the world dead or alive? And what does that mean for the daily lives of people? What is the place and status of the human being in a world filled with sentient and powerful spirits? Is the world a fallen world from the beginning of time or does it simply have a set of historical difficulties which have been nearly impossible to resolve? What are the purpose, task, and meaning of human existence? The questions and issues which divide traditional American Indian religions from the world religions are many and profound and not capable of resolution through reference to a pre-existing set of doctrines and dogmas.

The basic philosophical difference between the American tribal religions and the world religions, Christianity being the world religion most likely to come into direct contact with the tribal religions, is the difference between time and space, between times and places, between a remembered history and a sacred location. At this point Christianity, and by extension liberation theology, is in mortal danger. History is a highly selective interpretation of the events of our lives loosely strung in sequence to prove the validity of the argument. That is to say, by arranging certain kinds of facts in a certain sequence, it is not difficult to prove to the disbeliever that certain spiritual truths and realities exist. But in performing this arrangement of human memories and experiences, a good deal has to be omitted and a great many facts have to be given a specific twist in order to fit the pattern. We hear from the Christians that God works and is working in history. But this history does not reflect humanity's complete and comprehensive experiences. This history is valid only if the listener surrenders his or her critical sense of inquiry and accepts the many premises that history, any particular history, requires for validation.

The tribal religions, however, bound as they are to specific places and particular ceremonies, do not need to rely upon the compiled arguments of history. It is only necessary that people experience the reality of the sacred. The attraction of the Indian missionaries on the lecture circuit is that they do provide new kinds of experiences, and in the world today people crave their own experiences and judge the truth of a proposition by the manner in which it helps them understand themselves. Consequently in the conflict or competition between Christianity and the other world religions and the tribal religions, a competition that is approaching on the horizon, there is no question which tradition is capable of speaking meaningfully to the diversity of peoples. A Sweat Lodge, a Vision Quest, or a Sing performed in a sacred place with the proper medicine man provides so much more to its practitioners than a well-performed Mass, a well-turned sermon argument, or a well-organized retreat. Christian rituals simply have no experiential powers.

Ultimately religions ask and answer the question of the real meaning and purpose of human life. The fatal flaw in the world religions is their propensity to try to provide answers to these questions knowing full well that both questions and answers must come from honest and open participation in the world. The Apostle Paul, filled with the Spirit and zealous to pass on his received theological truths, found no audience in Athens because no one was asking questions. Consequently his answers, already pre-formed in his mind and pushing for expression, had no relevance to his situation. Tribal religions do not claim to have answers to the larger questions of human life. But they do know various ways of asking the questions and this is their great strength and why they will ultimately have great influence in people's lives.

American Indians should wish liberation theology well in its endeavors. There is no question that humanity needs liberation from the many ills that plague it. But even the sacralization of the institutions, governments, and economic systems that are represented in our various human societies could not answer the ultimate questions that we must answer in our lives. Sacralization would only provide a benign and comfortable context in which these questions could be asked. It would always be up to the Great Spirit and the higher spirits, to the community of living things and to the humans themselves to derive cooperatively the proper answers. Liberation theology, however, can and must clear out the underbrush which we have carelessly allowed to obscure our vision of the forest, and this task cannot be accomplished too quickly. All living things now stand on the brink of oblivion and extinction. Mass destruction cannot be allowed to be the answer to all of our other questions, or, for that matter, to foreclose the possibility of asking the proper questions.

An old Crow chief, asked about the difference between the Indian way of life and that of the whites, responded that for the Indian there were visions, for the whites there were only ideas. Visions, in the Indian context, require action and this action manifests itself in the community, enabling the people to go forward in confidence and obedience. The vision is complete, it is comprehensive, it includes and covers everything, and there is no mistaking its applicability. Ideas, on the other hand, have only a limited relevance. They explain some things but not all things; they are rarely comprehensive and there is great difficulty in finding their proper application. Most important, however, the idea never reaches the complete community — it only reaches those who have the ability to grasp it and it leaves the rest of the community struggling for understanding.

It is difficult to discern, at the present time, whether liberation theology is an idea or a vision. It has the requisite characteristics of praxis and community, and in the struggle for freedom from oppression it even has the experiences. But within its larger theological context it is tied to a narrow and historical understanding of the human experience. When and whether it can transcend this foundation and provide the context in which the ultimate questions can be asked is an exciting and perilous possibility that hangs over us today. Hopefully we can glimpse a vision of community through the praxis that liberation theology asks and demands of us.

6

Untitled

ANN-MARIE JOHNSON

I am the land of no shores or seas
a land of mountains and ravines
that echo the melodic names of
an Indian ancestry

I am the land of artists
who honor me with crafts and
musicians
who praise me with song

I am the land of black diamonds
buried beneath the earth and
black dust buried within the
lungs of my people

I am the land of no forgiveness,
a land whose harsh realities
have molded proud independent
generations of settlers

I am the land of rich beauty, natural
that overwhelms the eye
and soothes the soul
I am the land of Appalachia.

This Land Is Home to Me:
A Pastoral Letter on Powerlessness in Appalachia

THE CATHOLIC BISHOPS OF APPALACHIA

Many of our Catholic people,
especially church workers,
have asked us to respond
to the cries of powerlessness
from the region called Appalachia.
We have listened to these cries
and now we lend our own voice.

The cries come now from Appalachia,
but they are echoed
— across the land
— across the earth
in the suffering of too many peoples.
Together these many sufferings
form a single cry.

The living God hears this cry
and tells us,
what long ago
on a different mountain
God told Moses.
This living God said:

I have heard the cry of my people.
I will deliver them out of the hands of oppression.
I will give them a rich and broad land.

But before we turn
to this message from the Lord,

we must hear first
the cry of Appalachia's poor.

Their cry is a strong message,
not because we have made it that way,
but because the truth of Appalachia
is harsh.
In repeating this message
we do not put ourselves
in judgment of others.
The truth of Appalachia
is judgment upon us all,
making hard demands on us bishops,
as well as on others.

We know that there will be other opinions
about the truth of Appalachia,
other views than those of the poor.
But we must remind ourselves
that the poor are special
in the eyes of the Lord,
for he has told us,
in the voice of his Mother:

He has pulled down princes from their thrones,
and exalted the lowly.
The hungry he has filled with good things.
the rich sent empty away [Luke 1:52–53].

Even so,
we know that our words are not perfect.
For that reason,
this letter is but one part
of an unfinished conversation
—with our people
—with the truth of Appalachia
—with the Living God.

Yet we still dare to speak,
and speak strongly,
first,
because we trust our people
and we know
that those who belong to the Lord
truly wish to do his will;

and second,
because we believe
that the cry of the poor
is also a message of hope,
a promise from the Lord,
that there can be a better way,
for he has told us,
The Truth will make you free [John 8:32].

PART I
THE LAND AND ITS PEOPLE

Appalachia makes us think
of people who live in the hills,
who love nature's freedom
and beauty,
who are alive with song
and poetry.
But many of these people are also poor
and suffer oppression.

Once they went to the mountains
fighting to build a dream
different from the injustice
they knew before.
Until this day,
their struggle continues,
a bitter fight
whose sound still rumbles
across the hills.

Yes, the poor of the mountains
have been wounded,
but they are not crushed.
The Spirit still lives.
The sound of music
still ripples through the hills.
Continually the tears of song
burn in outrage,
and outrage lives in struggle.

But the hill folk of the mountains
are not the only ones who struggle.
Besides the struggle in hollows,
typical of the central region,

there are struggles in industrial centers,
grown gray with smoke and smog,
blaring with the clank and crash
of heavy machinery
and urban congestion
where working people,
and those who wish there was work,
white and black,
native and immigrant,
speakers of one and many languages,
battle for dignity and security,
for themselves and for their children.

So too there is the struggle in the farmland,
typical of rolling hills in the southern sector,
where little farmers and sharecroppers,
day laborers and migrant workers,
who help the earth
yield its food to the hungry,
battle for that same dignity and security,
for themselves and their children.

In all three areas—
—the center
—the north
—the south
in every labor—
—the mine
—the factory
—the farm
the struggle is different,
yet remains the same.
It is at once the struggle
—of all Appalachia
—of the whole nation
—of the whole family.

The Appalachian mountains
form the spiny backbone
of the eastern United States.
This whole stretch,
which the federal government calls
"The Appalachia Region,"
runs from southern New York
to northern Georgia and Alabama.

It contains 397 counties
in 13 states,
parts of
— Alabama,
— Georgia,
— Kentucky,
— Maryland,
— Mississippi,
— New York,
— North Carolina,
— Ohio,
— Pennsylvania,
— South Carolina,
— Tennessee,
— Virginia,
and all of West Virginia.

In the region there are:
— mountain folk,
— city folk,
— country folk,
— coal miners and steel workers,
— industrial workers and service workers,
— farmers and farm laborers,
— housewives and children,
— teachers and health workers,
— ministers and rabbis and priests,
— artists and poets,
— professionals and technicians,
— lawyers and politicians,
— lobbyists and interest groups,
— executives and managers,
— little business people and big business people,
— coal companies and chemical companies,
— industrialists and bankers.

So, you see,
Appalachia is not a simple place.
There are rich and poor,
big and little,
new and old,
and lots in between.

But somehow,
no matter how confusing it seems,

it's all tied together
by the mountain chain
and by the coal in its center,
producing energy within it.

Of course,
there is more than coal
in the region.
There are
— gas,
— timber,
— oil,
— farms,
— steel mills,
— cheap labor,
but coal is central.

COAL

There is a saying in the region
that coal is king.
That's not exactly right.
The kings are those who control big coal
and the profit and power
which come with it.
Many of these kings
don't live in the region.

A long time ago in this country
when big industry just got started,
Appalachian coal played a big role.
It fed the furnaces
of our first industrial giants,
like Pittsburgh and Buffalo.
The coal-based industry
created many jobs,
and brought great progress to our country,
but it brought other things, too,
among them
oppression for the mountains.

Soon the mountain people
were dependent on the coal companies
and on the company towns
that came with them.

An old song sings,
Another day older
and deeper in debt.
That was life for many people
who lived in the shadow
of the mountain's coal.
Many of our Catholic people
lived under this suffering,
—in the coal mines,
—in the steel mills,
—in the other harsh jobs
that surround coal and steel.

Then came the unions,
as men and women fought hard
to change their lot.
The unions did good work
and for that reason
they were bitterly attacked
by enemies of justice.
But seeds of injustice
were also sown
within the labor movement.

Sometimes criminal forces entered
to crush their democratic structure,
to prevent union growth in other areas,
or to turn contracts
into documents of deceit,
both for labor and management,
thus encouraging their breach
from both sides.
Sometimes workers allowed themselves
to be used for selfish ends,
like keeping out blacks,
or women,
or Indians,
or Spanish-speaking people.
Sometimes the labor movement
thought only of workers in the U.S.
and did not take seriously
their membership
in the global human family.
Sometimes, too,
some U.S. workers used the unions

to protect the relative advantages
of a few workers
with little concern for
the great disadvantage of the many.

The real power of the labor movement,
a power which has not been totally crushed,
is the vision that
an injury to one is an injury to all,
whether to white or black,
whether to male or female,
whether to worker or consumer,
whether to union member or nonmember,
whether to U.S. citizen or to citizen
of any nation.

But later on for many people,
whose lives were tied to coal,
the unions didn't matter so much anymore.
Coal gave way to oil,
and different suffering
came across the mountains.

The mines in the hills
began to close.
The industrial thunder
of cities near the mines
weakened.
The people from the mountains
fled to the cities
looking for jobs.
But in the cities,
the jobs were few.

It is a strange system
which makes people suffer
both when they have work
and when they don't have work.

THE WIDER PICTURE

The people had to fight one another
for the few jobs:
—mountain people against city people,
—white people against black people,

—Irish people against Polish and Italian people,
—skilled workers against unskilled workers,
—union workers against nonunion workers.

As the people were forced
to fight over jobs,
self-defense often became a way of life
—in wars,
—in sports,
—in movies,
—even sometimes at home.

Our country meanwhile
grew strong and powerful
because of
—exploding war-stimulated technology,
—cheap raw materials from abroad,
—lots of oil,
—and a large work force.

But many people stayed poor,
and suffered attacks on their dignity,
especially
—Indians,
—Blacks,
—Mexican Americans,
—immigrants,
—Puerto Ricans,
—and poor whites, like Appalachians.

The Worship of an Idol

The way of life
which these corporate giants create
is called by some
"technological rationalization."
Its forces contain the promise
of a world where
—poverty is eliminated
—health is cared for
—education is available for all
—dignity is guaranteed
—and old age is secure.

Too often, however,
its forces become perverted,

hostile to the dignity of the earth
and of its people.

Its destructive growth patterns
—pollute the air
—foul the water
—rape the land.

The driving force
behind this perversion is
"Maximization of Profit,"
a principle which too often converts itself
into an idolatrous power.

This power overwhelms the good intentions
of noble people.
It forces them to compete brutally
with one another.
It pushes people into
"conspicuous consumption"
and "planned obsolescence."
It delivers up control
to a tiny minority
whose values then shape
our social structures.

Of course technological rationalization
and the profit principle
have served important functions
in human development.
It is not they themselves
that form an idol,
but the idol is formed
when they become absolutes
and fail to yield,
when the time has come,
to other principles.

Appalachia as a Symbol

In a country whose productive force
is greater than anything the world has ever known,
the destructive idol
shows its ugly face
in places like Appalachia.

The suffering of Appalachia's poor
is a symbol
of so much other suffering
—in our land
—in our world.

It is also a symbol
of the suffering which awaits
the majority of plain people
in our society
—if they are laid off
—if major illness occurs
—if a wage earner dies
—or if any other major thing goes wrong.

In this land of ours,
jobs are often scarce.
Too many people are forced
to accept unjust conditions
or else lose their jobs.

Human services for the poor,
and for the almost poor,
are inadequate.
Safety standards
are often too weak,
or ignored.
Workers are injured
unnecessarily.
Legal and medical recourse
for claims for occupational injury
or occupational disease
is often too difficult
or unavailable.
Sometimes
those who should be helping people
in their claims
seem to stand in the way.
Black lung
and mine accidents
are the most famous examples,
but are not the only ones.

On the other hand,
powerful reform movements

are underway
—in the union movement
—in community organizing
—in the consumer movement
—in public interest lobbies
—in religious circles.

To these must be added
even forces from within the
business community:
—managerial personnel who are concerned not only with salaries and promotion, but also with the contribution of the economic order to social
  well-being, particularly the bringing of jobs to poor areas;
—small and medium-sized businesses that wish to operate justly but that
  struggle under the pressure of giant economic corporations ruthlessly
  trying to wipe them out;
—stockholders who rebel against the impersonal structure of ownership
  and try to make their voices felt for justice within large corporations.

Together these groups struggle
to achieve what must become
the foundational principle
of our common life,
namely citizen involvement
—in our productive base
—in our political institutions
—in our cultural life.

The main task for such citizen involvement
will be to build social structures
which provide full employment
and decent wages
for all people.

Despite abuses,
we feel that a strong and broad
labor movement
is basic,
one which can stabilize the labor market
North and South
East and West
and prevent groups
from playing off different sectors
of working people
against each other.

Even so,
these movements are just beginning
and reach too few people.

We know also
that as they grow stronger,
they will be attacked;
that other forces will try to crush them.

Unaccountable economic powers
will continue to use
democratic political institutions
for nondemocratic purposes.
Sometimes this shows itself brutally,
when the police act like company enforcers.
At other times, it's more complicated,
when lawyers and legislators
seem to get paid
to keep the people confused
and to find loopholes
for the benefit of the rich.

These same massive economic forces,
still accountable to no one,
will even use vehicles of our cultural life,
like communications media and advertising
and even the educational system,
to justify their ways,
and to pass off their values
as our national values.
This happens
when news that's important to people
can't get time or space,
or when school programs
are designed by experts
without incorporating the voice of the people.

We know that there are many
— sincere business people,
— zealous reporters,
— truthful teachers,
— honest law-enforcement officers,
— dedicated public officials,
— hard-working lawyers and legislators
who try to do a good job.

But we know too that,
the way things are set up,
it's hard for good people
to do a good job.

It's strange, for instance,
despite earlier reforms,
that a country which took such richness
from Appalachia
left so little for the people.
Great fortunes were built
on the exploitation of
Appalachian workers
and Appalachian resources,
yet the land was left
without revenues
to care for the people's social needs, like
—education
—welfare
—old age
—and illness.

Some may say
"that's economics,"
but we say
that economics is made by people.
Its principles don't fall down from the sky
and remain for all eternity.
Those who claim
they are prisoners of the laws of economics
only testify
that they are prisoners of the idol.

The same thing which is so obvious in Appalachia
goes on outside the mountains.
Plain people work hard all their lives,
and their parents worked hard before them,
yet they can't make ends meet.

—Food is too expensive.
—Taxes are too high for most.
—(Too low for the rich.)
—Sickness puts people into debt.
—College is out of reach for their children.
—Paychecks keep shrinking.

And it's worse still for those who can't work,
especially the elderly.

Meanwhile
corporate profits
for the giant conglomerates,
who control our energy resources,
keep on skyrocketing.

But now there is some promise
of fresh "economic development"
in the Appalachian region,
at least if our industry returns
to a substantial coal base.
From the rest of the world, however,
we know now, after hard experiences,
that "development" often brings little
to the poor,
or to the workers.

Often the reverse.
Yet even if it were to bring prosperity,
there is a question we must ask
about the new energy resources.

It is,
How will we use our energy?
as well as,
Where will we get it from?

If our present system keeps on growing and growing,
it will burn up ourselves
and our world.
The present pattern of energy use,
a great deal of which goes for military production
or else for the production of discardable junk,
is barbaric.

Some talk about a population problem
among the poor.
There's an even bigger consumption problem
among the rich —
consumption not just of luxuries,
but of power,
of the power to shape

—economic structures
—political structures
—cultural structures
all in the service of
—more waste
—more profit
—more power.

Even worse,
U.S. energy consumption is expected
to double in the next decade.
What kind of world would it be
where "Maximization of Profit"
destroys life
for so many today,
and for future generations?
Ironically,
most people in this country
are not satisfied with the consumer society.
It makes life a rat race,
where nobody feels they belong,
where all are pushed around,
where roots disappear.
With so much busy-ness
and clutter of things,
—things that don't work,
—things you have to keep fixing,
—no time to play or sing like folks used to,
we get lost in our busy-ness
and grow to hate and abuse
all our things.

Worse still,
swallowing us up in things
is the power of the idol
which eats away at our openness
to the living God.

It would be bad enough
if the idol tried only
to take the land,
but it wants the soul, too.

When it has its way,
the poet is silent.

Instead comes
noisy blare and din,
the chatter of a language
empty of meaning,
but filled with violence.

This struggle of resistance,
is a struggle against violence —
against institutional violence
which sometimes subtly,
sometimes brutally,
attacks human dignity and life.

Therefore,
although the Catholic tradition
fully acknowledges the legitimacy
of self-defense and force
as the final recourse
against injustice,
we must beware of the temptation
of too easy violence —
of a bitterness which can poison
that for which we struggle,
or which,
still worse,

can provoke from forces of injustice
an even more brutal and repressive
institutional violence,
whose first victim
is always the poor.

It is the mountain's spirit of resistance
which must be defended
at any cost,
for at stake is the spirit
of all our humanity.
There are too few spaces of soul
left in our lives.

Once we all
— knew how to dance and sing
— sat in mystery before the poet's spell
— felt our hearts rise to nature's cathedral.

Now an alien culture
battles to shape us
into plastic forms empty of the Spirit,
into beasts of burden
without mystery.

If the struggle's dream can be defended,
and we believe it can,
then perhaps the great instruments of attack,
—cable TV,
—satellite communications,
—ribbons of highway,
can become like so many arms,
which instead of crushing life,
reach out to make it fuller,
to bring to others
beyond the mountains,
the promise of their vision.

PART II
THE ANSWERS OF THE LORD AND THE CHURCH:
THE GOD OF THE POOR

The living God,
the Lord whom we worship,
is the God of the poor.

God revealed the divine self to the people of Israel
by liberating them from oppression
under the bondage of Egypt:

I have seen the miserable state
of my people in Egypt.
I have heard their appeal to be free
of their slavedrivers. . . .
I mean to deliver them
out of the hands of the Egyptians. . . .
And now the cry of the children of Israel
has come to me.

That day, Yahweh rescued Israel
from the Egyptians . . .
and the people venerated Yahweh [Exod. 3:7–9; 14:30–31].
Not only in the liberation of God's people
is the Lord revealed

as the living God,
but also within Israel
by defending all those
who are victims of injustice.

God will free the poor person who calls on the Lord,
and those who need help.
God will have pity on the poor and feeble. . . .
God will redeem their lives
from exploitation and outrage [Ps. 72:12–14].

Thus, the God of Israel,
who is also our God,
is the God of the poor,
because that God frees the oppressed.

The Messiah and His Kingdom

And there came among us,
a man from Israel,
whom we confess to be
God-with-us,
the messiah long promised.

And when he rose up
to speak in his native Nazareth,
he chose the words
from the prophet Isaiah:

The Spirit of the Lord has been given to me,
for he has anointed me.
He has sent me to bring the good news to the poor,
to proclaim liberty to captives
and to the blind new sight,
to set the downtrodden free,
to proclaim the Lord's year of favor [Luke 4:18–19].

And when like Moses of old,
this Jesus climbed a mount
to tell the people his Father's law,
he left no doubt
that he was indeed
the messiah of the poor:

How happy are you who are poor:
yours is the kingdom of God.

Happy you who are hungry now:
you shall be satisfied.

Happy you who weep now:
you shall laugh. . . .
But alas for you who are rich:
you are having your consolation now.
Alas for you who have your fill now:
you shall go hungry.
Alas for you who laugh now:
you shall mourn and weep [Luke 6:21, 24–25].

The messiah, his Father, and their Spirit
are the living God.
They are different from the dead idols
which clutter history,
because they,
and not the idols,
act for justice.
The dead idols prove
to be gods of oppression.

I am Yahweh your God who brought you
out of the land of Egypt,
out of the land of slavery.
You shall have no gods except me [Exod. 20:1–3].

The choice between the living God
and inert idols
is not only a choice between justice
and injustice.
It is also a choice
between life
and death.

Today,
I set before you life or death,
blessings or curse.
Choose life, then,
so that you and your descendants may live,
in the love of Yahweh your God,
obeying his voice,
clinging to him;
for in this your life consists,
and on this depends your long stay

in the land which Yahweh
swore to your fathers ... [Deut. 30:19–20].

The Church's Mission

Out of faith in the risen Jesus
a new community of people is born,
seeking to be united
in one mind and spirit
with him.
Upon this community
Jesus pours forth his Spirit,
the Spirit of truth,
who teaches us everything
and reminds us of all Jesus said to us.

Still the church
is not perfect.
Its early bishop James
had to remind the people:
It was those who are poor
according to the world
that God chose, to be rich in faith
and to be the heirs to the kingdom
which God promised to those who love God [James 2:5].

If you refuse to love, you must remain dead;
to hate your brother is to be a murderer ...
This has taught us love —
that he gave up his life for us;
and we, too, ought to give up our lives
for our brothers and sisters.
If a man who was rich enough in this world's goods
saw that one of his brothers was in need,
but closed his heart to him,
how could the love of God be living in him?
My children,
our love is not to be just words or mere talk,
but something real and active;
only by this can we be certain
that we are children of the truth [1 John 3:10–12, 15–19].

Through the ages,
the church has tried to be faithful
to this message.

At times it has begun to stray from it,
but always the Spirit is alive within it,
stirring up new voices
to call it back
to its mission for justice.

The Church's Social Teaching

For a long time now,
our church has been restless
with what many call
"The Modern World."
There is much in this modern world
which is good and beautiful:
—the sense of freedom
—the progress of science and technology
—the personal creativity unleashed from under stifling traditions
—the growing unity of the human family.

The Lord has challenged the people of God
to take up as God's own
whatever is good and beautiful
in the modern world
as in all of God's creation.
But the Lord has also challenged us
to resist what is evil,
especially injustice.

Since the industrial age,
we have been active,
speaking and acting
on behalf of the casualties
of the new economic spirit.

At the end of the last century,
Pope Leo XIII
wrote a great letter,
On the Condition of the Working Classes.
Our own past brother,
Archbishop Gibbons of Baltimore,
made a great plea that this letter
reflect the views of the common people.
He told the pope,

To lose the heart of the people
would be a misfortune

for which the friendship of the few rich and powerful
would be no compensation.

In the wake of Leo's letter,
as the destructiveness of the new economic order
continued unchecked,
the U.S. Catholic bishops
felt compelled themselves
to draft a letter to their people
on the question of social reconstruction.
While acknowledging that the American people
were not ready for major reconstruction,
and that the present industrial system was
destined to last for a long time . . .
the bishops condemned three grievous abuses:
— enormous inefficiency and waste in the production and distribution of
   commodities;
— insufficient incomes for the great majority of wage earners;
— and unnecessarily large incomes for a small minority of privileged capitalists.

Further,
they argued for an industrialism
based on cooperation,
rather than on competition:
The majority must somehow become owners,
or at least in part,
of the instruments of production.

Finally, in discussing remedies,
they laid down the following principle:

Human beings cannot be trusted
with the immense opportunities for oppression and extortion
that go with the possession of monopoly power.

Still the injustices continued,
so much so that Pope Pius XI felt obliged
to publish another letter,
forty years after Leo's letter,
On Reconstructing the Social Order
and Perfecting It Comfortably
to the Precepts of the Gospel.
Pius XI pointed out how,

In our days not alone is wealth accumulated,
but immense power and despotic economic domination
are concentrated in the hands of a few. . . .
This concentration of power has led to
a threefold struggle for domination.
First, . . . the struggle for dictatorship
in the economic sphere itself;
then, the fierce battle to acquire control of the state,
so that its resources and authority
may be abused in the economic struggles.
Finally, the clash between states themselves.

The Catholic bishops of the United States
again responded with their own letter,
The Church and Social Order,
in 1940.
They lamented that an unjust society
had caused many working people
to become alienated from religion
and to have lost faith and hope.
Reminding economic powers that
the earth is the Lord's and
the fullness thereof [Ps. 24:1],
they especially denounced
—concentration of ownership and control
—the anonymous character of economic interests.

Now, closer to our own day,
the popes have continued to speak
on the social question.
Many will remember the warm letters
of Pope John XXIII,
Peace on Earth, and *Mother and Teacher*,
and Pope Paul's letters
On the Development of Peoples
and *A Call to Action*.
In a more contemporary context,
with a view to the poor across the globe,
the popes have called us back
to the message of Jesus
and to Yahweh the God of JUSTICE.

We bishops have not been silent either.
At the Vatican Council

we spoke strongly for justice and the poor
in *The Pastoral Constitution on the Church in the Modern World.*

When we gathered in synod a number of years ago
with all our fellow bishops of the world,
scrutinizing the signs of the times
and listening to the word of God,
we were

able to perceive the serious injustices
which are building around the world
a network of domination, oppression, and abuses. . . .

But we also noted,

a new awareness which shakes [people]
out of any fatalistic resignation
and which spurs them on to liberate themselves. . . .
Action on behalf of justice
and participation in the transformation of the world
fully appear to us
of the preaching of the gospel,
or, in other words,
of the church's mission
for the redemption of the human race
and its liberation from every oppressive situation.

Thus,
there must be no doubt
that we, who must speak the message
of the God who summoned Moses
and who spoke with the mouth
of Jesus of Nazareth,
and who has kept the Spirit alive
on behalf of justice
for so many centuries,
can only become
advocates of the poor.

PART III
FACING THE FUTURE:
A PROCESS OF DIALOGUE AND TESTING

More and more people recognize
that a new social order is being born.

Indeed,
the Spirit of God
presses us to this recognition.
We do not understand it all,
but we know we are part of it,
—in Appalachia,
—in our nation,
—across the world.

While we have no answers,
we have some principles
to guide the process.
Our searching must carefully balance
the following three elements:
1. closeness to the people;
2. careful use of scientific resources;
3. a steeping in the presence of the Spirit.

Throughout this whole process
of listening to the people,
the goal which underlies our concern
is fundamental in the justice struggle,
namely, citizen control,
or community control.
The people themselves
must shape their own destiny.
Despite the theme of powerlessness,
we know that Appalachia
is already rich here
in the cooperative power
of its own people.

In regard to the second element,
we must be careful with science,
because scientific models are not value free.
So much of science has been used,
in the contemporary world,
to oppress rather than liberate,
but science is not itself evil.
Rather it is our task to take it up,
and to infuse it with wisdom and humility,
in the service of justice.

In regard to the third,
we note with joy

the renewed zeal
for the presence of the Spirit
in prayer and meditation
among our Catholic people.
We know that if this renewed presence
can mature into a convergence
with the thirst for justice,
a new Pentecost will truly be upon us.

Also,
as suggested by the letter of Paul VI,
A Call to Action,
we commend where they exist,
and recommend where they do not,
centers of popular culture
in every parish,
or in areas where there are no parishes,
as a sign of the church's concern,
linked to the broader action centers,
places where the poor feel welcome,
spaces for people to come and share
at all levels,
so that if a new society is to be born,
it will emerge from the grass roots.

Especially we stress
emphasis on the economic questions,
for these are the first and most basic
questions for all people.
We call attention
to the presence of powerful
multinational corporations
now within our region.
The fate and role of these institutions
is a major question
not only for Appalachia,
but for the whole world.
Pope Paul VI has warned us that:

The multinational enterprises, . . .
largely independent of the national political powers
and therefore not subject to control
from the viewpoint of the common good, . . .
can lead to a new and abusive form
of economic domination of the social, cultural,

and even political level.
The excessive concentration of means and powers
that Pope Piux XI already condemned
on the fortieth anniversary of *Rerum Novarum*
is taking on a new and very real image.

As a counter-force
to the unaccountable power
of these multinational corporations,
there must arise a corresponding
multinational labor movement,
rooted in a vision of justice,
rising above corruption
and narrowness,
with a universal concern
—for all workers
—for all consumers
—for all people.

We are happy to note
that some voices at least
are raising up such a vision
within the ranks of labor.

Conclusion

We ask you to weigh seriously with the Spirit
the matters we have put before you,
—in your own silence;
—in your families;
—in your work;
—in your parishes.

We ask you to share
in dialogue and testing
with the leaders of your local church
and with us bishops
what we have presented here.
There will be different views,
but let us test them together
—with the people,
—with one another,
—and with the Spirit.

Dear sisters and brothers,
we urge all of you

not to stop living,
to be a part of the rebirth of utopias,
to recover and defend the struggling dream
of Appalachia itself.
For it is the weak things of this world,
which seem like folly,
that the Spirit takes up
and makes its own.
The dream of the mountains' struggle,
the dream of simplicity
and of justice,
like so many other repressed visions,
is, we believe,
the voice of the Lord among us.

In taking them up,
hopefully the church
might once again
be known as
—a center of the Spirit,
—a place where poetry dares to speak,
—where the song reigns unchallenged,
—where art flourishes,
—where nature is welcome,
—where little people and little needs come first,
—where injustice speaks loudly,
—where in a wilderness of idolatrous destruction the great voice of God
    still cries out for life.

7

"From a Heart of Rice Straw" *(excerpt)*

NELLIE WONG

My heart . . . once
ashamed of your China ways.
Ma, hear me now, tell me your story
again and again.

Union of Ethical Walking
and Theological Beholding:
Reflections from an Asian American

KOSUKE KOYAMA

Does the vision of liberation in Jesus Christ shed any light on the lives of Asian Americans living in North American communities today? Can Asian Americans find in their ancient traditions any resources which will help them understand their situation within Western culture? I will suggest in this paper that Asian Americans can better understand their oppression if they see it in the light of the doctrine of *karman*, a time-honored Asian concept, the spirit of which in the West may be expressed by the English word "individualism."

In order to prepare for my discussion I must describe briefly how I understand the theology of liberation. I will then look at individualism as it has affected Western society. I will set it in the context of *karman* both to show its similarities and contrasts. I will suggest some direction for Asian Americans in light of the vision of liberation theology and the realities of North America.

I believe the foundation of liberation theology is best understood as the bringing together of two key texts from the Bible: Micah 6:8 and John 1:29. The words of Micah, "What does the Lord require of you but to do justice, and to love kindness, and to walk humbly with your God?" focus on "ethical walking," while those of John, "Behold the Lamb of God, who takes away the sin of the world!" call our attention to "theological beholding." Thus "ethical walking" and "theological beholding" are brought together in the biblical tradition. We are to "do justice" as we "look to the lamb of God," and we must "look to the lamb of God" only as we are about "doing justice." Redemption cannot be complete without justice, nor justice without redemption. In fact this is the foundation of all Christian theology. But for liberation theology it is the very essence and mission. The contribution of liberation theology has been to remind us of this foundational principle.

The positive social power of the union of ethical walking and theological beholding is demonstrated as the destruction of self-righteousness. Examples of this are the German Christian, Dietrich Bonhoeffer; the Indian Hindu, Mahatma Gandhi; the American Christian, Martin Luther King, Jr. Each of these heroic figures held the good of the community to be of such great importance that he was willing to lay his life on the line for its healing. The letter Martin Luther King, Jr., wrote from the Birmingham city jail in 1963 is a good example of what I mean by the union of ethical walking and theological beholding because of its selfless challenge in the midst of theological reflection.

Self-righteousness has its classic illustration in the words of the Pharisee in the parable of Jesus: "I thank thee that I am not like other men, extortioners, unjust, adulterers, or even like this tax collector" (Luke 18:11). This is clearly the language of self-idolatry. Self-idolatry, by raising the self to ultimate importance, takes the name of God in vain (Exod. 20:7). In fact, we take the name of God in vain whenever we use God's name to our own advantage. This is always done from a limited or parochial perspective. Self-righteousness, self-idolatry, parochialism, and the taking of God's name in vain are all bound together and are the soil in which injustice and oppression thrive. To eliminate self-righteousness is to eliminate idolatry.

With the elimination of self-righteousness comes the possibility of universality. Christian universality affirms that the redemptive love of God is universal, directed to all people, and even to all creatures and all of nature. This is expressed precisely in the words from Deuteronomy: "For the Lord your God is God of gods and Lord of lords, the great, the mighty, and the terrible God, who is not partial and takes no bribe" (10:17). And the God who takes no bribe, and thus refuses to become parochial, demands from us the pledge to take no bribe. We too are to practice universality of justice before God. "You shall not pervert justice; you shall not show partiality; and you shall not take a bribe, for a bribe blinds the eyes of the wise and subverts the cause of the righteous. Justice, and only justice, you shall follow, that you may live and inherit the land which the Lord your God gives you" (16:19, 20).

Such universality, rejecting all forms of bribery, is God's ecumenical orientation. In the ancient words of the Bible, ecumenicity means that "you may live and inherit the land which the Lord your God gives you" by doing "justice, and only justice." This call to do "justice, and only justice" (ethical doing) is rooted in the knowledge of God who takes no bribe (theological beholding). God's ecumenical outpouring of grace contradicts individualism that seeks personal advantage and prestige at the expense of the welfare (shalom) of the community. Individualism tempts us to take the name of God in vain. The theology of liberation, which stands upon the union of ethical walking and theological beholding, is the theology of the destruction of self-righteous individualism.

The Hindu and Buddhist doctrine of *karman* is generally familiar to Asians. The word *karman* means "deed" or "action." The fundamental thrust of the *karman* doctrine is that any human action will cause a reaction.

It means that if one acts against the order of the cosmos one will accordingly receive a negative reaction from the cosmos. In religious terms it means simply that evil will be met by evil and good by good. This thesis summarizes the fundamental spirit of popular Buddhism in Asia. It is an objective principle of retribution.

When we look at "Christian" North American communities it is puzzling to note that there is a strong element of something very similar to the spirit of the *karman* philosophy — so much so that one is tempted to speak of the "Hinduization" of Christian America. (I am not using the expression "Hinduization" in a derogatory sense. I am simply trying to point out what the individualism of the North American community looks like from an Asian cultural and social sensitivity.) Of course North American people have not taken up the Hindu and Buddhist concept of *karman* and "indigenized" it into their own spiritual and cultural soil. It seems rather that both East and West have made a similar observation of their common humanity and each has named it in its own way. Asians can better understand individualism if they observe how it is similar and different from the doctrine of *karman*.

One of the most pervasive elements of Western individualism is the retributive language of militarism. We are increasingly hearing from the American military the language of "retaliation" and "getting even," and worse in a culture that prides itself on its Hebraic-Christian roots. For those who come from Asia this is *karmic* language, but *karmic* language in a very violent mode. And it is not only the military establishment that is using this retributive language. It has become common in the general discourse and in everyday life as well. The language of retaliation is even employed by Christian evangelists, such as the Reverend Jerry Falwell. He writes, "The sad fact is that today the Soviet Union would kill 135 million to 160 million Americans, and the United States would kill only 3 to 5 percent of the Soviets because of their antiballistic missiles and their civil defense."[1]

In the area of our economic life, the concept of retribution has been brutally applied in the service of individualism. It is the doctrine of non-intervention in individual economic life. Any effort to alleviate the lot of the poor is interpreted as an interference in the free-market processes. Business should be "free" to sell wherever it can find a market and at whatever price it can command. The poor, on the other hand, must be "free," and therefore responsible for their own welfare. And even though in the present century political necessities have brought many programs which would provide for the poor, Western individualism has kept alive the "free-market" notion. The current political strategy is to move away from government "intervention" in social systems. The Reagan and Bush administrations have been devoted to individualistic principles and have been unable to recognize the nature of systemic economic oppression and its effects on people. Thus many people in this society live in extreme poverty almost within hailing distance of the privileged wealthy class. The concept of retribution (what you sow you shall reap) has been used in this country to justify the right to amass wealth. This has resulted in the exploitation of those who are at the mercy of the marketplace. The ideology of individualism with its interpretation of a free marketplace has permeated almost every aspect of American life.

In the area of medical care individualism expresses itself in the social requirement that each person make provision for any medical contingency that may occur. The ability to pay has become more fundamental than the cure or the prevention of illness. There is no strong community approach to the problems of public health. In the area of education, the ideology of individualism has had wide-ranging and devastating effects. Knowledge has been fragmented and retailed for individual consumption, and utilized for the acquisition of personal prestige and economic power, rather than for the building of community. Opportunity for study is becoming less accessible for the marginalized groups as educational institutions become more and more subject to market principles. The American public has been victimized by the advertising industry as it raises hopes and aspirations and appeals to individualistic impulses with its hard sell. Saturating the media, this propagator of the ideology of individualism has become an inescapable aspect of American life.

Why has this ideology of individualism been so pervasive and devastating in American society while its counterpart in Asia is relatively diffuse? One reason seems to be that ideologies take on greater intensity in Western cultures than in Asian cultures. I have often felt that this was true because of the West's historic Judeo-Christian understanding of the meaning of truth. It may, however, reflect the fact that Western individualism, through economic and political philosophy, has been more directly related to the social system, while the doctrine of *karman* in Asia continues to be a religious and cultural concept. There may also be a stronger sense of community in the traditional Asian societies than in the American communities. Nevertheless this harmful ideology has succeeded in what Asian Americans perceive to be a "Christian" nation. However, biblical theology cannot support the ideology of individualism as we have described it here. Obviously a different vision is needed to guide humanity into the future — a vision drawn from the union of ethical walking and theological beholding; a vision that seeks to destroy self-righteousness.

In light of the need for a new vision, how are Asian Americans to perceive their situation in the white-dominated American society? First, although Asians are an ethnic minority in the United States, they are not an economically repressed minority. We are told that the Asian population in this country will grow in the 1990s to 8.1 million. By the year 2000, Asians will represent 3 percent of the U.S. population, and by 2050 it is projected to be 6.4 percent. It is only recently that there has been a massive inflow of Asian peoples. Ninety-two percent of the Vietnamese Americans immigrated after 1970. Of the Korean Americans, 68 percent entered the country after 1970. In general, Asians are doing well economically in comparison with other ethnic minority groups. Asian Americans are also doing better in the area of education. "In the Ivy League they [Asians and Jews] are the two groups most heavily 'overrepresented' in comparison to their shares of the population."[2] "Whereas 17 percent of white Americans age 15 or older are college graduates, 33 percent of Asians have a college degree. An incredible 52 percent of adult Asian Indians in the United States are college graduates, and more than one-third of the Chinese and Filipinos."[3]

But if the statistics indicate that Asian Americans are doing well, that does not mean that they have not suffered at the hands of white America. The forced removal of U.S. citizens of Japanese ancestry from the Western states during World War II without due process of law was a traumatic and unjustified experience. Had the Japanese Americans looked like Caucasians it is doubtful that they would have been put in camps behind barbed wire. Today hardly anyone would disagree that the internment was a racist incident.

Another ugly incident, the killing of Vincent Chin, took place in 1982 in Detroit. It was motivated by the resentment of auto workers who lost their jobs because of the massive inflow of cars from Japan. Vincent Chin was Chinese, but to the dominant group all Asians look alike. The mob shouted, "Get Chinks! Because of you we're out of work!"

William R. Tamayo, an attorney with the Asian Law Caucus of California, began a speech on the "Root Causes of Anti-Asian Violence and Anti-Asian Agitation" with these lines:

> "Ching Chong Chinaman
> Tight-eyed Chink!
> Boy, you don't have a
> Chinaman's chance!"
> "Oh beautiful for spacious skies, for amber waves of
>   grain . . . "
> "Hey, Jap! Hey, Buddhahead!
> Mr. Senator, you've got to
> keep out those yellow hordes.
> They're heathens, they
> can't assimilate."
> "For purple mountain
> majesties,
> above the fruited plain . . . "
> "Those brown Filipino
> monkeys are taking away
> our jobs!
> Hey, monkey, don't touch our
> white women or we'll kill
> you!"

"America, America,
God shed his grace on thee ... "
"And you know, Martha, I shot fifty gooks
right in the head
back in 'Nam."
"George, those refugees are
moving into our
neighborhood. You better
lock up the dog and call the
realtor."
"And crowned thy good with
brotherhood from sea to
shining sea."[4]

Defining the root causes of anti-Asian violence in the United States, Tamayo highlights the realities of scapegoating. A scapegoat is "one who is blamed or punished for the sins of others" (*Oxford Dictionary*). In the scapegoat arrangement the real culprit is not punished: the punishment is taken by a substitute. This has been the experience of Asian Americans:

By the mid-1870s during a severe depression on the West Coast, Chinese laborers were 50% of the labor force in California. With many white miners and workers displaced by the shutting down of the industry, Chinese became the ideal scapegoat and victim of racial violence. For not only were the Chinese non-white; moreover, they were "foreigners," "aliens," "yellow heathens," little men with pigtails running around in pajamas, taking away the jobs of whites.[5]

White Americans, believing they had a position of privilege in the divine order of things, could not accept that their job opportunities were being lost to an "inferior" racial group. They had a "religious" sense of mission which in their eyes justified their making a scapegoat of the minority group when they were frustrated in reaching their own goals.

Scapegoating is not rare. In one form or another it is probably one of the most common strategies in human societies for dealing with the sins or failures of the dominant group. When the minority group is made the scapegoat, oppression takes place. Generally this happens when there is an irrational upsurge of mob psychology which cannot be pacified until some kind of sacrifice is made. In the mob a chaotic group passion is aroused which is irrational and closed to reasoned arguments. In time of war a society may be particularly prone to mob psychology. Hysteria, chauvinism, suppressed fear, and racial hatred characterize the mob. Some leader will persuade the mob with "absolute conviction" that a minority group or individual is guilty of infringing on the rights of the dominant group. Then someone, a person or persons of the despised minority, must be sacrificed to satisfy the anger of the mob. More than any other ethnic group in the history of humankind, the Jews have been singled out to play the role of the scapegoat.

Asian-American liberation theology must address the issue of the scapegoat from Asians' own experience in this country. Because of the long experience of the Jews in this area, it will be important to enter into dialogue with them on the subject. If such a dialogue can be advanced, it will have profound theological implications. But Asians who have experienced being made the scapegoat must be careful not to lay the experience on other minority groups. "You shall remember that you were a slave in Egypt and the Lord your God redeemed you from there" (Deut. 24:18).

Asian Americans can make a special contribution from their own doctrine of *karman*. What *karman* affirms is that the actor of an action, not someone else, must receive the reaction to his or her original action. The *karman* does not accept bribes. It insists upon just retribution. This idea is not foreign to the Bible. "There will be tribulation and distress for every human being who does evil, the Jew first and also the Greek, but glory and honor and peace for every one who does good, the Jew first and also the Greek. For God shows no partiality" (Rom. 2:9–11). The God who shows no partiality and the principle of *karman* both condemn the practice of scapegoating.

In the book of Leviticus (chap. 16) a solemn liturgy is described in which a goat, bearing all the iniquities of the people, is sent into a solitary land (vv. 20–22). This is probably the origin of the word "scapegoat." The ritual suggests that a sacrifice must be made to atone for sin, but also that the sin of the community must be removed, carried away, from the congregation. Here is suggested a theology for the disposal of the polluting sins of the community. Whatever the meaning of the ancient rite, the symbol changes its nature when a human person or group is put in the place of the scapegoat. Scapegoating involves unbearable injustices and suffering on the part of the victims. Even if it were possible that such injustices and suffering could restore social tranquility for a time, the society that uses scapegoating is basically unjust. There is certainly no redemptive force in scapegoating.

The idea of a punishment for sins is found in the idea of Jesus' death on the cross. Certainly parallels can be drawn between the scapegoat practice and the experience of Jesus, but there is an important difference. Jesus accepted crucifixion willingly. He went to Jerusalem knowing what the consequences would be. So we can say, "Behold the Lamb of God who takes away the sins of the world." He was not a passive recipient, but an active participant in those events. The redemptive value of this divine willingness has been a subject that no theologian in all the Christian centuries has been competent to describe. "For our sake he made him to be sin who knew no sin, so that in him we might become the righteousness of God" (2 Cor. 5:21). This passage by Paul must not be understood as a statement about fundamental injustice, but rather as one about fundamental love. The mysterious power of this active love is what separates the act of redemption from the experience of the scapegoat. Liberation theology can remind us of this distinction and suggest a way to counter the injustice of scapegoating.

Yet theologians must be careful when they apply biblical passages to a given sociological situation. They must make sure that their conclusion makes sociological sense. For example it is true that white people lost their jobs when Asians who would work for less entered the country, and so whites felt that an injustice was being done. In this kind of situation of competing resources, how does one realize the biblical injunction: "Justice, and only justice you shall follow"? This is a dilemma which can be faced only on the basis of careful sociological analysis of a given community. In fact careful analysis may even suggest that in the complexity of today's world Asian Americans are inadvertently making scapegoats of other minority groups or enjoying security by colluding with the dominant group against the minority groups.

The evil of racism must become a subject of critical reflection among the Asian Americans. In spite of having been subjected to racial injustice, have Asian Americans developed racist attitudes toward other racial or ethnic groups, such as the black or Hispanic communities? Have they adopted, to their own advantage, the life-philosophy of racial individualism? Or have they, learning from their own experience, been able to appreciate the position of groups set apart because of their different appearance? Have they publicly deplored the evils of racial discrimination in our society?

Ironically, at roughly the same time Asian Americans were suffering discrimination, Japan, possessed by the demon of national chauvinism, was oppressing the minorities within its borders. The minority that suffered the most in this particular context were the Koreans. Japanese Americans can hardly escape the responsibility of relating the experience of the "Japanese Empire" to their experience of national chauvinism in the United States. A careful study of the oppression of the Korean people in Japan during the war years should be brought into serious dialogue with the present situation of "patriotic chauvinism" in the United States.

Such searching theological examination will be deepened if Korean Americans who have gone through the bitter experience of Japanese imperialism are invited to participate. I would extend this invitation to Filipino Americans, Malaysian Americans, Indonesian Americans, Singaporean Americans, Burmese Americans, and others who were victimized by Japan during the war. Such an Asian-American "ecumenical" discussion on the relationship between patriotism and oppression is very much needed to document the close relationship between patriotism and parochial self-righteousness.

In conclusion I have three suggestions regarding the direction in which Asian liberation theology might move: (1) By understanding the nature of oppression that is rooted in American individualism, Asian Americans can seek to liberate themselves from the oppression directed against them, and can also engage in a critical self-examination to see whether they also share in the power which oppresses other minority groups. (2) Theological dialogue with Jewish people in the United States would be helpful for understanding scapegoating, and it thus would be helpful in the formation of Asian-American liberation theology. (3) Asian Christians representing various Asian groups in the United States must cultivate mutual dialogue to bring about the union of "ethical walking" and "theological beholding" as the fundamental Christian orientation of life.

8

"Para Un Viejito Desconocido Que Aun Conozco"

INES HERNÁNDEZ

Old man walking into Mi Tierra*
Famous Chicano restaurant in San Anto,
Old man, with the worn and gleaming pants,
the softly faded shirt, the thin belt
Old man, old man
Why, when you enter, do you walk so cautiously?
Why do you barely whisper to your compadre?†
Why do you wish to go unnoticed?
Your own people would not belittle you because
    you're poor
They would not cast sly, demeaning glances at you
They would not turn you away—
Or would they?
This is "Mi Tierra"—nuestra tierra,‡ no?
As I watch you and your compadre
As I count the lines and see the ravages, the suffering
    you have known
And I sense deep within me what courage you have
    shown each day
I smile at you and nod
Hoping you will know
That my heart reaches out to you
And my soul embraces you.

---

*My country
†Companion; literally, godfather
‡Our country

Mujeristas:
A Name of Our Own

ADA MARÍA ISASI-DÍAZ

To name oneself is one of the most powerful acts any human person can do. A name is not just a word by which one is identified. A name also provides the conceptual framework, the mental constructs, that are used in thinking, understanding, and relating to a person. For many years now, Hispanic women in the United States—who struggle against ethnic prejudice, sexism, and, in many cases, classism—have been at a loss as to what to call ourselves. The majority of Hispanic women have simply called themselves *cubanas*, *chicanas*, or *puertorriquenas*, and most probably will continue to do so. Some of us have called ourselves *feministas hispanas*. Though *feministas hispanas* has been an appellation riddled with difficulties, we have felt the need for a name that would indicate primarily the struggle against sexism that is part of our daily bread while also helping us identify one another in the trenches as we fight for our survival within Hispanic communities and U.S. society at large. But using *feministas hispanas* has meant giving long explanations of what such a phrase does not mean.[1]

Feministas hispanas have been consistently marginalized in the Anglo-feminist community because of our critique of its ethnic/racial prejudice and lack of class analysis. At the same time, when we have insisted on calling ourselves *feministas*, we have been rejected by many in the Hispanic community because they consider feminism a preoccupation of Anglo women. Yet Hispanic women widely agree with an analysis of sexism as an evil within our communities, an evil that plays into the hands of the dominant forces of society and helps to repress and exploit us in such a way that we constitute the largest number of those at the lowest economic stratum. Likewise, Hispanic women widely agree that, though we make up the vast majority of those who participate actively in the Hispanic churches, we do the work but do not participate in deciding what work is to be done; we do the praying but our understanding of the God to whom we pray is ignored.

As Hispanic women we, therefore, continue to search for a name that will call us together, that will help us to understand our oppression, that will identify the specificity of our struggle without separating us from our communities. And in our search we turn to our music—an intrinsic part of the soul of our culture. In love songs as well as in protest songs we are simply called *mujer*—woman. "Yo soy mujer en busca de igualdad, / no aguantare abuso ni maldad. / Yo soy mujer y tengo dignidad, / y pronto la justicia sera una realidad,"[2] proclaims a song composed by women in the South Bronx. "Mujer, tu eres mujer, / porque supiste ver, / la realidad de tu poder,"[3] sings Rosie Sánchez. "Hoy canto al Dios del Pueblo en mi guitarra, un canto de mujer que se libera," sings Rosa Marta Zarate. She continues, "Dios escucho el clamor de nuestro pueblo / se alio al expobrecido y explotado / y a la majer libera de cadenas / impuesta con crueldad por tantos siglos."[4] And the song ends by repeating time and again, "la mujer, la mujer, la mujer" (for the full text of the song see n. 6).

Yes, we are *mujeres*, and those of us who make a preferential option for *mujeres* are *mujeristas*.[5] As Rosa Marta's song says so clearly, a *mujerista* is one who struggles to liberate herself, who is consecrated by God as proclaimer of the hope of her people. A *mujerista* is one who knows how to be faithful to the task of making justice and peace flourish, who opts for God's cause and the law of love. In the *mujerista* God revindicates the divine image and likeness of women. The *mujerista* is called to gestate new women and men: a strong people. *Mujeristas* are anointed by God as servants, prophets, and witnesses of redemption. *Mujeristas* will echo God's reconciling love; their song will be a two-edged sword, and they will proclaim the gospel of liberation.[6]

At the same time that we name ourselves *mujeristas*, we want to rename our theological enterprise. What we called up to now Hispanic women's liberation theology will henceforth be called *mujerista* theology. *Mujerista* theology, a concept which is beginning to be articulated, is part of the daily voice of *mujeristas*, for Christianity is an intrinsic element of Hispanic culture. *Mujerista* theology articulates religious understandings of Hispanic women. It always uses a liberative lens, which requires placing oneself radically at the core of our own struggling pueblo. *Mujerista* theology brings together elements of feminist theology, Latin American liberation theology, and cultural theology—three perspectives that intertwine to form a whole. These three perspectives critique and challenge each other; they inform each other, giving birth to new elements of a new reality.

Like other liberation theologies, *mujerista* theology is indebted to the generative theological work of Gustavo Gutiérrez. This essay, which is a further development of the articulation of *mujerista* theology that I have already published,[7] deals with two *mujerista* understandings that engage specific themes of Gutiérrez's theological writings. Here I further develop the *mujerista* position that the real theologian is the community and not exclusively those of us with academic training. I will demonstrate that this is firmly rooted in the epistemological privilege of those who are oppressed and in the fact that all liberation theologies are about "doing theology," which cannot be done but as a member of a community. Secondly, after suggesting a nonoppressive way of using the Bible, I will propose the story of Shiphrah and Puah at the beginning of the Book of Exodus as a biblical interpretive key to the *mujerista* struggle. A third theme this article deals with has not been explicitly addressed by Gutiérrez but is a must for *mujerista* theology because of the twofold and at times threefold oppression Hispanic women suffer. It is the issue of power.

HACE TEOLOGÍA— A COMMUNAL TASK

Mujeristas are increasingly aware of how false and evil is any attempt to separate action from reflection. The physical participation of Hispanic women in programs and action is often sought, but they are seldom asked to be involved in deciding or designing content. Hispanic women are seldom invited to reflect on the reasons and motivations for their actions. But *mujeristas* will always insist on the need to be actively involved in the reflective moment of praxis. Without reflection there is no critical awareness, no conscientization and, therefore, no possibility of self-definition and liberation.

One of the most pervasive themes of *mujerista* theology is the preferential option for the poor and oppressed. This preferential option is based on the epistemological privilege of the poor because they can see and understand what the rich and privileged cannot. It is not that the poor and oppressed are morally superior or that they can see better. No, their epistemological privilege is based on the fact that, because their point of view is not distorted by power and riches, they can see differently: "The point of view of the poor, . . . pierced by suffering and attracted by hope, allows them, in their struggles, to conceive another reality. Because the poor suffer the weight of alienation, they can conceive a different project of hope and provide dynamism to a new way of organizing human life for all."[8]

The epistemological privilege of the poor should be operative in a very special way in the theological enterprise. It is the understandings of the divine and the way of grappling with questions of ultimate meaning in the daily lives of grass-roots Hispanic women which constitute *mujerista* theology. Theological reflection cannot be separated from theological action in the doing of theology. Therefore *mujerista* theology is a praxis which consists of two interlinked moments: action and reflection. *Mujerista* theology is a doing theology, which does not place reflection and articulation above action. Neither does *mujerista* theology see the theological enterprise as a second moment following the praxis, for all action, at the moment that it is taking place, has a reflective quality. Because *mujerista* theology is a praxis, it is, therefore, the community as a whole that engages in the theological enterprise.

Among liberation theologians who are academically trained, there seems to be concern about their role and title. If the community as a whole is the one that does theology, what is the task of those of us who call ourselves theologians? I believe there is no way of averting this identity crisis once the epistemological privilege of the poor is recognized and theology is understood as a praxis, a doing theology. The only way for academically trained theologians to resolve their dilemma is to participate fully in a community of struggle and to do theology as members of that community. The gifts of the academically trained theologian who is part of a community of struggle will not be wasted. The theological community needs some of its members to be enablers and facilitators during the reflective moment of praxis—which does not happen only when one is sitting down! Those who are trained academically can well put their gifts at the service of the community at this time. They can indeed be very instrumental in enabling the community to understand that its daily struggle for existence is not separate from its religious understandings, sentiments, beliefs. They can take responsibility for gathering what the community is saying and writing it down so the community can benefit from it in the future, so that it may be shared with other communities of struggle, and so that one day those voices may be an intrinsic element of the society norm.

Elsewhere, following the lead of Carlos Abesamis, I have proposed calling the enablers/writers of the theological reflection of the community "theological technicians."[9] Several of my colleagues have objected to such a title. Maybe we are not ready to name ourselves. But what *mujerista* theology insists on saying is that the community of struggle is the one that does theology, and not individuals who are not intrinsic members of the community. Those of us who are academically trained and are intrinsic members of a community of struggle must do theology with our community and not as separate individuals. The theological articulations we write, therefore, should always be birthed by the community, discussed in the community, understandable to the community. Because the theological articulations we write are but a moment in the praxis of the community, such an articulation must always be open, in flux. It must always welcome revision and be evolving.[10]

SEFORA Y FUA—AN INTERPRETIVE KEY

For *mujeristas* the primary role of the Bible is to influence the "horizon or ultimate way in which the Christian looks at reality."[11] This biblical influence yields mainly an ethical model of relationality and responsibility that is/can be/should be operative in the struggle for liberation. The way liberation theologies have used the Bible up to now, however, will not effectively contribute to building a model of relationality and responsibility. Most liberation theologies' use of the Bible is limited to a "simple learning."[12] What liberation theologies have promoted are "certain exemplary themes such as exodus, prophetic criticism of society, ... Jesus' confrontation with authorities,"[13] Jesus as a member of a marginated group—the

Galileans—[14] and so forth. Or liberation theologies have also reworded biblical stories using popular terminology in order to make them relevant to different situations of struggle in the world today.[15]

Instead, the Bible should be used to promote a critical consciousness, to trigger suspicion, which is the starting point of the process of conscientization. The Bible should be used to learn how to learn—"to involve the people in an unending process of acquiring new . . . information that multiplies the previous store of information."[16] This new information becomes a source that can be consulted "in order to solve new problems the people have not faced before."[17] The Bible must not be directly applied to a problem—it does not offer a solution to any given problem. Instead the Bible must become a resource for learning what questions to ask in order to deal appropriately with the problem at hand.

This way of using the Bible liberates the Bible—frees it from becoming a mere guidebook about the correct thing to do. The Bible cannot be the only tool, nor is it always the main tool, which *mujeristas* use to reflect on who we are, on our "attitudes, dispositions, goals, values, norms, and decisions."[18] The Bible should always be seen as only *one* of the traditions through which the community can remember its past, its roots, the source of its values, customs, and practices. Any and all sources that help "to nurture and reform the community's self-identity as well as the personal character of its members"[19] must be seriously engaged by *mujeristas*. Furthermore, the Bible as well as any other text to which the community of Hispanic women gives authority should be used only as an integral part of a process that helps Hispanic women to be self-determining. This way of using the Bible makes it clear that each person has to decide how she is to participate in the struggle for liberation.

Specific biblical stories can and should serve as interpretive keys in the struggle for liberation of Hispanic women. In looking at specific biblical passages as interpretive keys, I intend for us to use them to help us understand the questions we need to ask, questions that shed light on the oppressive situations we *mujeristas* face today. An interpretive key does not demand compliance to a given archetype or prototype, but rather helps us to be critical about the situation at hand. An interpretive key helps us ask questions instead of providing us with definitive answers. When we use the Bible in this way we claim that the starting point is always the situation at hand and not the Bible. As an interpretive key, no biblical passage can be *the* deciding factor in our lives. Seeing certain passages of the Bible as interpretive keys allows *mujeristas* to be self-determining—to be the ones who decide what to do and how to do it.[20]

Shiphrah and Puah stand at the beginning of the most formidable and formative event for the Hebrew people, the exodus event. And yet, little attention has been paid to them. The action of these two women is indeed an interpretive key for *mujeristas* today and it needs to be explored at length. Their story in Exodus 1:15–22 helps raise questions about what should be our role as *mujeristas* in the struggle for our own liberation and the liberation of our pueblo.

Exodus 1:15–22[21] starts with an order from the pharaoh: Shiphrah and Puah[22] are to kill sons born to Hebrew women. Though a man, the pharaoh, stands at the beginning of the narrative, it is not his action but rather the actions of these women that are of primary concern.[23] The pharaoh attempts to deal with the growing number of Hebrews.[24] However, had he been able to foresee the persistence of the women in thwarting his decree, he might have been more successful in his attempt to check the Hebrew population growth by ordering all female infants to be killed![25]

Were these two midwives Egyptian or Hebrew? The Masoretic text reads, "Hebrew midwives."[26] But a minor variation in the grammatical forms yields "midwives of the Hebrews," which is the way the Septuagint and the Vulgate read.[27] The ambiguity of the text introduced by the variation can be seen as a way of moving "beyond nationalistic concerns to bear witness to the power of faith to transcend ethnic boundaries."[28] Uncertainty, then, about the midwives' nationality allows us to suggest that the main moving force and motivating principle of their action was the fear of God.

Fear in this text is not fear of punishment. The fear of God that Shiphrah and Puah felt was generated by a sense of *mysterium tremendum*, "a mystery in divine holiness which produces . . . a sense of terror."[29] This sense of terror is not merely negative but is also an expression of faith, trust, love, and communion, based on God's unmerited, gratuitous, and unearned love. The defiant act of Shiphrah and Puah makes life for the Hebrews possible, and their risky, clever answer to the pharaoh, which puts them in immediate danger, is born out of their own relationship with God. Their fear of God "becomes the principle of human behavior and the beginning of wisdom,"[30] making them mothers, life-givers of the Hebrew people.

A literary analysis of this pericope further strengthens the image of the midwives as life-givers. The pericope portrays the pharaoh as the source of death. In contrast, the midwives are portrayed as the source of life. Between the role of the pharaoh and that of Shiphrah and Puah "stands the fear of God as a motivating factor (v. 17) and as an attitude of faith which reaps its reward (v. 21a)."[31] This reward, though there is no clear way of reading verses 20–21, is a reward that corresponds to Shiphrah's and Puah's deed.[32] They are blessed with a progeny. Furthermore, Shiphrah and Puah, as verse 20 seems to indicate, "are credited with building up the house of Israel."[33]

The story of Shiphrah and Puah foreshadows the exodus event. Their defiant attitude toward the pharaoh foreshadows the attitude of Moses and Aaron. Like the pharaoh with whom Moses and Aaron will have to deal, this pharaoh becomes increasingly stubborn. The midwives' brave stance forces the pharaoh to escalate his strategy. His attempt to finish with the Hebrews will "force God's hand." Remembering the covenant made with the Israelites, God will intervene in their behalf. The exodus movement has started. Further, Shiphrah and Puah save the Israelites. Their actions make the exodus possible. No liberation is possible without life; these women are indeed givers of life. No liberation is possible without courage to act and willingness to risk; these women are indeed risk-takers, agents of their own history and of the history of their people.

As an interpretive key which can be used by *mujeristas*, the story of Shiphrah and Puah raises many questions that we apply to our situation today. Often caught against our will between the oppressor and the oppressed, how can we, Hispanic women, be self-determining? How can we be about liberation, no matter what our role in life is? When we do not have power or strategic advantage, do we give in or do we find a way to resist? Can we sacrifice one for the sake of many? Can a few be liberated at the expense of others? What is the critical lens that *mujeristas* must use all the time: Hispanicness or liberation? How does the God of *mujeristas* differ from the God of the pharaohs of our days, or the God who the pharaohs of our world believe themselves to be? How do we as oppressed persons remain faithful to our God?

Each *mujerista* must allow Shiphrah and Puah to ask her many different questions. These questions will produce not jarring pieces but rather elements that will come together to form a tapestry of the whole. Such a weaving will depict a vision of justice that is not possible without liberation, and this is precisely that task of *mujeristas* today: to be about the task of liberation.

PODER MUJERISTA — REINVENTING POWER

One of the most important and at the same time most difficult understandings to keep in the forefront of *mujerista* theology is the difference between equality and liberation. Equality has to do with participation by the oppressed in the structures that exist today. Liberation, on the other hand, is about radical change of the oppressive societal structures. To think that equality for all is possible within the present structures of society is a mistake. The structures of society today, all of them linked and controlled or at least heavily influenced by patriarchy, necessitate someone at the bottom, someone to be oppressed, someone from whom others can benefit. Those in control, those who benefit from present societal structures, wish to maintain those structures at all cost. Therefore, though they may not like it, they are willing to allow the marginated of society to gain equality — to participate in the structures that the powerful control — but they will oppose liberation with all their might.

Liberation demands that we bring about a new order of relationship among persons, whether that relationship is a personal or a business relationship. The powerful of today cannot hold on to their power with one hand and extend an invitation to the poor and oppressed with the other. Liberation, therefore, is most threatening to the powers that be because by insisting on redefining power, liberation does away with their privileged position. But those who insist on liberation must understand that a redefinition of power also challenges the way the poor and the oppressed themselves structure and participate in the struggle of liberation. The way we carry out our struggle will be an integral part of the outcome. Therefore, we must move away from authoritarian, hierarchical structures of power in our communities of struggle. We must work to operate out of a circular model of leadership and use a consensual process when the community has to make decisions.

For us *mujeristas* power is the ability to enable all persons to become the most they themselves can be. It must be clearly understood that in the Hispanic culture persons can become fully themselves only in relation to the community and not as isolated individuals who look out only for themselves. Our understanding of power demands that we work incessantly to create the political, economic, and social conditions needed for the self-realization of all persons. It also requires establishing relational structures and operational modes in all spheres of life which facilitate and promote the self-realization of all persons. Finally, our understanding of power requires promotion of the creativity of all persons so they can contribute efficaciously to the common good.[34] *Mujerista* theology struggles to bring up the question of power in every single moment of the doing of theology. Furthermore, *mujerista* theology challenges all liberation theologies to place the question of power at the heart of their theological enterprise. The focus might be different but the questions about power must always be asked. For example, what do we mean when we say that God is all-powerful? Is our God an enabling God or a controlling God made to the image and likeness of the males who control the society in which we live? If power as understood today in our society is good, then it should be shared by all. Then why has Mary been portrayed exclusively as a submissive woman and why is this submissive Mary proposed as the main example for Roman Catholic women? What would reinventing power mean for the "power of orders" so very central to the present understanding of priesthood in the Roman Catholic church? What would priestly ministry entail if power is understood as enablement and fostering creativity instead of control and domination? What happens to our ethics and morality if we raise the question of power when making decisions? In conclusion, how do our theological discourse and the structures of our churches bless and sanctify the understanding of power as control and domination?

The struggle for liberation of Hispanic women is being carried out in many different ways by many different *mujeristas* all around the United States. *Mujerista* theology is one of the voices of such a struggle — a struggle which is life for us because we have learned from our grandmothers and mothers that *la vida es la lucha*.

PART III

PRAXIS

9

"Turning of the World" (excerpt)

RUTH PELHAM

Let us sing this song for the turning of the world
  that we may turn as one
With every voice, with every song
  let us move this world along
And our lives will feel the echo of our turning

Case Study of a Black Parish in Detroit: Developing a Small Christian Community Model of Church

JOSEPH G. HEALEY, M.M.

How does a revolution in a black inner-city parish take place? This is the story of St. Agnes parish's revolution.

1961. St. Agnes, in the center of Detroit, was a thriving, middle-class, white parish. Twelve hundred Catholic families belonged to the parish and eight thousand people attended the six Masses on a typical Sunday. The many parish organizations and activities were booming. St. Agnes had given more priests (35) and more Sisters (55) than any other parish in the Detroit archdiocese.

1967. By 1967 most white people had moved to the Detroit suburbs and St. Agnes was a predominantly black parish. The terrible city riots started just two blocks from St. Agnes church and left the neighborhood scarred with burned-out buildings and alienated hearts. Radical conflict and dissension abounded in Detroit. Parishioners were afraid to walk on the streets and even mistrusted some of their neighbors.

1978–81. After eighteen years as spiritual director and professor at the nearby Sacred Heart Seminary, Father Edward J. Farrell became pastor of St. Agnes parish. A well-known spiritual writer and lecturer, he had traveled to many places in the world. Now he listened to the people and assessed the needs of Detroit's inner-city black community, and a new model of evangelization evolved.

First, Father Farrell formed a pastoral team composed of five white Sisters, a black minister of service (similar to a permanent deacon), a retired, black Internal Revenue Service worker, and two Irish lay volunteers. The team formed a small community themselves. Some members lived together; all prayed, reflected, and planned together regularly. The pastoral team wanted to be a community itself before going out to form and animate other small communities.

Farrell and the team reflected on different models or styles of evangelization for a black inner-city parish in the late 1970s and 1980s. They found

132

that black Catholics are as varied and individual as white Catholics. Some prefer the structure, discipline, and tradition of the Catholic church. A purely charismatic style is not appealing to many black Catholics today.

Door-to-door evangelization (home visiting on a one-on-one basis) has not been that successful in black neighborhoods in the inner-city. Dedicated Catholic Sisters have been visiting apartments and homes in the parishes in Detroit's center for a number of years without many pastoral break-throughs.

St. Agnes parish was really a mission situation. Pastoral work in 1961 became missionary work by 1978. There were only about one hundred Catholic families in a total population of twenty thousand people. Only ten families were intact, that is, father, mother, and children living together. Young people were few and the committed ones even fewer. Crime and violence were frequent. Detroit's inner-city life included fear, distrust, and individualism.

While at Sacred Heart Seminary, Farrell had developed small communities or "fraternities" among the students and faculty. During trips through Africa and Latin America he had learned about the small Christian community (SCC) model of church. So he and the pastoral team designed a new pastoral plan for St. Agnes parish that stressed grass-roots, urban evangelization based on SCCs. The team divided the mile-square parish into seven SCC zones. Farrell said: "By dividing the parish into sections you move from the church of the anonymous multitude to smaller disciple groups—you're creating small communities in neighborhoods." The goal was for St. Agnes parish itself to become a communion of seven SCC zones and each zone a neighborhood of families.

Parish council members became the leaders of each zone, and members of the pastoral team became animators in this grass-roots model of evangelization. The SCC zones tried to meet weekly in the homes of members to pray, discuss, and socialize together. Zone members tried to reach out to needy people in the wider community through practical action and service.

How did black Catholics in St. Agnes parish respond to the SCC model of church? Some were enthusiastic and immediately began to form an ongoing community. Yet reluctance and hesitation were the most common responses. After several valiant attempts to discover some common bonding, members of one zone honestly admitted that no natural cohesion existed at a level sufficient for them to build upon. Of critical importance were the patience and persistence of the animators of the SCC zones. Leadership and co-responsibility emerged extremely slowly.

Perhaps the black Catholics' strongest desire has been for a more intense and dynamic community. But most St. Agnes parishioners preferred larger community gatherings (the larger assembly model) to the SCC model. Some experienced isolation in the SCC prayer groups. Some preferred homogeneous groups rather than neighborhood groups. The best SCC zone is composed of professional people.

During several trips to Africa, Farrell became very interested in African customs and traditions, especially as they related to the black experience in the United States. He took a course at Wayne State University called "African Retentions in the New World after 400 Years." As he observed the customs of the black people in St. Agnes parish he wondered about the depth of their African roots. One day he was visiting a black parishioner in her apartment. When Farrell prepared to leave, the woman insisted on walking him not only down to the front door of the apartment house, but also the two blocks back to the rectory. Later Farrell learned about the common African custom of *kusindikiza* (to accompany or escort a friend or visitor back to his or her home). Without realizing it, the black woman in Detroit's inner-city had been living out a practice from her African roots.

St. Agnes parish began using *Kwanza* (the Swahili word for "First"), a program for developing black consciousness and heritage in the United States as part of the celebration of festivals that commemorate the first fruits of the African harvest. Along with other parishes and schools in Detroit, parishioners in St. Agnes used *Kwanza* to celebrate their African heritage, to give thanks to their ancestors, and to reinforce the black value system which is closely related to gospel values.

The pastoral team saw the possibilities of integrating African Christian values with black Christian values in America—in the context of the development of the SCC zones. This became a reality during an eight-day mission retreat at St. Agnes in March 1980. The theme of the retreat was "Experiencing African Christian Values," and the retreat focused on those values that have universal meaning: community, waiting, familyhood, sharing, joint responsibility, faith, self-determination, and call to unity in action. For each value there was a Swahili code word (for example, *jumuiya* for community), a short African story, an African proverb, a relevant Bible reading, and suggestions for concrete action, such as sharing with neighbors and helping needy persons in the community. After each talk and audiovisual presentation the parishioners met for discussion and sharing in their seven SCC zones.

During the mission retreat, a key insight was the importance of a community response. It became clear that risk and outreach by individuals were not enough; what was needed was the joint action of the seven SCC zones and the whole parish. Parishioners began to realize that to really live gospel values means to reach out and break down fear, mistrust, and isolation. This could best be done together through the SCCs. Zone One Christians supported a member in a protest against the negligence of a slum landlord. Zone Seven members decided to prepare Christmas gifts for needy families in their neighborhood.

At the end of the mission retreat, the seven SCC zones started concrete follow-up actions. Several zones decided to meet weekly in their neighborhood groups for prayer, discussions, and informal sharing. Others planned specific social action to help the sick, mentally retarded, and lonely. Zone One leader Thomas Grove said that the zone members wanted to put into practice the African saying that "Christianity is living for others." Ines Jenkins, the leader of Zone Four, decided to link her SCC with an SCC in Nyabihanga, Tanzania. She wrote Thomas Kidende, a Tanzanian lay leader, and suggested this "twinning" plan. Thus, a black Christian community in Detroit's inner-city joined hands with an African Christian community in rural western Tanzania.

Through 1980 and into the first months of 1981, St. Agnes parish tried various ways to develop its SCC zone model of church. One member of the pastoral team participated in a workshop on "Basic Christian Communities" at Maryknoll, New York, and other parishioners attended a similar workshop in July 1981. The St. Agnes Renovation Campaign from July to October 1980 was organized through the seven SCC zones. The zone captains coordinated the distribution of raffle tickets. For the St. Agnes Eucharistic Week, each zone was responsible for one day of prayer.

During this time the seven SCC zones searched and struggled for their identity. Rotating the prayer meetings among different homes in the zone was always difficult. Some people didn't want to meet in certain homes. One parishioner asked: "Why not meet in the church until everyone becomes comfortable with each other?" Some zones felt isolated if the Christians always remained in their small communities. So the SCC zones planned to meet at the parish for sharing and exchange every third week.

Zone members still hesitated in their social outreach. Fear and mistrust remained deep-seated in the inner-city. A seminar was organized for August 1981. It concentrated on the spirituality that underlies our Christian risk and outreach, especially in justice and peace issues.

So this SCC model of evangelization has its good days and bad ones. But it brought "small communities with a human face" into Detroit's inner-city and an opportunity for black Catholics to take responsibility for their church. As one black parishioner of St. Agnes parish said: "We are the mustard seed of the archdiocese. But we are already growing. We are experiencing a new trust, warmth and concern for each other. We are going to take more responsibility with the parish team for the parish. Evangelization is one of our priorities. We plan to reach out to the young and the old and all the unchurched people of our neighborhood."

Several other parishes in Detroit began adapting the SCC model of church, including one white, urban parish that has "satellite communities." This is part of the signs of the times calling us to develop "small communities with a human face."

AFTERWORD FROM ST. AGNES PARISH, BY FATHER EDWARD J. FARRELL

Update to October 1987. In 1987 St. Agnes church, though still small in number, was very much alive and active. Though a poor (from a financial viewpoint) parish, it cares for and about its people, as demonstrated by its raising funds for an elevator so that the handicapped could participate more fully in the life of the church. Between 1981 and 1987, several significant programs emerged in St. Agnes's continuing mission of outreach: A Montessori school for the parish children, where parents are offered classes in parenting and domestic skills and are encouraged to continue their own education, has proven so needed and so beneficial there is always a waiting list. A retreat team made up of St. Agnes parishioners, Father Farrell, and one or two Sisters began to go out on occasion (especially during the Lenten season) to interrelate with white, suburban parishes. This prayerful communication with people of varying social, ethnic, and economic backgrounds was one small step in breaking long-standing barriers and diminishing the fears that create separation. The old two-story flat on St. Agnes's property was remodeled by volunteers from the Catholic Alumnae Club of Detroit. And St. Marcella's vision of low-cost, alternative community-living for the elderly became a reality in September 1987 when the first resident moved in.

Between 1981 and 1987 people became more rooted in their African heritage through black studies programs at St. Agnes and the sending of individuals to study black history, liturgy, and theology at Xavier University's summer program. Peoples from all over the city (including many people from different cultures) gathered at St. Agnes for Thanksgiving Harvest Festivals in the African tradition with native dress, native music, food, art, and praying together in native tongues.

Sister Helen came to St. Agnes for seven months and Father Emanuel for five weeks—both are from Nigeria—to teach, share, and live with the people. As individuals have begun to claim their tradition, their own saints, and their unique and important contributions to the world, a new sense of pride, self-esteem, and positive identity has emerged. People who once shied away from contact with one another have begun to walk hand-in-hand. This was literally lived out during the Week of Remembrance that was organized to commemorate the twentieth anniversary of the Detroit riots; as part of the commemoration we of St. Agnes initiated a remembrance walk along the route of the riots. It was a solemn occasion, yet one filled with new hope and new visions. Reconciliation from so many facets can be felt, can be seen.

The zone groups, which fostered community in the 1960s and 1970s, have remained as check-points for prayer, concern, and communication through the parish team. In January 1985 we began the Contemplative Community at St. Agnes. Jesus' love of the city and his compassion and concern for the multitudes, for the "little ones," are imperatives for a contemplative prayer parish in the heart of the city. A contemplative parish provides an oasis to the thousands of people who work and live in what is virtually a Via Dolorosa, a Way of the Cross, a way so many are compelled to walk each day. This contemplative parish is anchored in a parish of ordinary and faithful people who have chosen to continue to live in the heart of the city. Through their own experience of the hardships of city life with its alienations, its struggles, its works, its restraints, its anonymity and violence, they know the stress, the noise and pollution, the joys and sorrows, the evil and the goodness of the city. They live in solidarity with the people of the city and wish to offer them some kind of Nazareth or Bethany or Emmaus freely open to all, a place of welcome and hospitality, a place of deep silence alive with prayer, a place of rest and healing, a home where all people, whatever their social or religious background, age or outlook on life, are invited to come and share in a common search for contemplation in Christ.

The violence and fear in the inner city has become an appropriate and favorable environment for contemplation. The ominous worldwide threats can only be counterbalanced by a power greater than destruction. The new sanctuary is contemplation in community. The human heart will submit to only so much psychic numbness. Then tremors begin to be felt in the depths, an irruption builds up and pressures forth. The Spirit-quake may be "underground," but its seismic effects circle the globe. Contemplation initiates a continuous conversion, a *transformation*. A transcendence, an exchange is demanded. Doing something is not enough. We must become some *one*. Contemplation creates an abandonment, a freedom to love, a freedom to die, a freedom to be nothing, a freedom to be all things, a freedom to be like God, like Jesus. The price we must pay is nothing less than everything!

St. Agnes, on Rosa Parks Boulevard, is a renaissance neighborhood . . . a light . . . a hope . . . a promise of today.

10

From the Fields of California: Rising Hispanic Consciousness

CÉSAR CHÁVEZ

All my life I have been driven by one dream, one goal, one vision: To overthrow a labor system that treats farm workers as if they are not important human beings.

Farm workers are not agricultural implements; they are not beasts of burden, to be used and discarded.

My motivation comes from my personal life: from watching what my mother and father went through when I was growing up, from what we experienced as migrant farm workers.

All Hispanics are connected to the farm workers' experience. They or their parents lived through the experience of the fields. They shared a common humiliation. . . .

How could our people believe that their children could become lawyers, doctors, judges, and business people while this shame and injustice continued? . . .

The United Farm Workers of America has struggled to attack the historical source of the shame and infamy with which our people lived in the country. . . .

By addressing this historical problem, we created confidence, pride, and hope in a people's ability to create the future. . . .

The union's existence sent a signal to all Hispanics that we were fighting for dignity; we were challenging and overcoming injustice; we were empowering the least educated and poorest among us. The message was that if it could happen in the fields, it could happen in cities, schools, courts, city councils, and in state legislatures. . . .

Times are changing; the political and social environment has changed. . . . The rise of Hispanic influence in California is part of a force of history.

... It is inevitable. Once social change begins, it cannot be reversed.

You cannot uneducate the person who has learned to read; humiliate the person who feels pride; oppress people who are not afraid.

It is not just a union we have built. For nearly twenty years our union has been on the cutting edge of a people's cause; you cannot stamp out a people's cause.

Regardless of what the future holds for farm workers, our accomplishments cannot be undone. *La Causa* doesn't have to be experienced twice. The consciousness and pride that were raised by our union are alive and thriving inside millions of young Hispanics who will never work on a farm.

Like other immigrant groups, the day will come when we win the economic and political rewards that are in keeping with our numbers in society.

That day may not come this year. That day may not come during this decade. But it will come, someday.

And when that day comes, we shall see the fulfillment of a passage from the Book of Matthew in the New Testament: That the last shall be first and the first shall be last.

On that day, our nation shall fulfill its creed.

Editor's note: To draw attention to the plight of United Farm Workers, César Chávez spent 23 days in July and August 1988 fasting and praying. For Chávez and his more than 3,000 supporters, including the Rev. Jesse Jackson, the fast was a time of spiritual cleansing for the continuation of la causa.

11

Liberation Theology Comes
to the South Bronx

ARTHUR JONES

"I see the possibility of the beginnings of a liberation theology in the South Bronx. It will begin, I think, to use liberation theology terms, with praxis and reflection. It will be ecumenical from the very ground up, which is tremendous."

Slender, fifty-one-year-old Father Peter J. Gavigan was not at his parish, Our Lady of Victory in the South Bronx, when he spoke, but in a convent retreat house in suburban, upper-class White Plains, New York, where South Bronx Christian ministers were gathered for a three-day session to get to know one another and to strategize.

This retreat is one more stage in a drawn-out, two-to-three-year process to bring to fruition the organizational stage of empowering the people of the South Bronx. The starting point is the people of the Christian churches, the tens of thousands among the hundreds of thousands who call the South Bronx home.

SBC, as the South Bronx Churches' organization is known, has already had member churches agree to put up almost $700,000 to finance the organizational stage; SBC has the example of neighboring East Brooklyn Churches (EBC) to draw on. . . . And SBC knows that if empowerment can be seen to work in the South Bronx, then that becomes a national breakthrough offering hope elsewhere, for "South Bronx" has become the preeminent synonym for urban decay.

Gavigan is neither naive nor a newcomer. Ordained in 1962, he is back for a second tour at South Bronx's Our Lady of Victory on Webster Street. Gavigan was at Our Lady's for six years in the 1970s (when there were eight hundred parishioners) and returned in 1983 to minister to the fewer than four hundred Hispanics and blacks for whom Our Lady's is both a spiritual home and a physical refuge.

The New York diocesan priest describes South Bronx churches as "little islands of hope surrounded by waters of fear and violence." He has watched the South Bronx's continual physical deterioration, but it is a deterioration contradicted by individual Protestant and Catholic churches that have rehabilitated housing, opened senior centers, and kept schools and day-care centers going.

Said Gavigan, "You could look around and say, 'Oh, this looks nice,' but the neighborhood around us is hostile. The neighborhood around us is drug pushers, muggers, crack dealers.

"So my little island, I mean the people, they step outside and look right and left and say, 'I can't come out at night.' So what good is this little island? It is a prison. A fortress."

There is an attempt to break out of that fortress. The SBC coalition has brought in the Saul Alinsky-founded Industrial Areas Foundation that assisted with EBC community organizing in East Brooklyn.

Said Gavigan, "We, as Christian ministers, do not want to become just another secular power organization. We want this grounded in the gospel, in the tradition of the scriptures, in Catholic and other Christian social teaching.

"Many of us, including myself, did this in the 1960s and 1970s in individual parish social action programs and had limited success. Now we've come to realize that unless we join together — Catholics, Protestants, blacks, Hispanics, whites — we're not going to have the power, the clout necessary to do what needs to be done.

"I think, I hope, this is the way God is drawing us together, knitting the churches together, not through navel-gazing or theological conferences, but through meeting the needs of God's people."

SBC is an attempt both to "link up the islands through bridges of mutual respect" so that the "inhabitants really know each other" and to "fight off the predators." The South Bronx is valuable real estate, blighted though it may be. "Developers want our islands, our streets, our empty lots, want to make them a desert and call it an 'industrial park'; that's the euphemism they use, 'park,' " Gavigan said. "They want whole tracts of land and would displace already displaced people in the name of 'progress.' "

Gavigan undoubtedly is speaking for many South Bronx ministers when he says, "Someone said war is too important to be left to the generals. Well, we have come to the conclusion that public business in the Bronx is too important to be left to the politicians — we have to return it to the people."

Given that Bronx politicians under indictment still find ways to be re-elected in an area plagued by political scandals, SBC's hope to reinvigorate the area politically means sheer hard work ahead.

"The people basically don't know how the system works," said Gavigan. "They are apathetic and they have given up on it. That's a dangerous thing. We Christian ministers want to give the people hope, to educate people in how the system works so they can confront that system with their power. But we don't want to be David going up against Goliath, and David not even having a slingshot."

In the summer of 1986, Gavigan took "a bus-man's holiday" spent with the poor in Chile, Bolivia, Argentina, and Venezuela. He was on vacation with another priest.

He said, "Some of us have been kind of wondering why we don't have what the Latin Americans have: their methodology and all these theologians writing. A Chilean friend, a layman, said the North American situation is so different we have to create our own theology and methodology."

Gavigan sat back in his comfortable stuffed chair in the relaxed atmosphere of the retreat house. There was the gentle buzz of conversation coming through the walls from next door, where the South Bronx pastors were deep into their retreat's first session.

Gavigan, the South Bronx Catholic priest, leaned forward again in his chair and said, "The oppression here in North America is more subtle. The more we observe, the more we realize that our people in the United States are hurting, too. Especially the poor; they are paralyzed. We have been paralyzed. But we sense that now is the time to shift.

"We don't have a worked-out theology yet for the North American situation. Some people, like John Coleman, have written on it. Yet, we have been reformed, and reinformed, by Vatican II, and we are going to come to grips with what's happening to our own poor people.

"Here in the South Bronx, through the methodology of this SBC organization, we think we have a vehicle. Out of this, and out of what's happening in East Brooklyn and elsewhere, the theology will be written.

"I haven't been this excited in twenty years."

12

Prison Statement from Sing Sing

NEW YORK THEOLOGICAL SEMINARY STUDENTS WITH INSTRUCTOR JOHN EAGLESON

OUR CONTEXT

1. We are fifteen students of theology, of various racial and ethnic backgrounds, incarcerated in the Sing Sing maximum security prison, Ossining, New York.

2. Our situation is dehumanizing on every level: physical, psychological, emotional, sociological, spiritual.

3. Twenty-four hours a day, seven days a week we are stripped of our identity, warehoused.

4. Prison causes a chilling effect on our self-image, a continuous crisis of identity, a castration of self-purpose, an undermining of the foundations of compassion, loyalty, and respect for society and for each other.

5. The psychological harassment, the condescending, authoritarian abuse, has many expressions, for example:

6. —Those who confront the penal system intellectually are labelled troublemakers, are transferred to distant facilities, or are isolated from the general population on trumped-up charges.

7. —Family ties are damaged, as visitors are harassed.

8. —Our families are expected to be "humble," humorous, and diplomatic, never asserting their human rights or righteous indignation over the harassment they suffer.

9. From society's perspective we are mere numbers, caged statistics, tax dollar expenditures. Ironically, it costs society more to imprison us than it would to support and educate us and our families.

10. Wealth in this country is not equally distributed, and poverty is one of the factors responsible for crime. Our society is one of injustice enforced

by law; we live under a kind of American apartheid, made all the worse inside the walls.

11. The vast majority of the imprisoned are disadvantaged people, usually members of minority groups. Those who have no money, who are poorly educated, who are unemployed, are much more likely to end up in prison. The indigent are often forced to stand trial represented by incompetent lawyers using plea-bargain incarceration tactics.

12. Black and Hispanic youths are imprisoned while white youths, especially middle- and upper-class whites, guilty of the same crimes are often placed on probation or released outright.

13. Sentences are excessive, frequently exceeding the ages of young persons.

14. The beneficiaries of this billion-dollar incarceration business are largely white communities and white businesses in proximity to the prisons.

15. In the face of an oppression that would have us no longer exist as ourselves, we have struggled to preserve our own identities, self-confidence, and faith.

16. Under this psychological assault, many of us rely very heavily on the love, the care, and the support of our families. Others have no strong family ties and must rely only on themselves if they are to survive.

THEOLOGICAL REFLECTION

17. Our present situation in large part is due to individual and societal disregard for the principles of the kingdom of God.

18. We are sinners in the eyes of God, but repentant sinners . . . forgiven and blessed by God, as surely as the repentant thief was blessed by Jesus on the cross (Luke 23:39–43).

19. Society, however, is not so forgiving. We are sinners in society's eyes, but we are not allowed to demonstrate repentance. We are cast aside and considered beyond salvation. We owe a debt to society and have no choice but to "give unto Caesar what is Caesar's."

20. But we believe that no matter what the circumstances in which we find ourselves, if we seek God, God is there to help us (Ps. 121).

21. In the word of God, we are all created in God's image and likeness (Gen. 1:26-27).

22. Whether black, white, or Hispanic, whether Jew or Greek, young or old, male or female, we are all one (Gal. 3:28). God has chosen the color of our skin, and race is not an issue with God. God gives to each of us "a body as he has chosen. . . . For not all flesh is alike . . . " (1 Cor. 15:38–39).

23. We are in exile, deported from our homes and families. Incarcerated and oppressed, we nevertheless believe in a God of liberation and justice.

24. Our God is fully involved in human affairs, a God who delivered Israel from the slavery of Egypt, who protected Daniel in the lion's den.

25. The gospel is good news proclaimed to the poor, the captives, the blind, and the oppressed.

26. The Qur'an, the holy book of some of us, states that God does not change the condition of a people until the people change their own condition. God works with the people, through the people, for the people.

27. These are some of the changes we would like to see:

28. —We address the prison administration, the courts, the parole boards, and society at large. If we exhibit responsible, rehabilitated conduct while in prison—either by educating ourselves or dealing with our situation in intelligent, mature, and nonviolent ways—we believe that our changed behavior should be rewarded by early parole.

29. —Counselors, psychiatric staff, and facility educators must work together to educate and assist inmates toward the goal of early release for demonstrated modification of behavior.

30. —Concrete criteria for parole eligibility and release should replace the arbitrary determinations of the parole board members, who make such determinations on the basis of personal biases.

31. One possibility is "contract parole," in which an inmate is given a specific list of obligations to fulfill. Once these obligations are fulfilled, the inmate is paroled; rehabilitative needs are addressed and rewards and punishments are administered more objectively.

32. Some of us are gifted as apostles or mentors, as educators or administrators or musicians. Whatever our gifts or talents, we are a people called to serve. The following are examples of the ways we intend to live out our commitments:

33. —We believe it is our responsibility to work for change by educating both our prison peers and the general public as to the structural defects and systemic abuses inherent in the present criminal justice system. Whether inside prison or out, we plan to work where we can best use our experience and abilities to become catalysts for constructive change.

34. —We intend to teach, lecture, and write on issues that will raise the level of consciousness among the inmate population, first, to help liberate ourselves and others from the bondage of distorted thinking, and, second, to help instill a sense of our own worth as human beings.

35. —One example of the kind of organization with which we can work effectively is FIST (Families and Inmates Serving Time). This is a religiously based self-help group of inmates and family members who seek positive change through petitions, law suits, legislative enactments, and political pressure. At present FIST exists only at Sing Sing, but two new chapters are being established at other New York state prisons.

36. This is our understanding of our situation, our reading of God's word for us, and our discernment of the commitment we are called to make.

13

Empowering the Poor with Housing

CHUCK MATTHEI

If you had chanced to cross Government Center Plaza in Boston on a certain cold, windy day in 1988, you would have encountered several hundred nuns, priests, and laypeople—and Mayor Ray Flynn and City Councilor Rosario Salerno—and representatives of ICE (Institute for Community Economics) gathered around a semicircle of banners bearing the names of twenty-eight Catholic religious orders. And from the stage you would have heard Sister Kathleen Popko, president of the Leadership Conference of Women Religious in New England, say:

> We are here today to demonstrate our concern for the housing crisis, and to show that ordinary people with ordinary resources can do something about it. . . . We are Catholic religious who feel that we can no longer remain comfortable in our convents and rectories while thousands of men, women, and children have no place to call home. It is not that we have not responded in the past . . . but we believe that the current crisis demands that we do more and do it collectively to ensure a greater impact.
>
> We are responding to the gospel challenge to be just stewards of our resources and we invite all of you to join us. . . . ICE is our bridge.

It was a prayer service, it was a press conference, it was a political demonstration. It was the dedication of the "Collaborative Investment for Housing." Already more than $700,000 has been received, with more loans pending. The participating orders had made not only an initial investment, but a commitment to a process of reflection and deepening involvement—with the affirmation that these community investments best reflect religious values and should be the standard against which every investment opportunity is measured. They have transformed a traditionally private business decision into a powerful moral and political statement, reaching out to others in the church and in the community and saying, "Join us!"

It had been, you might say, a banner year for ICE's Revolving Loan Fund (RLF), the year in which we first passed the $10,000,000 mark in cumulative loans to community development projects, and then substantially exceeded $10,000,000 in cumulative loans from investors as well!

The year 1988 had seen the most dramatic growth in the RLF's history. As of the end of the year, 147 new investors had committed $2,625,000 — twice as much as the best previous year. Major loans came from the Mac-Arthur Foundation and the National Coop Bank Development Corporation. The Calvert Social Investment Fund made its first foray into community investment, and the Franklin Companies of Boston, the leading management firm in the social investment field, significantly increased its participation, transferring client funds from money-market accounts into the RLF. And, as always, individual investors, one by one, formed the backbone in the RLF.

We had been able to make thirty-four loans to community groups that year, with others pending. Eleven CLTs (Community Land Trusts) — from Glenwood City, Wisconsin, to Albany, New York, from Durham, North Carolina, to Trenton, New Jersey — had received one or more loans . . . and loans had supported an agricultural coop in Puerto Rico, an emergency shelter in New York City, a home for developmentally disabled adults in Washington, D.C., the Federation of Southern Cooperatives in Alabama, and a mobile home park in Palmer, Massaschusetts.

Let me tell you very briefly about that mobile home park, because it so blatantly illustrates not only the need but the injustice many of these groups confront. . . . We received an urgent call from the president of the residents' association, who had been notified that the out-of-state corporation that owned the park would sell it to a developer who planned to evict all of the residents and build condominiums. Many residents had lived in the park for fifteen to twenty years, had landscaped and built additions, and were anything but mobile. There were no alternative sites available for the park, and individual lots in the area were going for an unaffordable $40,000 each.

Under Massachusetts law, the residents' association had a right to purchase the park if they could match the developer's offer. The price was high, but then so were current lot rents, and the residents discovered that they could afford to amortize a conventional mortgage in less than fifteen years. In this, they were so much more fortunate than most of our borrowers! So they assembled a down payment and approached the banks — but the only bank that indicated any willingness to lend wanted 4 percent on closing, a rate of 2 percent over prime, an adjustable monthly rate with no upper limit, and a four-year balloon rate . . . and they refused to close in time to meet the deadline.

In desperation, the residents approached ICE. We were able to make the loan, and to provide advice and technical assistance. The homes of these ninety-two families were saved, and both the residents and ICE were committed to opening new sources of financing for mobile home parks.

That was good news. And similarly, the RLF was instrumental in saving or creating homes for hundreds of other families that year, and protecting and strengthening critical community organizations and local leadership. ICE's loans, technical assistance, and personal encouragement help to bring down barriers that deny access to decent, affordable housing, employment, and basic human service to so many.

But for so many others, the barriers persist. The corporation that sold that mobile home park announced plans to sell ten others across New England. After that successful purchase, ICE received requests from four more parks, but our lending resources were exhausted.

Over and over again, we see the injustice. In the same week that we closed that loan, I found a copy of the *Wall Street Journal* left behind on a New York-to-Boston Amtrak train by a departing businessman. There was a full-page photo of a middle-aged white man, standing on the expansive lawn of a huge, white-pillared house—and superimposed in big letters the caption: "FOR OUR PRIVILEGED CLIENTS: A 7% MORTGAGE." Underneath it said, "If you are purchasing a house for $200,000 or more, call the Boston Company and speak to your personal banker" . . . and I was tempted to go home and pick up the phone and say, "Boston Company, I'm looking at a home (for ninety–two families) for $1.3 million; let's do business."

It reminds me of the story my friend Dorothy Day—co-founder of the Catholic Worker movement, with its soup kitchens and shelters, its dedication to the "works of peace and the works of mercy"—told of a trip to Mexico. As she crossed the border, she saw:

> . . . one long line of shacks made of packing boxes, that melt away in the rain—and there's a tall fence that separates the United States and its opulence from this shacktown on the other side. And you see on this fence places where the Mexicans have tried to climb over, and you see garments hanging where they've been caught, and they couldn't get them back, maybe a piece of shirt was ripped off of one or another of them. And it's a sad sight. I thought to myself, "This is our Berlin Wall!"

So many barriers still remain, around us and among us.

14

The Feeding of a Multitude: Loaves and Fishes at Grand Central

ROBERT HIRSCHFIELD

The man in the suit and tie with the carton of sandwiches, fruit, and milk knocked on the phone booth door, as though it were the front door of someone's home. The old black woman sleeping lightly inside the booth opened the door, took the food, then went back to sleep. She is one of the approximately three hundred people who live in New York's Grand Central Station and who are fed each night by the Coalition for the Homeless.

The coalition's Grand Central project got under way after a thirty-four-year-old homeless woman was found dead in the station, a victim of malnutrition. The coalition, a Manhattan-based advocacy group, decided to purchase meals prepared for the school lunch program from the Board of Education at a cost of ninety-five cents each and distribute them to Grand Central's homeless. A donation of $10,000 from a well-known cartoonist helped meet the cost of feeding three hundred people a night for a year.

The sight that greets the driver of the coalition van as it pulls into Vanderbilt Avenue (Grand Central's western flank) at ten o'clock sharp comes straight out of a Third World refugee camp. A line of hungry, homeless men and a few women extends in the shadows of the station's walls for almost a block. They are mainly black or Hispanic, and young. The elderly, the mad, and the lame remain inside the station for the most part. The mark of dispossession, that emblem of the 1920s and 1930s, indents almost every face in the line.

While the meals are being distributed outside the terminal, inside another line has formed, this one leading to the ChemBankcard Center's all-night cash machine. The people waiting for their money and those waiting for their food seem totally unaware of each other's presence. The narrow space that separates them might as well be a mountain. But occasionally, a passerby will stop and stuff bills into the hands of a coalition volunteer. David Beseda, the project director, estimates that hundreds of dollars have come to the coalition in this way.

By serving free meals inside the terminal, the coalition has brought down upon itself the wrath of station authorities who fear that, as word gets out about free food, Grand Central's homeless population will soar. "The station," in the words of officials who run Grand Central's commuter railroad, Metro North, "is for passengers. It is not a shelter." While the station master himself has warned Beseda not to distribute food inside the station, no action has yet been taken to stop the distribution. Fear of public obloquy is sometimes a serviceable substitute for conscience.

A tough, young Puerto Rican, asked why he chose Grand Central Station over a city-financed room in a Bowery hotel, replied, "It's better to sleep on a bench than in the flops where you have to spend the night fighting off lice." Others complain of the violence in the city shelters and the contempt of the guards for shelter inmates. (Some New York churches and synagogues, in coordination with the city's shelter program, do provide overnight accommodation for a few men at a time in church basements, etc. But such beds are few, and the congregations' interest is difficult to maintain.) The terminal's vastness allows for anonymity, for the possibility of eluding danger among milling crowds. If the needs of the homeless were merely spatial, Grand Central would be ideal.

From 1:30 A.M. to 5:30 A.M. the station closes down. Police briskly scatter the homeless, who drift from the phone booths and benches to the streets or the ramps leading down to the subway, each in his or her own solitude. The nightly migrants include the lame, the mad, and the elderly. None is spared.

For New York's homeless, Grand Central Station is one wilderness among many. It is neither the most nor the least parched. At ten o'clock sharp, the coalition van arrives with bread. Manna on wheels. In other wildernesses throughout the city, vans do not appear at appointed hours like bountiful chariots. Seldom does anything appear to break the cruel circuit of hunger and isolation. The condition of Grand Central's homeless is at once dreadful and privileged.

15

Justice House

STEVE VANDERSTAAY

In 1985 David Hayden and his family drove a pick-up truck into Roanoke, Virginia, with $200 and a dream: to create a radical Christian community among homeless Virginians.

The Haydens found their "house": a vacant, worn Baptist sanctuary and adjoining, dilapidated half-way facility. Homeless people quickly found Justice House, filling all available space even before the community had funding, furniture, gas, or heat.

In the intervening years, Justice House has emerged as a U.S. version of the base Christian communities (BCCs) of Latin America. Reflecting together on relevant biblical passages from their context as poor, homeless Americans who follow the "liberator Jesus," community members strategize for themselves and other homeless people. This process of action and reflection called "hermeneutical circle" in the argot of liberation theology has generated a controversial and cohesive community engaged in nonviolent action. Justice House members have shown remarkable success in reestablishing control over their own lives.

"We're not really a shelter," explains Will, pausing from his repair of the front steps of Justice House. "People don't live in shelters; they just stay there at night. We live here. More than seventy of us: men, women, and children. All races. Sharing life together."

Completing the hole and tightening the screw to reinforce the old wood, Will continues, "Take me, I'm an alcoholic. Homeless for years, I live and work here now. I haven't had a drink in four months, and I'm starting to work downtown, too, thanks to God and Justice House."

Others share their stories. A young stonemason explains how a skin disease caused by overwork and the chemical hazards of his trade keeps him unemployed. An elderly woman speaks of life in a company town, now deserted with the closing of the mines.

Injustice, tragedy, layoffs, bad luck, lack of housing and good jobs, stories all too common among homeless people. But there is also a sense of rebirth, of rejuvenation, with most ending their stories with a postscript: happening upon Justice House, and the experience of healing, empowerment, and a radical Christian commitment to social change, for which Justice House is known.

This commitment has led community members to interrupt governmental budget hearings with laugh boxes and occupy an abandoned apartment building located on Episcopal church property.

During a forty-eight-day fast in Washington, D.C., by Hayden, Mitch Snyder, and Carol Fennelly, Justice House members were the first of thirty-one support groups to be arrested as they demonstrated for fuller access to housing. Hayden considers it "theologically significant" that Justice House residents led the protest.

"We are a community of the poor, an incredibly radical thing. Hurt and angry, we are now doing something about it. 'God has chosen what the world counts weakness. He has chosen things low and contemptible, mere nothings, to overthrow the existing order.' We believe that's what we're doing."

RADICAL PILGRIMAGE

The son of a displaced farm worker who moved north to work in an auto plant, Hayden grew up disdained for his southern heritage and background of poverty. Working his way up the corporate ladder of a pharmaceutical company, he became disillusioned and quit the job, deliberately putting himself on a "downwardly mobile" track and opening his suburban Gainesville, Florida, home to homeless people.

Hayden has garnered a reputation for his campaigns on behalf of the homeless, and his harangues against the "institutional church," which he likens to the Antichrist.

"That may sound extreme," he admits, "but the longer my pilgrimage continues, the more radical I see Jesus to be; and the further removed I see the institutional church to be from the kingdom of God. The church, I believe, is the most oppressive structure in our country, crushing the spirits of the poor with its charity.

"Now we are considering the idea of occupying a rich, establishment church, and to actually run the money-changers out. Jesus condemned the rich categorically, and so do we."

As if to illustrate this point, a large banner which reads "WOE UNTO THE RICH!" hangs in front of the apartment building now housing Justice House. Hayden defends it as part of Christ's challenge to the affluent to divest themselves of their wealth and give to the poor.

Some of his detractors object to the revolutionary bent of Hayden's theology, while others insinuate that he may be seeking martyrdom through his fasts. The *Roanoke Times & World News* has likened Hayden's approach to that of the black power advocates in the Civil Rights movement, calling his tactics "childish blackmail."

Hayden dismisses the criticisms as society's fear of the homeless. He affirms the Justice House commitment to life in community with the poor. He believes the church is at the threshold of a second reformation, a reformation by the poor.

Justice House represents a radical theological manifestation of what Larry Rasmussen has called the vibrant and empowering "community-creating religion among lower socioeconomic classes or other marginalized groups."[1] This movement, based on liberation theology, emphasizes Christ's concern for the poor, insisting upon justice as "the moral test of God-claims and spirituality."

Justice House residents believe Christian obedience demands that they move yet further from the mainstream of society, for Christ's aim, they insist, was not to influence Caesar but to oppose him. In Hayden's view this can be done only by poor people taking control and directing the movement. Toward this end Justice House residents plan to establish a network in the South, the goal being other religiously based communities of poor people.

"For me this originated from an understanding of the incarnation," explains Hayden, describing the role liberation theology played in the development of Justice House and his own views.

"I was a liberationist before I had ever heard of liberation theology because, as a poor person, it was apparent to me that God came to earth a poor man. Later, after we had established Justice House, I read Jon Sobrino, probably the closest to my thinking; José Miranda; and Gustavo Gutiérrez. You can't use someone else's model to create your own community; you simply build community with poor people. The result will be very similar to a BCC in Latin America."

COMMUNITY LIFE

There are numerous groups in the United States, especially among Hispanic Catholics, currently coming together as BCCs and employing the "hermeneutical circle," the process whereby political praxis and biblical reflection influence one another. Justice House differs from these groups in that members live together, share a common history of homelessness, and choose to remain poor.

Community time spent in biblical reflection, group therapy, and planning reduces conflict and strengthens cohesiveness. All decisions are by consensus; and Justice House has no staff or hierarchy, other than Hayden, who serves as the community pastor and spokesperson.

Attendance at community meetings is not mandatory, and members have few obligations. Some long-term residents join fully in community life, while others remain at Justice House only a few months, taking advantage of community stability to save money, find work, and establish a permanent address. For a community that does not attempt to reintroduce people into mainstream society, its success in doing so is remarkable. Former members often maintain contact with the community after reentering the job market or finding housing.

As a new and legitimate expression of the "community-creating religion among lower socioeconomic classes," Justice House raises challenging questions about the direction of such a movement.

The theological underpinning of the community, that the affluent cannot know who God is, is exclusive and class-based by definition. It advocates increased confrontation with mainstream churches. Implicit, too, is a wholesale denouncement of capitalism as an economic system incompatible with Christianity.

The first question, then, is whether Sobrino's and Gutiérrez's analysis of the BCC movement in Latin America, which has found wide acceptance in the United States, can also apply to the Justice House situation. That is: Have the class injustices of our societal institutions, both religious and secular, reached the point that they can be cleansed only by a new movement outside the parameters of the old?

Second, if such a new movement continues in the direction of the Justice House model, what can be expected of community and church support? Many Mennonites—who have historically borne a "silent witness" to their faith—are uncomfortable with the increasing demands and righteous assertiveness of Justice House and its leader. When the Virginia Mennonite Board of Missions was reluctant to increase contributions to Justice House, Hayden fasted to achieve his end, promising more of such actions in the future.

The Virginia Mennonite Conference, nevertheless, has remained cautiously supportive of Hayden and Justice House. A Virginia Conference bishop, Glendon Blosser, says that despite objections to Hayden's means he feels Justice House ministry to be important in sensitizing the church to its own values.

Justice House also stands as a challenge to the present system of shelters and feeding programs, established in response to the crisis of homelessness.

In sharp contrast to the short-term nature of most shelters, Justice House offers a model community which allows members to achieve personal stability and dignity. A shower, meal, and bed for the night may be feeding the hungry and sheltering the poor, but it does not equal justice; nor does it assist people in rebuilding their lives. Only with the guarantee of a place to stay, an address, and adequate food, can homeless people be expected to find suitable housing and work.

A MODEL OF EMPOWERMENT

Most important, Justice House stands as a model of empowerment. Shifting homeless people from shelter to shelter and meting out inequality to persons sharing a common tragedy are techniques used for centuries to render oppressed and disenfranchised persons ever more powerless.

While visiting Justice House, I saw a taxi, paid for by an evicting landlord, pull up to the curb to deposit a single mother and her three children at the front door. Their personal belongings remained behind, piled in front of their former apartment house. Justice House could not accommodate the displaced family; cots covered the floor of the church, and the fire marshal was threatening closure should more people be admitted.

Hayden loaded the family into the Justice House car to go in search of housing. The Salvation Army, already filled to capacity, agreed to take them in for one night.

"Do you know what it feels like?" asked a man standing next to me. "Do you know what it feels like to see this happen every day, just like it happened to you? Well, let me tell you: It makes you want to do something!"

16

Sanctuary in Chicago

RENNY GOLDEN AND MICHAEL McCONNELL

The late August Sunday service was not typical for the congregation of the Wellington Avenue church. In their midst, blinking back tears, a young Salvadoran refugee, wearing a sombrero and bandanna to conceal his identity, and still bearing scars and burns from six months of torture, faced television cameras. For the Wellington congregation, the war in Central America had come home.

When "Juan" was presented to the congregation, its thunderous applause dissolved any previous doubts. Juan whispered his gratitude to a translator and silently lifted his left fist in the traditional Latin American symbol of solidarity and resistance. The congregation answered his salute with hundreds of raised fists.

Reverend David Chevrier, sensing the deep community recognition of the holiness of their harboring action, then invoked the ancient tradition of sanctuary: "We live in a time of encroachment . . . violation of the holiness of even the most basic of human rights. A demonic domination has been unleashed that is profaning the human through torture and terror. It is time to provide a safe place and cry out Basta! Enough! The blood stops here!"

Upstairs in a makeshift room where the congregation was barely able to coax the plumbing to work, Juan spent his days with twenty-four-hour companionship. We visited him there.

When we knocked, he was asleep, exhausted from his overnight ride on the underground railroad from Tucson to Chicago. Our first impression was that of a child awakened too suddenly. Clearly he was bewildered—the long trip, a tumultuous reception, strange surroundings. But even several hours later, when he had warmed to us and told us his story of eight months of torture and a two-year journey to this precarious freedom, there remained a certain innocence. He was a shy country boy from La Libertad.

156

It was during his student days at the University of San Salvador that Juan was picked up. One day after class, while he was waiting for a bus, a security policeman came up behind him, yanking his hair and throwing him to the ground. At first, because he was not "political," he was bewildered and hoped that mistaken identity would be established when his papers were checked.

But the police did not ask for his papers. They threw him on the floor of a jeep; a policeman pressed one boot against his head and another on his back. When he tried to move, one of them slammed a rifle butt against the side of his face.

Next they blindfolded him, and he felt terror lock a muscle in his neck. He began to breathe deeper to loosen the cramp. Like a drowning person, his whole life spun before his eyes. Had he somehow been a subversive? But how? Of what was he accused? Juan was never to find out. No charges. No trial.

He felt the thud of two more bodies jar the jeep floor. "They piled up like potato sacks, only they respect food a little more." When the jeep started, he felt terrible sorrow for his mother, then stabbing anxiety when he remembered the pattern of arrest, followed by rape and murder of the prisoner's family.

During Juan's imprisonment, his father "disappeared." Neighbors saw the security forces come to the house. Three months later his mother died of a heart attack. Juan never has located any of his six brothers.

When Juan began telling about his first day of torture, I felt him distance himself slightly; his voice flattened. It was sad suddenly that all we offered was horrified silence — none of us knew, we could barely imagine, what he had been through. Though safe now, he was still alone. He seemed to know it, so he smiled a lot to reassure us, except when he told about his parents' deaths.

They began his torture in a place that was not a jail. He remembered hallways and torture rooms. He never saw other prisoners, because he was always blindfolded when taken from his room, but he heard screams daily. For eight months he held on; others went mad or committed suicide. Near the end he was delirious, and his hope was waning.

They pounded his hands with heavy metal rods, demanding responses to questions he could not answer. They asked for names. When he would not answer, they hit him on the chest over and over. He still has continual pain in his chest and occasional lack of sensation in his spine. They used electric shock, pulled out his fingernails, hung him by his wrists, burned him with acid, broke his arms.

"But what were they after?" we asked. "Was it your student activities?" His answer:

No, it wasn't that. It's true I was part of a student movement demand-ing curriculum change, an overhaul of the educational system, and student participation in university decisions. But their interest was in my truck-driving years before the university. I had a route that ran into Guatemala toward the Atlantic coast. In both El Salvador and Guatemala I saw many cadavers lying on the roads. Back then, when they bothered to disguise things, they threw the bodies in the road so that high-speed trucks or cars would run over them, making their death appear to be accidents. But if you stopped, you could see the bodies had been tortured. I think they thought I knew something from my travels.

Juan was unaware that a general amnesty had been granted prisoners when they blindfolded him and drove him to what was clearly a jail. The next day he was released in San Salvador. It was 1979.

He dwelt on that day somewhat, how friends and relatives came to greet the prisoners, but he waited in vain for one of his brothers to step through the crowd. Then he began a ten-block walk to a friend's house. He laboriously pulled his ninety-six pounds through the streets. The lonely walk took him six hours. "I was weak, looked awful. . . . When I got to my friend's house, he did not recognize me."

He stayed there three days before the National Guard came looking for him. He learned later that four of the five prisoners released with him had been apprehended and their decapitated bodies thrown into the streets. When the guard came to his friend's front door, Juan leapt out a back window, scampered over a row of rooftops toward Rio Acelhuate, a city drainage river, where he dropped into the water and covered his tracks.

He slept on the riverbank when he could walk no longer. Under the sun, and under the stars, he forced himself to walk toward Aguilares, where friends would feed him and he could move on toward the mountains to hide. For months he traveled from town to town in the Chalatenango area, seeking the whereabouts of his brothers. He was taken in by friends. Then he made his way to the mountains where time healed his wounds.

Juan finished his story, telling of his escape to Honduras, then Mexico, and finally his connection with the underground railroad created by religious groups on both sides of the Mexican-American border and extending now to Chicago. He had had to go about it slowly, carefully, because in Honduras and Guatemala Salvadoran refugees are targets for military and right-wing death squads. In Mexico Salvadorans are jailed or extorted. Mexican border guards demand payments from families carrying life savings in hidden pockets.

As a final question to Juan, almost as an afterthought, we asked him why he came here, prepared for possible arrest by the Immigration and Naturalization Service.

"It is because of the children," he said, the same innocence in his eyes. "They don't die just from guns. They are hungry. I don't want them just to grow up to a strong adulthood; I want them to have an infancy. That's part of why I'm here, to demonstrate that all of us must be willing, not just one person, to stop this suffering. It's a call."

17

Sanctuary Community:
"We Will Continue"

VICKI KEMPER

It is the first Sunday after Easter, and Reverend John Fife is preaching to children. "Sometimes, to be a disciple of Jesus means to go places you would rather not go," Fife says, accentuating Jesus' words to Peter.

A few minutes later, Fife is preaching a slightly harder message to a somewhat older group: "The risen Christ is to be found in the persecuted and the suffering who live in the faith and die in the faith. . . . To experience the risen Christ, you must stand with the persecuted who live and die in the faith. . . . That's not us, folks," he interjects. "Don't be fooled by what's going on in a federal courtroom."

It is a regular Sunday morning service at Tucson's Southside Presbyterian church, the congregation John Fife has pastored for seventeen years. But less than four weeks later, the hearing and preaching of the word on the Eastertide Sunday had taken on a new and far more personal application.

Because a federal jury had found John Fife and seven other sanctuary workers guilty for standing with the persecuted of Central America, Southside's pastor faced the prospect of being led to prison, where he would rather not go.

The jury's verdict, and its serious implications for Fife, marked an important juncture in the journey Southside had been on in the four years since all but two members of the congregation voted to make Southside the first sanctuary church in the United States. The worst case scenarios the congregation had prepared for had become realities, but members of Southside did not despair. The night after the jury rendered its shocking verdict, the congregation had a special service — and a party. For with the guilty verdict, and all the spiritual trials it would mean, came a promise: a fuller knowledge of the risen Christ.

For all the publicity it has received, Southside remains a simple and humble congregation, a church whose building is on a scraggly corner in one of Tucson's poorest and bleakest neighborhoods. On any given Sunday the gospel is read in English and Spanish; and blacks, Hispanics, Native Americans, and whites, along with a former Catholic nun, a retired Baptist preacher, single mothers, laborers, families, and professionals serve communion to one another.

But the trial has left its mark—on Fife and on the congregation. Commenting on this, Fife says:

It's been a very difficult time for the congregation. They haven't had a pastor now for a year, a year and a half. I mean, I have been preoccupied with the trial, spending all but two or three days a week [on it], sometimes more than that. And that's difficult in the life of any congregation.

It's meant that many people in the congregation who would have expected and who would have received pastoral care in times of their own crises have not had those services, on behalf of the church and the community of faith. And I'm sure that's placed a lot of strain on people. . . . The grace of God really is—had better be—pretty broad for folks like me in that situation. So those times have been very difficult for all of us.

But on the other hand, it's been a profound time of spiritual renewal for this congregation. They have looked at the indictment and possible conviction and imprisonment of their pastor, and it has meant for them being together as a community of faith, a uniting around a decision, a commitment to ministry, to refugees, of saying, "Look, no matter what happens to John, our ministry and our call to the ministry goes on."

So they have selected a pastor to succeed me [if I go to jail], Rev. Marguerite Reed [a Southside member involved in sanctuary work]. They have arranged for that with the presbytery, and they have put in her job description, "You can probably expect to be indicted or arrested in this position." And we are going to continue to provide sanctuary for Central American refugees—no matter what. Because we believe that we are called to that particular mission by God, and we cannot sell our souls. And if they put our pastor in prison, we will call another pastor, and we will continue to provide leadership and ministry in that particular mission. We will continue.

Fife went on:

All of that has been wonderful. It's been delightful to see a congregation which has understood that kind of commitment and has come together as one around that decision, which has not been afraid in the face of a threat from the civil authorities, which has understood that faith is that important to them and is common to them, and which can discover that and celebrate it — and have a sense of humor about it.

The spiritual joy of that congregation at worship is something that has kept me on track and grounded through all the emotional ups and downs of the trial. And I never expect to have such an experience in ministry again.

18

Hammers and Blood:
Hope and Plowshares-Disarmament Actions

ART LAFFIN

On September 9, 1980, the "Plowshares Eight" carried out the first "plowshares" action. They entered a General Electric plant in King of Prussia, Pennsylvania, where the nose cones for the Mark-12A nuclear warheads were manufactured. With hammers and blood they enacted the biblical prophecies of Isaiah (2:4) and Micah (4:3) to "beat swords into plowshares" by hammering on two of the nose cones and pouring blood on documents. They were subsequently arrested, tried, convicted by a jury, and sentenced to prison terms ranging from one and a half to ten years. As of May 1989 their case was under appeal in the Pennsylvania courts and had been so since 1981. In February of 1988 the Pennsylvania Supreme Court denied a hearing of any further issues in the case and the eight were ordered to be resentenced. However, a motion to stay the sentence pending a final appeal to the U.S. Supreme Court was granted in late March, and on April 10, 1990 the eight were resentenced to the time they had already served.

Since the Plowshares Eight action, other communities and individuals have entered military bases and weapons facilities and with hammers, blood, and other symbols have symbolically, yet concretely, disarmed components of U.S. first-strike nuclear weapon systems: the MX, Pershing II, Cruise, Minuteman, ICBMs, Trident II missiles, Trident submarines, B-52 bombers, P-3 Orion antisubmarine aircraft, the ELF communication system, and the Navstar system. Disarmament actions have also been carried out against combat aircraft, nuclear-capable battleships used for military intervention, as well as at an "Arms Bazaar."

In each case, people who have engaged in plowshares-disarmament actions have undertaken a process of spiritual preparation and nonviolence

162

training, and have given careful consideration to the risks involved in such an action. Accepting full responsibility for their actions, plowshares activists have always peacefully awaited arrest following each act.

Resonating closely with this spirit of nonviolent direct disarmament, other people, though not seeing their action arising specifically out of a biblical tradition, have been compelled by their consciences to disarm nonviolently components of nuclear and conventional weapons.

As of May 1989, over one hundred individuals have participated in twenty-seven plowshares actions and six other related disarmament actions. In addition to the United States, plowshares and other disarmament actions have occurred in Australia, Germany, Holland, and Sweden. The backgrounds of plowshares activists vary widely. Parents, grandparents, veterans, former lawyers, teachers, artists, musicians, priests, Sisters, housepainters, carpenters, writers, health care workers, students, advocates of the poor and homeless, and members of Catholic Worker communities have all participated in disarmament actions.

In my view, the basic hope of the plowshares actions is to communicate from the moment of entry into a plant or base — and throughout the court process and prison witness — an underlying faith that the power of nonviolent love can overcome the forces of violence; a reverence for the sacredness of all life and creation; a plea for justice for the victims of poverty and the arms race; an acceptance of personal responsibility for the dismantling and the physical conversion of the weapons; and a spiritual conversion of the heart to the way of justice and reconciliation. Thus our resistance is not just to a particular weapon system, law, or policy, but to the web of violence, fear, and greed that underlies the policies of the national security state and which also lies in the very depths of our own hearts.

The main symbols used in plowshares actions are hammers and blood. Motivated by the prophetic call, participants use hammers to literally begin the process of disarmament that thousands of arms talks have failed to accomplish. The hammer is used to take apart as well as to create, and to point to the urgency for conversion from war production to products that enhance life. The blood symbolizes the mass killing nuclear and conventional weapons can inflict, as well as the murderous cost they now impose on the poor. Blood speaks too of human unity, and the willingness to give one's life rather than to take life.

Plowshares activists believe that nuclear weapons and all weapons of war are anti-God, antipoverty and antilife, and, therefore, have no right to exist. In the Trident Nein plowshares action that I participated in, we hammered and poured blood on missile hatches and sonar equipment of the first-strike Trident submarine. With spray paint we renamed the Trident "USS Auschwitz," because of our belief that such a weapon has no more right to exist than the Nazi gas ovens. The real crime being committed is not hammering upon weapons but the U.S. government's first-strike nuclear war preparations, its commitment to wage a war of aggression throughout the Third

World to protect U.S. economic interests, and its interventionist policies.

Seeking to expose the violence, secrecy, and idolatry of the national security state, many plowshares defendants have tried to present a "justification" or "necessity" defense during their trials. During their defense they have tried to show that their actions were morally and legally justified and that their intent was to protect life and prevent a crime, not commit a crime. In most cases, the courts have shown their complicity in protecting the interests of the national security state and have disallowed this defense. Most judges in plowshares trials have also refused to allow the jury to hear and apply the elements of the justification defense. Some plowshares groups have also presented a defense declaring that a state religion of "nuclearism" has been established which is unconstitutional, in violation of the First Amendment. Moreover, nuclearism is in violation of God's law which forbids the worship of "gods of metal." Plowshares defendants have moved for dismissal of all charges brought against them; for the law, as applied in these cases, is used to protect this unconstitutional state religion. Such motions have been constantly denied.

To date, there have been twenty-nine disarmament trials where people have been convicted of trespass and/or conspiracy and property destruction. Also, five people have been convicted of sabotage. The "Epiphany Plowshares" were tried an unprecedented five times in Philadelphia Federal Court — two trials ending in hung juries; the third trial ending in a mistrial; and the fourth trial ending in a conviction. During their fourth trial Lin Romano and Greg Boertje's *pro-se* rights were revoked and court-appointed lawyers were ordered to represent them. Lin and then Greg appealed this ruling from jail and their convictions were overturned after nine months. The government prosecuted Lin a fifth time and she was convicted on a reduced charge of trespass. (Charges against Greg were dropped though he remains in prison, failing to appear at his sentencing after the fourth trial.)

Trial tactics by the courts in plowshares cases have become increasingly repressive. *In limine* motions, which call for the complete prohibition of any "affirmative" defenses by defendants, have been introduced in a number of disarmament cases. For example, prior to the third and fourth trials of the Epiphany Plowshares, the trial judge, complying with the U.S. prosecutor's request, imposed a "gag" order forbidding any mention of such subjects as the Bible, God's law, international law, U.S. military intervention in Central America, nuclear weapons, and the poor. (For speaking about these subjects, Greg and Lin were cited for contempt of court and were given twenty-five-day jail sentences in addition to long prison terms.)

Nine people are now serving prison sentences ranging from thirty months to seventeen years for plowshares-disarmament actions. The witness of these sisters and brothers along with that of other imprisoned peacemakers worldwide are beacons of light and hope for our world. Their witness in captivity challenges each of us to deepen our commitment to the abolition of war and all forms of injustice. Despite attempts by the courts and the powers that be to suppress the truth and discourage acts of resistance, plowshares actions and other actions for peace and justice continue. The nonviolent resistance movement continues to grow. In the face of the U.S. empire's pervasive violence and oppression, acts of amazing grace and hope continue to flourish.

19

I Was Thirsty:
Recalling August 6 and 9, 1945

MARYA BARR

August 6. August 9. Days that human memory wants to forget, but deep down knows it has to remember.

It is August 8. I am standing in a circle with one hundred or so other people. It's ninety-two degrees, blistering hot for the Pacific Northwest. Our circle crosses several railroad tracks leading into the Bangor submarine base. We are expecting a train transporting Trident missile motors to arrive within the next two hours. Fifteen of us have prepared to resist this shipment of nuclear weapons components by placing ourselves in the path of this train. For several years our Agape Community has been asking Burlington Northern Railroad and the Navy to consider their roles in the preparations for nuclear war; but weekly leafleting, vigils, and requests for meetings have produced little response from them and we feel obligated to take further steps.

I am jolted back to the circle by a large picture being held in front of me of a terribly burned Japanese woman holding her heat-blackened child. I hear the voice of a reader describing the days after the bombing of Nagasaki. The bomb had been dropped close to noon, August 9. Midsummer temperatures that week in 1945 were in the nineties. In that heat, people dealt with the pain of excruciating burns with little medical help and no water. I remember Mary Fugita, a Seattle resident who was in Hiroshima at the time of the bombings, telling us that she never saw a doctor. She said, "You know, you see pictures of doctors bandaging people. I don't know where that was. I never saw a doctor or nurse. We did the best we could helping each other out. We had no medical supplies, no medicine. Mostly we just comforted one another."

I feel the perspiration running down my face and back. Mothers in the circle are trying to shade babies; older folks are using umbrellas for protection. How, I wonder, could people cope with burns from an atomic explosion in such heat? Somehow today's temperature is a gift of re-membering; to recall—and then to re-member; to put back together that which has been rendered apart. To remember the past is to become part of it in such a way as to commit oneself to the future through the present.

My mind jumps back to a term paper I wrote in high school. It was 1955, the tenth anniversary of the bombings. I read about the destruction of buildings, roads, and bridges, and about the lack of electricity, gas, and water. I saw pictures of almost miraculous clean-up efforts, of rebuilding a modern city. But no one showed pictures of the people or told stories of what really happened to them. It is only now, forty years later, that I see the people.

The photos from Hiroshima and Nagasaki have been posted on a large cloth mural near the tracks. There have been songs, sharings from people as to what brought them to the tracks today, time for a cool drink and a short talk with friends. Strands of peace cranes have been distributed. The cranes are folded from brightly colored paper—symbols of hope in honor of a young Japanese girl, Sadako, who folded cranes in an effort to live, despite the lethal effects of radiation sickness in her body.

The train is due in about fifteen minutes. I realize people are moving out from under the trees to form a line of vigil next to the railroad tracks. It's time to take the next step—a step of breaking the silence, of saying no to the preparations for a war with nuclear weapons.

Six people have started out toward the tracks to resist the train's shipment on tracks that are still within the county's jurisdiction. Four others proceed down the tracks toward the gate of the base. Mary and I carry a large banner reading "Trident is a crime against humanity." We walk with another group of five who will be on the tracks about one hundred feet onto federal property.

I'm ready for naval security to block our path, but no one appears. A man is standing on top of a small shed inside the base fence taking pictures of us, but he is the only indication that the Navy notes our presence. We walk slowly past the last rail switch and decide to stop. I watch the four continue along the tracks right up to the locked gate where the train will enter the base. As we sit down on the ties between the rails, I try to avoid big globs of tar, soft and sticky from the heat. The six people sitting ahead of us on the county side of the line are barely visible. The vigil line, too, seems far away, but their singing drifts down to us and we join in; the volume is weak, but somehow the connections are strong.

I'm startled by the train's whistle. I expected to be waiting here longer. The whistle repeats and a bright headlight is clearly visible as the engine rounds the curve about a quarter of a mile away. Another whistle.

Today's train is one more in an ongoing cycle. Trains loaded with nuclear warheads, boxcar after boxcar of nuclear bombs . . . trains loaded with solid fuel missile motors. . . . Since 1982 we've witnessed the movement of these trains, the steady flow of Trident weapons components into the Bangor base to be readied for deployment on Trident submarines. We try to be present often, to let sink into our bones the reality of what it means to prepare for nuclear war. We have come to realize that we each carry the responsibility to say *no* to these preparations.

There are many ways to raise the question. Today it's straightforward. We're asking people from Burlington Northern Railroad, Kitsap County law enforcement, and the U.S. Navy to consciously confront their own involvement in the preparation for nuclear war.

The train has stopped in front of the first group on the tracks. I know from previous experiences that the under-sheriff is telling people to leave or they will be arrested. I know, too, that those on the tracks are insisting on their responsibility to remain, compelled by their Nuremberg obligation not to cooperate with crimes against peace. For the fourth time in five months, Kitsap County deputy sheriffs are removing people from the tracks and taking them to a waiting vehicle and subsequent booking.

The train is now moving slowly toward us. Will it stop or inch its way right up to us in an effort to frighten us off the track? Before I have time to really think about this, the engine has stopped at least fifty feet in front of us. Clearly it's across the white line and into what the Navy calls U.S. government property. The engine towers above us, taking on enormous proportions from where I sit. Yet I feel calm and grounded. The sun continues to beat down its midday heat.

For the first time in all the nonviolent resistance to weapons shipments at Bangor, no one is objecting to our presence on the tracks. No sheriff, no Burlington Northern security is impeding our access to the tracks or removing us from the path of the train. The train with its load of missile motors sits motionless on the track. The five of us sit on the track before it. I look back and see the four others, ten or so feet behind us, sitting backed to the fence. Their banner, stating the illegality of Trident weapons under Nuremberg, hangs from the fence gate. For what seems like a long time, we all just sit. Vigilers told me later how the refrigerated boxcars with their big "Explosives A" sign sat right in front of the vigil line. All during this wait, the vigilers could hear the refrigeration units going on and off— a constant reminder of the volatile cargo inside.

Gradually news reporters and photographers move in a bit closer. A man in uniform with a walkie-talkie walks inside the base fence down toward the vigil line. The sheriff and under-sheriff and several Burlington North security guards are now visible near the vigil line. They, too, seem to be watching and waiting. Finally the realization sinks in: the sheriff and the Burlington North guards are not going to cross onto federal property to take responsibility for this train.

We continue to sit in the sun. I bend down to wipe my forehead on my sleeve. As I look up I see one of the men in the engine cab climb down and walk toward us. He good-naturedly asks us to move — we're causing him to miss his lunch break. Anne and Jim, sitting first in the group, explain to him why we're here. He replies with suggestions of other ways to raise the questions, like writing our congressional representatives, but then agrees that hasn't reversed the arms race. He accepts Jim's offer of a string of peace cranes, and carries them back to hang in the engine.

Within a few minutes a second man climbs off the train and starts toward us. He is juggling something in his hands. It isn't until he's handing a container to Anne and to Jim that I realize he has brought us four cartons of cold water.

For a few moments everything seems unreal. My mind is a swirl of images of people in Hiroshima begging for water, and there is none; of the gospel story of the Good Samaritan — of someone from "the other side" showing such kindness without even a request; of the refreshment of this cool liquid — I can feel the cold "all the way down."

I hear the man telling us he is an engineer, but is functioning today as the brakeman on this train. Anne thanks him for not running over us. His response is that of course they'd stop; human life is precious. I know he'd also make every effort to stop for a cow or a car on the tracks. I wonder why it is so hard to stop carrying that which can totally destroy land and life.

Anne asks the brakeman if he would take the other half of the container of water down to those sitting on the tracks by the gate. "No," he says, "you keep that. I'll get some more." He goes back to the engine and returns, not only with cartons for the others, but drops one more off for me so Mary and I won't have to share one. Again I'm overwhelmed by his thoughtfulness.

Karol told me later that as he approached her group, the words, "I was thirsty and you gave me to drink" flashed through her mind. She spoke the words to him as he handed her a carton of water, and he smiled warmly, saying "Amen."

The train remained stopped for thirty-five minutes. The Navy did eventually unlock their gate and come out to take responsibility for this train. Pan American security guards removed and booked the nine people on the federal portion of the track, though to this date no charges have been filed.

The train did eventually deliver its cargo of Trident missile motors to the Bangor base, but not in silence and not without a small postscript to history. Who would have expected that it was from the very train we stopped that someone would emerge to help us? Amid the burning memory of Nagasaki and Hiroshima we drank from the cup of human kindness.

20

Refugee Rights:
The Cry of the Refugee

GREGORY BOYLE S.J.
LUIS OLIVARES, C.M.F.
MICHAEL KENNEDY, S.J.

On more than one occasion, in response to activities that take place at our two churches, which offer sanctuary to undocumented immigrants and refugees from Central America—the Western Regional Commissioner of the Immigration and Naturalization Service (INS), Harold Ezell, has stressed that "no one is above the law." He emphasizes with each declaration that if he discovers that we are "aiding, abetting, and harboring" the undocumented we will be held to answer to the law.

We write, then, to clarify our position: that although we are not above the law, the struggle of undocumented people to assert their rights as human beings is.

What we are doing in our ministry to these people is an attempt to approximate what Jesus would do in the same circumstance. This is not guesswork on our part: the gospel is clear and abundantly full of Jesus' concern for the poor, the fearful, the persecuted, those who hunger for peace and justice. It is our strong belief that if he were in our situation, he would find himself aiding, abetting, and harboring the sisters and brothers who have come to our community in hope and instead are hunted because they lack the papers that would allow them to stay.

Jesus, of course, would seek to do even more: he would publicly denounce unjust policies and laws so that hearts would change and so that such personal conversion would result in the radical transformation of policy and law.

It is our sincere hope to act toward the undocumented as Jesus would. To do otherwise would be to deny a tradition that has been respected ever since the Lord commanded: "When aliens reside with you in your land, do not mistreat them. You shall treat the aliens who reside with you no differently than the natives born among you; have the same love for them as for yourselves" (Lev. 19:33–34).

As a response to that call, we clothe, feed, and provide shelter for those undocumented whose only crime has been the desire to pursue their fundamental human right to work and thus feed themselves and their families. We do this knowing that in caring for "the least" we opt for Christ's poor and oppressed.

In the light of the gospel call to justice, we find ourselves unable to remain silent in the face of what is denied the undocumented community.

This is why we condemn employer sanctions and the INS's employee-verification protocol as immoral in their intent to deprive so many of their God-given right to work.

This is why we denounce the street sweeps of day laborers and continue to encourage employers to hire them and pay them honest wages for their labor.

This is why we deplore practices of physical aggression and psychological abuse perpetrated by the INS against the undocumented, especially those being held out of sight in detention centers.

This is why we publicly call on all people of faith to join the undocumented in their struggle.

And this is why we oppose laws and policies that would legitimize the designation of people without documents as nonpersons, subhuman, not worthy of the respect and dignity afforded the rest of us.

In preferentially opting for the poor in Los Angeles, we have sought to align ourselves with the undocumented, denouncing laws and attitudes that seek to deny their basic rights and calling all citizens of moral courage to care for these culturally disparaged and oppressed women and men. For, as Archbishop Roger Mahony states, such laws and attitudes would tell us "that these people are now outside the framework of our concern as a society; our Christian tradition tells us the opposite."

When laws trample human rights, they must not be obeyed. When policies subordinate the needs and rights of people to order and convenience, they must be denounced.

To the extent that we openly aid, abet, and harbor the undocumented, we indeed are breaking the law. The gospel would have us do no other.

We do so fully aware of the consequences of our actions. And yet we cannot help but feel that what little we are able to say and do remains insignificant compared to the depth of suffering and commitment of our sisters and brothers struggling to assert their rights as human beings. Our integrity as ministers of the word could never be kept whole were we to remain immobile and transfixed by the law's claim and deaf to the cry of the poor.

In seeking to make public again the private and intense pain of the undocumented, we pray that God's grace will break through all hearts of stone so that, finally, cold indifference will give way to compassionate justice for the poor.

21

Refugee Rights:
To Walk in the Shoes of Another

MICHAEL KENNEDY, S.J.

Ten P.M. Tuesday, June 14. The lights of the Church of La Placita in Los Angeles were turned off. I lay down on the wooden pew. For four years my place had been near the altar in front, so I had never noticed the narrowness of the pews until I tried to find a position to sleep. One hundred men were trying to get comfortable that night in La Placita.

The Commission of Human Rights had decided to spend the night here after a press conference denouncing the violations of human rights we had documented, a Mass, and a dinner.

Soon a youth nearby began to snore. The long night began. I lay looking at the ceiling of the church, thinking that the last thing I felt like doing was sleeping. So I sat up on the bench and glanced around and saw a number of young men praying in the stillness of the church. I began to reflect on the numerous, painful stories that I had heard during these days. Their pain, their desperation were palpable as they hung their heads low, praying, praying that maybe, maybe tomorrow there would be some work.

I lay back down on the pew and tried to tell myself I was tired. I stared at the nothingness and listened to the stirrings around me. I was thinking that the last time I was this uncomfortable was when I was trying to sleep in a jail in El Salvador, after being shot at and almost killed because we were working with the poor. I remembered well the feeling of being imprisoned and powerless.

At the end of the press conference that evening at Placita all these men, now sleeping in the church, had broken the chains around their hands in a gesture that they have the right to work, to live, and this country is denying them this right.

I thought back on the liturgy that followed. We listened to the gospel passage where Jesus spoke in the synagogue of Nazareth and declared that his good news was to bring freedom to the captives, liberation from bondage.

I was now listening to the sounds of a hundred men sleeping—men who were in a jail that in many ways was different from the one in El Salvador but that in other ways was very similar. Because they have no papers, their hands, desperate to work, are chained—hands yearning to do the most humbling work; hands that are full of desire to gain something in order to send it back to their families so they can stay alive, these hands with great necessity, expressing life or death.

At two A.M. a small group silently left the church. They would go and work to the middle of the day distributing fliers. This is one of the only types of work they can obtain. I thought about how cynical this law was for thousands of people in Los Angeles. There are countless business owners who are looking for workers like these in the church. But at the present they are scared to hire them. Who is really gaining from this law as we see the exodus of businesses from Los Angeles to Mexico? How long is it going to take us to see how detrimental to our economy this law is? I began to think about the jail in El Salvador again and the sounds of torture I heard. I realized, sleeping that night in La Placita, that unless you try somehow to walk in others' shoes it is almost impossible to understand. I know owners of businesses say they are afraid of being fined. I also know that when university students from El Salvador came to our office the previous week and told about what happened to their families, or when Juan, from southern Mexico, came and explained how his family was starving to death, it became clear to me that no law can deny them the right to survive, especially after all they have been through.

But perhaps if one has never been in jail for helping displaced persons, never heard the cries of those being tortured, or seen people dying of hunger, then it is hard to take any risk and give serious consideration to what compliance with this law means. Owners tell these men: "Do you have papers? Sorry, no job."

One day we will wake up to the fact of what we are doing. We are sending almost $2,000,000 a day to El Salvador so the military and death squads can remain in power, and as a result thousands of people flee to this country. They arrive here and we close the door. Mexico has to pay back so much in interest on its debt to the United States that it cannot pull itself out of its crisis. This absurdity, this injustice, kept me awake all night.

I was perhaps overanxious about being cold and not being able to sleep, but at the same time, that night in the church, there was a sense of satisfaction that the members of the Commission of Human Rights of La Placita, who continually work with the undocumented, were willing to fight alongside their brothers and sisters, for their rights and to tell the truth—the truth of what it is like to have your hands chained, to feel you are in jail.

Five A.M. . . . The lights of the church were turned on; the men silently sat up in the pews. Slowly they began leaving the church, wandering out into the dark. I hope that soon our country will see more clearly the injustice it is doing by denying new immigrants the right to work and survive.

Part IV

Connecting Beyond

22

Images of Mother-God

As an eagle stirreth up her nest,
fluttereth over her young,
spreadeth abroad her wings,
taketh them, beareth them on her wings:
  So the Lord alone did lead.
Deuteronomy 32:11–12

O Jerusalem, Jerusalem, . . .
how often would I have gathered
thy children together,
even as a hen gathereth her chicks
under her wings.
Matthew 23:37

Can a woman forget the infant at her breast
or a loving mother the child of her womb?
Even these may forget,
yet I will not forget you.
Isaiah 49:15

It was I who taught Ephraim to walk,
I who had taken them in my arms, . . .
harnessed them with cords of compassion
and led them with bonds of love. . . .
I lifted them like a little child to my cheek,
I had bent down to feed them.
Hosea 11:3–4

You shall suck, you shall be carried
upon her hip
and dandled upon her knees.
As one whom his mother comforts,
so I will comfort you.

Isaiah 66:12–13

For Women in Men's Worlds:
A Critical Feminist Theology
of Liberation

ELISABETH SCHÜSSLER FIORENZA

This is a poem for me
and women like me
we who live in men's worlds
like the free spirits of birds in the sky. . . .[1]

Feminist writers and poets explore the experiences of women in androcentric culture and patriarchal society. They seek for a new voice, a "common language" that could express the meaning and significance of women's
lives and could articulate the religious experience of "trying to be in our
souls."[2] In 1896 Alice Meynell—who was one of the greatest English poets
of her time but is virtually forgotten today—likened one such woman
thinker to the biblical figure of the Good Shepherd: "She walks—the lady
of my delight—a shepherdess of sheep." She guards the flock of her
thoughts "so circumspect and right: She has her soul to keep."[3] In a similar
vein the black poet Ntozake Shange ends her choreopoem *for colored girls
who have considered suicide, when the rainbow is enuf* with an affirmation
born out of the exploration of black women's pain and oppression: "i found
god in myself . . . & i loved her fiercely."[4]

Like feminist poets, feminist theologians seek to articulate what it means
that women have found God in their soul. This experience should not be
understood as being over and against body and world but as the finding of
a true religious and spiritual self, and the articulation of that experience is
the feminist vision of self-affirmation and freedom lived in men's worlds
and expressed in the oppressor's language. Within the patriarchal context
of Christian religion, women's spirit has continued to explode from time to
time proclaiming truth and justice. However for the most part such articulations of women's spiritual experiences were swallowed up by historical
forgetfulness and covered up by androcentric language.

For the first time in Christian history we women no longer seek to express our experience of God's Spirit within the frameworks of androcentric spirituality but attempt to articulate that we have found God in our soul in such a way that this experience of her presence can transform and break through the traditional frameworks of androcentric theology and patriarchal church. For the first time in Christian history women have achieved sufficient theological education and economic-institutional independence to refuse to be just the objects of men's theologizing and to become the initiating subjects of theology and spirituality.

We Christian women have begun to formulate our own theological questions, to explore our own Christian history, and to chart our own spiritual visions. The theology which we have learned has left us out, the history of the church is not written as women's history, and the clerical-patriarchal structures of the church identify it as a men's church.[5] In her article "Im Schatten des Vaters" (In the Shadow of the Fathers) Hildegunde Woller has articulated this alienating experience of women studying theology: "Theology and life remained unmediated in myself. A dream plagued me several years, again and again the same dream: I came home and found in my bed a child about whose existence I had known nothing and whom I had forgotten. It was starved and frozen to death. Nobody had heard it crying. I felt innocent."[6] Only when she attempted the journey inward to take care of the lost child did she realize that the gospel addressed herself. But when she began to communicate this experience, those whom she had called her "theological fathers" did not understand her and labeled her religious experience of self "dangerous, subjective, or irrelevant."

FEMINIST THEOLOGY

Feminist theology is often misunderstood as a genitive theology, as the theology of woman. It is misconstrued as "feminine" theology, a theology that perpetuates the cultural-religious stereotypes of femininity and masculinity. Establishment theologians usually qualify feminist theology with the adjective "so-called" — suggesting it is a somewhat dubious and academically suspect enterprise. Such prevalent misrepresentations of feminist theology are, of course, not accidental. By qualifying feminist theology as "woman's" or as "feminine" theology it can be restricted to women who are marginalized, trivialized, and considered of no importance in a patriarchal church and society. While the "pro-feminine" expressions in theology are lauded, the characterization "feminist" is labelled "radical, abrasive, fanatic, and unwomanly." Naturally such a misrepresentation of feminist theology invites its rejection as a "particularistic" theology restricted to a tiny minority in society and church — militant women — with whom no "real" woman should want to be associated.

The early feminists assumed that the intellectual frameworks as well as the contents of academic education and scientific knowledge available to men but not to women were valid, true, humanistic, and objective. If women just could overcome their exclusion from academic institutions and the professions they could fully participate in the production of human knowledge and art. One of the first to question this assumption was Virginia Woolf, who insisted in *Three Guineas* that women must raise the question whether they should join the "processions of educated men."[7] They had to decide under what terms and conditions women should join them and to inquire where the processions of the sons of educated men would lead them. The feminist studies movement within the second wave of the women's movement has explicitly addressed these questions.

The resurgence of the women's liberation movement has not just revived women's political struggles for equal rights and full access to academic institutions, but has also inaugurated an intellectual revolution that engenders a paradigm shift[8] from an androcentric world view and intellectual framework to a feminist comprehension of the world, human history, and Christian religion. While androcentric scholarship takes man (male) as the paradigmatic human being, feminist scholarship[9] insists on the reconceptualization of our intellectual frameworks in such a way that they become truly inclusive of women as subjects of human scholarship and knowledge on the one hand and articulate male experience and insights as a particular experience and perception of reality and truth on the other hand.

Thus feminist scholarship throws into question the dominant cultural mind-set articulated in male language and classical male texts, scholarly frameworks, and theories of men that make invisible, marginalize and trivialize women. Such an androcentric world view perpetuates a popular and scientific consciousness that declares women's experiences, cultural contributions, scientific knowledge, and artistic or religious expressions as less valuable, less significant, or less worthy than those of men. Feminist studies challenge male symbolic representations, historical interpretations, and our habitual consciousness of sexism as a classificatory given in our language and thought-world. They point to the interaction between language and society, sexual stereotypes and economic exploitation, gender and race as social constructs and political oppression; they point to the interface of sexism, colonialism, and militarism in Western society. Sexism, racism, colonialism, and militarism are thereby unmasked as constitutive of the language of oppression in our society,[10] a language that is declared as value-neutral and objective in academic discourse.

However, it must be noted that feminist studies articulate the feminist paradigms in different ways and with the help of varying philosophical or sociological-political analyses.[11] While liberal feminism insists on the autonomy and equal rights of the individual, socialist or Marxist feminists see the relationship between social class and gender within Western capitalism as determinative of women's societal oppression. Third World feminists in turn insist that the interactions of racism, colonialism, and sexism are defining women's oppression and struggle for liberation.[12] Such a variety of analyses and theoretical perspectives results in different conceptions of feminism, women's liberation, and of being human in the world.

Such a diversity in approach and such polyphony in feminist intellectual articulations are also found in feminist theology and in feminist studies in religion.[13] It is therefore misleading to speak of feminist theology as such or of any feminist theology without recognizing many different articulations and analyses of feminist theologies.[14] These articulations do not only share in the diverse presuppositions and theoretical analyses of women's experiences but also work within diverse theological frameworks — e.g., neoorthodoxy, liberal theology, process theology, evangelical theology, or liberation theology. As theological articulations they are rooted in diverse ecclesial visions and political-religious contexts. I have defined my own theological perspective as a critical feminist theology of liberation which is indebted to historical-critical, critical-political, and liberation-theological analyses and is rooted in my experience and engagement as a Catholic Christian woman.[15]

A CRITICAL FEMINIST THEOLOGY OF LIBERATION

Such a feminist theology conceives of feminism not just as a theoretical world view and analysis but as a women's liberation movement for societal and ecclesial change. Patriarchy is not just a "dualistic ideology" or androcentric world-construction in language, not just the domination of all men over all women, but a social-cultural-political system of graded subjugations and dominations. Sexism, racism, and militaristic colonialism are the roots and pillars of patriarchy. Although this patriarchal system has undergone significant changes throughout its history, it survives as "capitalist patriarchy"[16] in modern societies. It has found its classic Western definition in Aristotelian philosophy, which has decisively influenced not only Western political philosophy and legal systems but also Christian theology.[17]

Patriarchy defines not just women as "the other" but it also defines subjugated peoples and races as "the other" to be exploited and dominated in the service of powerful men. It defines women not just as "the other" of men but also as subordinated and subjected to propertied men. It conceives of women's and colored, Third World peoples' "nature" in terms of their "function" for patriarchal society, which, like the patriarchal household of antiquity, is sustained by female and slave labor. Women of color or poor women are doubly and triply oppressed in capitalist patriarchy. Patriarchy however does not just determine societal structures but also the hierarchical male structures of the church,[18] which support and often sustain the patriarchal structures of society that specify women's oppression not just in terms of race and class but also in terms of heterosexuality and motherhood. The right-wing backlash against the women's movement in society is legitimated and fuelled by a patriarchal church and theology. Over and against capitalist patriarchy in society and church, feminist theology insists that the victimization and dehumanization of the "poorest and most

despised woman on earth" exhibit the full death-dealing powers of patriarchal evil while poor and Third World women's struggle for survival and
liberation expresses the fullest experience of God's grace and power in our
midst.

Feminist theology therefore challenges all forms of liberation theology
to take their preferential "option" for the poor and oppressed seriously as
the option for poor and Third World women because the majority of the
poor and exploited today are women and children, the latter being dependent on women for survival. The African theologian Amba Oduyoye has
pointed out that feminist theology is:

> not simply a challenge to the dominant theology of the capitalist West.
> It is a challenge to the maleness of Christian theology worldwide,
> together with the patriarchal presuppositions that govern all our rela-
> tionships as well as the traditional situation in which men (male
> human beings) reflected upon the whole of life on behalf of the whole
> community of women and men, young and old.[19]

Insofar as feminist theology does not begin with statements about God
and revelation but with the experience of women struggling for liberation
from patriarchal oppression its universal character comes to the fore in the
voices of women from different races, classes, cultures, and nations.[20] Insofar as the primary theological question for liberation theology is not "How
can we believe in God?" but "How can the poor achieve dignity?", the
hermeneutical privilege of the poor must be articulated as the hermeneutical privilege of poor women. Liberation theology must address the patriarchal domination and sexual exploitation of women.[21] Moreover a critical
feminist theology of liberation must articulate the quest for women's dignity
and liberation ultimately as the quest for God.

TOWARD A WHOLE THEOLOGY

Feminist theology in the United States has insisted on the importance
of "wholeness" as a basic category in theology:[22] the integration of body
and soul, world and church, earth and heaven, immanence and transcendence, female and male, nature and human technology. Elisabeth Moltmann-Wendel has pointed out that the category of "wholeness" did not
play a role in German academic theology but is found in the religious
expression of women in the last one hundred years or so.[23] A feminist
theology of liberation strives for the overcoming of theological dualisms but
at the same time insists that a "whole theology" is possible only when the
structures of hierarchical domination in theology and church are overcome.

As long as women suffer the injustice and dehumanization of societal
and religious patriarchy, a feminist theology must remain first and foremost
a critical theology. It must theologically name the alienation, anger, pain,

and dehumanization which women bear and which are engendered by patriarchal religion. At the same time it must articulate an alternative vision of wholeness by exploring women's experiences of survival and salvation as well as by assessing Christian texts, doctrinal traditions, moral injunctions, ecclesiastical pronouncements, and ecclesial structures in terms of women's liberation from patriarchal exploitation and oppression. A whole theology will become possible only when the source of dualistic theology—consisting in the contradiction between the liberating-inclusive vision of the gospel and the cultural-patriarchal structures of the hierarchical church—is overcome.

How difficult it is for women to sustain this hope of the gospel over and against their own experience of patriarchal oppression. The pain and anguish that patriarchal liturgies and androcentric God-language inflict on women can be understood only when theologians and ministers realize the patriarchal dehumanization of women in our society and church.

Therefore a feminist theology that conceives of itself as a critical theology of liberation must sustain a creative but often painful tension. In order to remain feminist and faithful to women's experiences it must insist that Christian theology, Biblical tradition, and the Christian churches are guilty of the structural sin of sexist-racist patriarchy which perpetuates and legitimates the societal exploitation and violence against women. Patriarchal religion and theology perpetuate and legitimate rape, wife-battering, child-abuse, sexual exploitation of women, second-class citizenship, and many more injustices against women. At the same time, if a critical feminist theology of liberation wants to remain a Christian theology, then it must be able to show that the Christian faith, tradition, and church are not inherently sexist and racist. In order to sustain this creative tension such a feminist theology has to move critically beyond androcentric texts, traditional teachings of men, and patriarchal structures by centering on the historical struggle of self-identified women and women-identified men against sexist-racist-militarist patriarchy and for liberation in the power of the Spirit.

Such a feminist theology does not ask for the integration of women into patriarchal ecclesial structures; it does not advocate a separatist strategy; rather, it works for the transformation of Christian symbols, tradition, and community as well as for the transformation of women. It does not derive its liberating vision from a special feminine nature or from a metaphysical feminine principle or divinity. In exorcising the internalized sin of sexism as well as in calling the whole Christian church to conversion, feminist theology reclaims women's Christian "birthright" of being church, fully gifted and responsible members of the "body of Christ" who have the power to articulate their own theology, to reclaim their own spirituality, and to determine their own and their sisters' religious life. As women-church we celebrate our vision and power for change; we ritualize our struggles; we articulate our own theological insights; and we share our strength by intellectually and spiritually nurturing each other. At the same time we remain fully aware that the church of women is always the *ecclesia reformanda* in need of conversion and "revolutionary patience" with our own failures as well as with those of our sisters.

To advocate that the women's liberation struggle in society and religion be the "hermeneutical center"[24] for a feminist critical theology of liberation, to speak of the *ekklesia* of women, does not mean to advocate a separatist strategy or to mythologize women. It means simply to make women visible as active participants and leaders in the church, to underline women's contributions and suffering throughout church history, and to safeguard women's autonomy and freedom from spiritual-theological patriarchal controls. Just as we speak of the church of the poor, the churches of Africa or Asia, of Presbyterian, Anglican, or Roman Catholic churches without relinquishing our theological vision of the universal Catholic Christian church, so it is also justified to speak of women-church as a manifestation of the universal church. Since all Christian churches suffer from the structural evil of sexist-racist patriarchy in various degrees, the church of women is a truly ecumenical movement that transcends traditional "man-made" denominational lines. As a feminist movement of self-identified women and women-identified men, women-church defines its commitment in and through solidarity with women who suffer from the triple oppression of racism, sexism, and poverty and who yet struggle for survival and human dignity.

I have refrained here from defining feminist theology either in terms of the traditional topics of theology (God, Christ, church, sacraments, anthropology, moral theology, etc.)[25] or in terms of an academic religious studies approach. Both approaches are valuable and necessary but they attempt to chart new visions and roads with the old maps of ecclesiastical or academic theology. Certainly, feminist theology could not have been born either without the women's movement for the integration of women into church ministry and academic theology or without the pluralism and autonomy of liberal theology. Nevertheless, a critical feminist theology of liberation cannot remain within the paradigm of the "equal rights" movement and the paradigm of liberal theology—but it must call for a paradigm shift in theology and ecclesial self-understanding.

As a theology by and for women committed to the feminist liberation struggle, its theoretical explorations and methodological approaches must be critically evaluated in terms of how much they are able to articulate religious visions as well as to make available theological-spiritual-institutional resources for women's liberation struggle in society and the church. Feminist theology therefore does not define itself primarily in terms of either traditional theology or ecclesial spirituality but in terms of women's struggle against societal, cultural, and religious patriarchy. As a critical theology of liberation, feminist theology hence challenges all androcentric forms of liberation theology to become more consistent and universal in their "option for the oppressed," the majority of whom are women. At the same time, as a liberation theology it unmasks the pretense of established academic theology to be universal, objective, and value-neutral. Finally, as a theology committed to the *ekklesia* of women as the gathering of free and fully responsible "citizens," feminist theology challenges the ecclesiastical theology of seminaries and divinity schools to abandon its clerical particularistic self-understandings and to become a theology for the whole church.

In short, such a feminist theology is not limited to women's interests and questions, but understands itself as a different way and alternative perspective for doing theology. At the same time it insists that the androcentric-clerical theology produced in Western universities and seminars no longer can claim to be a Catholic Christian theology if it does not become a theology inclusive of the experiences of all members of the church, women and men, lay and clergy. Finally, it cannot claim to be a liberative theology proclaiming the "good news" of salvation if it does not take seriously its call to become a theology for the poor—women, men, and children—a theology subversive of all forms of sexist-racist-capitalist patriarchy. The feminist Catholic poet and social activist Renny Golden expresses this challenge to all establishment theology and churches so well:

> Our freedom is your only way out.
> On the underground railroad
> you can ride with us or you become the jailer.
> Harriet Tubman never lost one entrusted to her
> Neither will we.[26]

23

Song of Exiles (Psalm 137)

By the rivers of Babylon
there we sat down,
yea, we wept
when we remembered Zion.
We hanged our harps
upon the willows
in the midst thereof.

For there they that carried
us away captive
required of us a song;
and they that wasted us
required of us mirth, saying
Sing us one of the songs of Zion.

How shall we sing the Lord's song
in a strange land?

The Palestinian Uprising and the Future of the Jewish People

MARC H. ELLIS

Since December 1987, as the twenty-year occupation of the West Bank and Gaza erupted into a veritable civil war, the Jewish community in North America and Israel awakened with a start. An outpouring of anger ensued over the betrayal of our ethical witness and a commitment arose to end the occupation. Michael Lerner, editor of the progressive Jewish journal *Tikkun*, summed up these feelings with an editorial titled, "The Occupation: Immoral and Stupid." In passionate and unequivocal language he called on Israel to "Stop the beatings, stop the breaking of bones, stop the late night raids on people's homes, stop the use of food as a weapon of war, stop pretending that you can respond to an entire people's agony with guns and blows and power. Publicly acknowledge that the Palestinians have the same right to national self-determination that we Jews have and negotiate a solution with representatives of the Palestinians!"[1]

In a sense, Lerner and many other Jews are moving toward a position almost unthinkable before the Palestinian uprising: solidarity with the Palestinian people. The uprising brings to mind Johann Baptist Metz's reflection on the Christian and Jewish journey after the Holocaust: "We Christians can never go back behind Auschwitz: to go beyond Auschwitz, if we see clearly, is impossible for us by ourselves. It is possible only together with the victims of Auschwitz." In light of the uprising, these words assume a new meaning, relating to the common journey of Jew and Palestinian. For Jews the challenge might be stated thusly: "We Jews can never go back behind empowerment: to go beyond empowerment, if we see clearly, is impossible for us by ourselves. It is possible only with the victims of our empowerment."[2]

Thus the question facing the Jewish people in Israel and around the world involves, and yet moves far beyond, negotiation of borders, recognition of the P.L.O., the cessation of the expropriation of human, land, and water resources in the occupied territories, and even the public confession of Israeli torture and murder. For in the end the Israeli-Palestinian conflict involves the political, military, and economic spheres of Jewish life while

190

at the same time addressing the deepest theological presuppositions of post-Holocaust Jewry. Without addressing the implicit and explicit theology of our community, any adjustment of political, military, or economic borders will represent superficial moments to be transgressed when the opportunity presents itself. Surely political settlement of any significance in Israel and Palestine without a movement toward solidarity is, by the very nature of the conflict, impossible.

As the uprising has made clear, the normative theology of the Jewish community today — Holocaust theology — is unable to articulate this path of solidarity. Nor can the most well known of Jewish spokespersons, some of whom helped to create this theology and others who operate within it, speak clearly on this most important issue. There are many reasons for this inability to address concisely the subject of solidarity. Holocaust theology, emerging out of reflection on the death camps, represents the Jewish people as we were, helpless and suffering; it does not and cannot speak of the people we are today and who we are becoming — powerful and often oppressive. Holocaust theology argues correctly for the Jewish need to be empowered; it lacks the framework and the skills of analysis to investigate the cost of that empowerment. Holocaust theology speaks eloquently about the struggle for human dignity in the death camps, and radically about the question of God and Jewish survival, but has virtually nothing to say about the ethics of a Jewish state possessing nuclear weapons, supplying military arms and assistance to authoritarian regimes, expropriating land, and torturing resisters to Israeli occupation.[3]

Although this information is readily available and accepted as documented by the world community, written about or even discovered by Jews in Israel and in the United States, Holocaust theologians often refuse to accept it, as if the suggestion that Jews could support such policies, rather than the policies themselves, is treasonable and grounds for excommunication from the community. Because of the power of Holocaust theology in mainstream Jewish institutions, media, and organized Jewish religious life, these "facts" are deemed outside of Jewish discourse *as if they are not happening, because it is impossible that Jews would do such things.* Thus a community which prides itself on its intelligence and knowledge is on its most crucial issue — the behavior of our people — profoundly ignorant.[4]

That is why the dialectic of Holocaust and empowerment, surfaced in Holocaust theology, needs, more than ever, to be confronted by the dynamic and dangerous element of solidarity. Solidarity, often seen as a reaching out to other communities in a gesture of good will, at the same time necessitates a probing of one's own community. To come into solidarity, knowledge of the other is needed; soon, though, we understand a deeper knowledge of self is called for as well. If we recognize the national aspirations of the Palestinian people, that is only a step toward the more difficult and critical question of how Israeli policy has interacted with those aspirations. If we support the struggle of South African blacks, the relationship of Israel and the South African government needs a thorough and continuing investigation. What we find today is a powerful and flawed Jewish community which has become something other than that innocent victim abandoned by the world.[5]

Because of the Palestinian uprising, increasing numbers of Jews are beginning to understand that our historical situation has changed radically in the last two decades and that something terrible, almost tragic, is happening to us. With what words do we speak such anguished sentiments? Do we feel alone with these feelings so that they are better left unspoken? Do such words, once spoken, condemn us as traitors or with the epithet, self-hating Jew? Or does articulating the unspeakable challenge the community to break through the silence and paralysis which threaten to engulf us? And those of us who know and empathize with the Palestinians, can we speak without being accused of creating the context for another holocaust? Can we be seen as emissaries of an option to halt the cycle of destruction and death?[6]

This is the challenge which faces the Jewish people. And with it is the task of creating a new Jewish theology consonant with the history we are creating and the history we want to bequeath to our children. When all is said and done, should it be that we are powerful where once we were weak, that we are invincible where once we were vulnerable? Or would we rather be able to say that the power we created, necessary and flawed, was simply a tool to move beyond empowerment to a liberation that encompassed all those struggling for justice, including those we once knew as enemy? And that our power, used in solidarity with others, brought forth a healing in the world which ultimately began to heal us of our wounds from over the millennia?

New movements of renewal within the Jewish community which have developed or expanded during the uprising point the way to this theology. In Israel, the Committee Confronting the Iron Fist, made up of Israelis and Palestinians whose first publication carried the provocative title "We Will Be Free In Our Own Homeland!" creates dialogue situations and stages demonstrations to end the occupation. Members of the anti-war movement *Yesh Gvul*, or There Is A Limit, made up of Israelis who refused to serve in the Lebanese War and today refuse to serve in the West Bank and Gaza, are courageous in their willingness to say "no" to the oppression of others, even at the expense of imprisonment. Women in Black, made up of Israelis who vigil in mourning dress, and Women Against Occupation, who adopt Palestinian women political prisoners and detainees, are just two more of many Jewish groups protesting the occupation and expressing solidarity with the Palestinian uprising.[7]

Since the uprising North American Jews are increasingly vocal in relation to the pursuit of justice in the Middle East. New Jewish Agenda, a movement of secular and religious Jews, continues to argue for Israeli security and the just demands of Palestinian nationhood. *Tikkun*, the progressive

Jewish magazine, is in the forefront of vocal argument and organizing for a new understanding of the Israeli-Palestinian situation. And now with the recent crisis, Jewish intellectuals, such as Arthur Hertzberg and Irving Howe, and institutions, including the Union of American Hebrew Congregations, have voiced their horror at Israeli policies in the occupied territories.[8]

What these individuals and movements represent is a groping toward a theological framework which nurtures rather than hinders expressions of solidarity. It is almost as if a long repressed unease is coming to the surface, breaking through the language and symbol once deemed appropriate. Of course the risk is that if the crisis passes without fundamental change, the language of solidarity will recede and the more familiar patterns will reassert themselves. And it is true to state that even the movements cited are often limited in their scope and vision, equivocating where necessary to retain some credibility within the Jewish community.

Still the drift is unmistakable and the task clear. The theological framework we need to create is hardly a departure, but a renewal of the themes which lie at the heart of our tradition, the exodus and the prophetic, interpreted in the contemporary world. A Jewish theology of liberation is our oldest theology, our great gift to the world, which has atrophied time and again only to be rediscovered by our own community and other communities around the world. A Jewish theology of liberation confronts Holocaust and empowerment with the dynamic of solidarity, providing a bridge to others as it critiques our own abuses of power. By linking us to all those who struggle for justice, a Jewish theology of liberation will, in the long run, decrease our sense of isolation and abandonment and thus begin a process of healing so necessary to the future of the Jewish community.

If it is true that we cannot go back behind empowerment, we now know that we cannot go forward alone. Could it be that the faces which confront us are those of the Palestinian people and that somehow in these faces lies the future of the Jewish people? This is why a two state solution is only the beginning of a long and involved process that demands political compromise and a theological transformation which is difficult to envision. For if our theology is not confronted and transformed, then the political solutions will be superficial and transitory. A political solution may give impetus to this theological task; a theological movement may nurture a political solution. However, a political solution without a theological transformation simply enshrines the tragedy to be repeated again.

Here we enter the most difficult of arenas; for the presupposition is that in the faces of the Palestinians lies the future of what it means to be Jewish, that at the center of the struggle to be faithful as a Jew today is the suffering and liberation of the Palestinian people. Despite the uprising, such a thought is still hardly considered in Jewish theological circles. At some point, though, an essential integration of Jew and Palestinian in a larger arena of political, cultural, and religious life is integral to a Jewish future.

But this assumes that a fundamental confession and repentance of past and present transgressions is possible and a critical understanding of our history uncovered.

THE OCCUPATION IS OVER

Since the beginning of the uprising we have awakened to reports of beatings and the deaths of Palestinian people, mostly youth, in the occupied territories. But this raises a strange and disturbing question: if Palestinians cease to die, will the uprising — at least for North American Jews and Christians — cease to matter? A horrible thought follows: for the Palestinian cause it is crucial that they continue to die in ever increasing numbers if we are to understand that *the occupation, as we have known it, is over*. Unable to accept this conclusion, I approached Palestinians and church workers who have returned from the West Bank and Gaza. All have the same thoughts. It is true, and the Palestinian leadership — as well as the Palestinian villagers — understand this tragic fact: the uprising is dependent on the continuing death of children.

But can Jewish Israelis continue to beat and kill Palestinian children *ad infinitum*? Can North American Jews continue to support these horrible acts? And can Christians, especially those who have chosen to repent the anti-Jewishness of the Christian past and who have accepted Israel as an integral part of the contemporary Jewish experience, remain silent on the uprising and Israeli brutality? Or, are we all hoping that somehow the situation will dissipate, go unreported, or better still, disappear? This much seems clear: the willingness of Palestinians to endure torture and death, and the willingness of Israel to inflict such acts of brutality, point to the most difficult of situations which many would choose to ignore — that some basic themes of post-Holocaust Jewish and Christian life are being exposed in a radical and unrelenting way.

If it is true that the occupation of the territories is in fact over, that it has moved beyond occupation to uprising and civil war, then the theological support for the occupation in Jewish and Christian theology must end as well. The focus of both theologies in their uncritical support of Israel has been shattered. The uprising, therefore, is a crisis on many fronts and is at its deepest level a theological crisis. Of course, like any crisis the uprising presents us with both tragedy and possibility. By uplifting the truth at the price of broken bones and lives, the children of Palestine force us to think again and to break through ignorance, half truths, and lies. But will we have the tenacity and courage in safe and comfortable North America that the Palestinian children have on the streets of Gaza and the West Bank? Or, will the inevitable allegations of Jewish self-hate and Christian anti-Jewishness deter us? Are we willing to reexamine our theological presuppositions as particular communities and in dialogue with each other, or will we attempt to pass over the question in silence?

It is not too much to say that the uprising poses the future of Judaism in stark and unremitting terms. The tragedy of the Holocaust is well documented and indelibly ingrained in our consciousness: we know who we were. But do we know who we have become? Contemporary Jewish theology helps us come to grips with our suffering; it hardly recognizes that today we are powerful. A theology that holds in tension Holocaust and empowerment speaks eloquently for the victims of Treblinka and Auschwitz yet ignores Sabra and Shatila. It pays tribute to the Warsaw Ghetto uprising but has no place for the uprising of ghetto dwellers on the other side of Israeli power. Jewish theologians insist that the torture and murders of Jewish children be lamented and commemorated in Jewish ritual and belief. It has yet to imagine, though, the possibility that Jews have in turn tortured and murdered Palestinian children. Holocaust theology relates the story of the Jewish people in its beauty and suffering. Yet it fails to integrate the contemporary history of the Palestinian people as integral to our own. Thus, this theology articulates who we were but no longer helps us understand who we have become.

So Jews who are trying to understand the present become a contradiction to themselves while others simply refuse to acknowledge the facts of contemporary Jewish life. A dilemma arises: awareness of Jewish transgressions has no framework to be articulated and acted upon; ignorance (albeit preferred rather than absolute) insists that what is occurring is impossible, that torture and murder are not in fact happening at all, that Jews could not do such things. Jews who become aware have few places to turn theologically, and the ignorant become more and more bellicose in their insistence and in their anger. Meanwhile, despite increasing dissent, Holocaust theology continues as normative in the Jewish community, warning dissident Jews that they approach the terrain of excommunication and continuing to reinforce the ignorance of many Jews as a theological prerequisite to community membership.

As we become more and more powerful, the neoconservative trend is buttressed by fear, anger, and by a deepening sense of isolation. Anyone who works in the Jewish community recognizes this immediately, the almost uncontrollable emotional level that criticism of Israel engenders. To be accused of creating the context for another holocaust is almost commonplace, as are the charges of treason and self-hate. Yet on a deeper level one senses a community which, having emerged from the death camps, sees little option but to fight to the bitter end. It is as if the entire world is still against us, as if the next trains depart for Eastern Europe, as if the death camps remain ready to receive us after an interval of almost half a century. This is why, though the entire world understands Yasir Arafat to be a moderate, there is no other name linked by the Jewish community so closely to Adolf Hitler. This is why Prime Minister Shamir spoke of the plans to launch a ship of Palestinian refugees to Israel as an attempt to undermine the state of Israel, as an act of war.[9]

Years after the liberation of the camps, Elie Wiesel wrote, "Were hatred a solution, the survivors, when they came out of the camps, would have had to burn down the whole world." Surely with the nuclear capacity of Israel, coupled with the sense of isolation and anger, Wiesel's statement remains a hope rather than a concluded option. Is it too much to say that any theology which does not understand the absolute difference between the Warsaw Ghetto and Tel Aviv, between Hitler and Arafat, is a theology which may legitimate that which Wiesel cautioned against?

Christians who have entered into solidarity with the Jewish people are similarly in a dilemma. The road to solidarity has been paved both by Christian renewal, especially with regard to the Hebrew scriptures, and by Holocaust theology. Understanding the beauty and suffering of the Jewish people as a call to Christian repentance and transformation hardly prepares the community for a confrontation with Israeli power. How do Christians respond now when, over the years, the centrality of Israel has been stressed as necessary to Christian confession in the arena of dialogue, and no words of criticism against Israel are countenanced as anything but anti-Jewish? Too, Christian Zionism, fundamentalist and liberal, is ever present. What framework do Christians have to probe the history of the state of Israel, to understand the uprising—to question the cost of Jewish empowerment? Can Christian theologians articulate a solidarity with the Jewish people which is a critical solidarity, one that recognizes the suffering and the power of the Jewish people? Can Christian theologies in the spirit of a critical solidarity open themselves to the suffering of the Palestinian people as a legitimate imperative of what it means to be Christian today?

The uprising continues to push Christian theologians to rethink their theology and move beyond frightened silence or paternalistic embrace. A critical solidarity is increasingly called for, especially in the works of feminist theologian Rosemary Radford Ruether. As a friend of the Jewish people, Ruether is calling attention to attitudes and behavior which can only lead to disaster. Repentance of Christian anti-Jewishness and the promotion of Jewish empowerment can only be authentic today within the context of a recognition of the legitimate rights of the Palestinian people.[10]

Clearly the Palestinian struggle for nationhood poses more than the prospect of political negotiation and compromise. For Jews and Christians it presents fundamental theological material which lends depth to the inevitable (though long suffering) political solutions. Without this theological component a political solution may or may not appear. However, the lessons of the conflict would surely be lost and thus the political solution would tend toward superficiality and immediacy rather than depth and longevity. A political solution without a theological transformation would simply enshrine the tragedy to be repeated again. An important opportunity to move beyond our present theologies toward theologies of solidarity, which may usher in a new age of ecumenical cooperation, would be lost. Could it be that the struggle of the Palestinian people—their struggle to be faithful—is a key to the Jewish and Christian struggle to be faithful in the contemporary world?

The torture and death of Palestinian children calls us to a theology which recognizes empowerment as a necessary and flawed journey toward liberation. It reminds us that power in and of itself, even for survival, ends in tragedy without the guidance of ethics and a strong sense of solidarity with all those who are struggling for justice. Today, the Palestinian people ask the fundamental question relating to Jewish empowerment: can the Jewish people in Israel, indeed Jews around the world, be liberated without the liberation of the Palestinian people? Once having understood the question posed by the Palestinian people, the occupation can no longer continue. What remains is to build a theological framework which delegitimates the torture and the killing—a theology of liberation which sees solidarity as the essence of what it means to be Jewish and Christian.

A NEW THEOLOGICAL FRAMEWORK

The development of a theological framework is crucial to delegitimate torture and murder—that is, to end theologies which promote a myriad of occupations including, though not limited to, that of the Palestinian people. In this case we focus on the Israeli occupation as the breakthrough point for Jewish theology. The theological framework which legitimates occupation also, if we look closely, forces Jews to take positions on other issues which would be questioned, even abhorred, if the framework were different. If our theology did not support the occupation, its vision of justice and peace would be transformed. Thus we turn again to the prospect that the uprising represents a culmination and a possibility, if we will only seize the moment.

An essential task of Jewish theology is to deabsolutize the state of Israel. To see Israel as an important Jewish community among other Jewish communities, with an historical founding and evolution, is to legitimate theologically what the Jewish people have acted out with their lives: the continuation of diverse Jewish communities outside the state. Thus the redemptive aspect of Jewish survival after the Holocaust is found in a much broader arena than the state of Israel, and must be critically addressed rather than simply asserted in unquestioning allegiance to a state where most Jews do not live. Deabsolutizing Israel hardly means its abandonment. Instead it calls forth a new, more mature relationship. Jews cannot bilocate forever and the strain of defending policies implemented by others, of criticizing without being able to influence directly, of supporting financially and being made to feel guilty for not living in Israel, is impossible to continue over a long period of time. With this new understanding responsibilities between Jewish communities assume a mutuality which includes a critical awareness of the centrality of our ethical tradition as the future of our community. Therefore, the present crisis and any future crisis moves beyond the call for unquestioned allegiance or disassociation from Israel to a critical solidarity with responsibilities and obligations on all sides.[11]

A second parallel task is to deal with the Holocaust in its historical context and to cease its application as a possible future outcome to issues of contemporary Jewish life. The constant use of the Holocaust with reference to Israel is to misjudge and therefore refuse to understand the totally different situation of pre- and post-Holocaust Jewry. Pre-Holocaust European Jewry had no state or military; it was truly defenseless before the Nazi onslaught. Israel is a state with superior military ability. Pre-Holocaust European Jewry lived among populations whose attitudes toward Jews varied from tolerance to hatred. Post-Holocaust Jewry, with its population concentrations in France, England, Canada, and the United States, resides in countries where anti-Jewishness is sporadic and politically inconsequential. Pre-Holocaust Jewry lived among Christians who had as a group little reason to question Christian anti-Jewishness. Post-Holocaust Jewry lives among Christians who have made repeated public statements, writings, even ritual affirmations of the centrality of the Jewish people and Christian culpability for an anti-Jewish past. The differences between pre- and post-Holocaust Jewry can be listed on many other levels as well, which is not to deny that anti-Jewishness continues to exist. As many Jewish writers have pointed out, the paradox is that the most dangerous place for Jews to live today is in the state of Israel rather than the Jewish centers of Europe and North America.

Even in relation to Israel the application of Holocaust language is clearly inappropriate. Israel has been involved in two wars since 1967 and can claim victory in neither; no civilian life was lost outside the battlefield. The great fear, repeated over and over again, is that one day Israel will lose a war and that the civilian population will be annihilated, i.e., another holocaust. It is important to note here that if the situation continues as it is today it is inevitable that one day Israel will lose a war and face the possibility of annihilation. No nation is invincible forever, no empire exists that is not destined to disappear, no country that does not, at some point in its history, lose badly and suffer immensely. Can our present theology exempt Israel from the reality of shifting alliances, military strategies, and political life? *The only way to prevent military defeat is to make peace when you are powerful.* Of course, even here there is never any absolute protection from military defeat, as there is never any absolute protection from persecution. But if military defeat does come and if the civilian population is attacked, the result, though tragic, will not by any meaningful definition be another holocaust. And it would not, by any means, signal the end of the Jewish people, as many Holocaust theologians continue to speculate. It would be a terrible event, too horrible to mention. And perhaps the differences between the Holocaust and any future military defeat of Israel are too obvious to explore, and would hardly need exploration if our present theology was not confused on this most important point.

To deabsolutize the state of Israel and distinguish the historical event of the Holocaust from the situation of contemporary Jewish life are imperative to the third task of Jewish theology: the redefinition of Jewish identity. This is an incredibly difficult and complex task whose parameters can only be touched upon here. Yet it is the most crucial of areas raising the essential question that each generation faces: what does it mean to be Jewish in the contemporary world?

There is little question that Holocaust theology is the normative theology of the Jewish community today and that at the center of this theology is the Holocaust and the state of Israel. Rabbinic theology, the normative Jewish theology for almost two millennia, initially sought to continue as if neither the Holocaust nor the state of Israel were central to the Jewish people, and Reform Judaism, the interesting, sometimes shallow nineteenth-century attempt to come to grips with modern life, also sought to bypass the formative events of our time. Yet after the Holocaust, and especially since the 1967 Six Day War, both theological structures have been transformed with an underlying Holocaust theology. Secular Jews, as well, often affiliated with progressive politics and economics, have likewise experienced a shifting framework of interpretation. Though not explicitly religious, their aid has been solicited by Holocaust theologians to build the state of Israel as the essential aspect of belonging to the Jewish people. In sum, both those who believed in Jewish particularity and those who sought a more universal identification have increasingly derived their Jewish identity from the framework of Holocaust and Israel. And there is little reason to believe that any of these frameworks—Orthodox, Reform, or secular humanism—can ever again return to their pre-Holocaust, pre-Israel positions.

We can move ahead only by affirming the place of Holocaust and Israel as important parts of Jewish identity while insisting that they are not and cannot become the sum total of what it means to be Jewish. The point here is to take the dynamic of Holocaust and Israel and understand it in new ways. In both events there is, among other things, an underlying theme of solidarity which has been buried in our anger and isolation. This includes solidarity with our own people as well as others who have come into solidarity with us. As importantly, if we recover our own history, there is a theme of Jewish solidarity with others even in times of great danger. The latter include some of the early settlers and intellectuals involved in the renewal of the Jewish community in Palestine, well-known figures like Albert Einstein, Hannah Arendt, and many others.[12]

Even during the Holocaust there were voices, Etty Hillesum, for one, who argued that their suffering should give birth to a world of mutuality and solidarity so that no people should ever suffer again. As she voluntarily accompanied her people to Auschwitz, Hillesum was hardly a person who went like a lamb to her slaughter. Rather, she chose a destiny as an act of solidarity with her own people and the world. Is it possible that those who affirmed human dignity where it was most difficult — and those who argued, and continue to argue today, for reconciliation with the Palestinian people even with the risks involved — represent the only future worth bequeathing to our children? By emphasizing our dignity and solidarity we appropriate the events of Holocaust and Israel as formative in a positive and critical way. Thus they ask us to once again embrace the world with the hope that our survival is transformative for our own people and the world. The key to a new Jewish identity remains problematic unless we understand that deabsolutizing Israel, differentiating Holocaust and the contemporary Jewish situation, and recovering the history of solidarity within our tradition and with those outside it, lead us to a critical confrontation with our own empowerment. To celebrate our survival is important; to realize that our empowerment has come at a great cost is another thing altogether. Can we, at the fortieth anniversary of the state of Israel, realize that the present political and religious sensibilities can lead only to disaster? Can we argue openly that the issue of empowerment is much broader than an exclusive Jewish state and that other options, including autonomy with confederation, may be important to contemplate for the fiftieth anniversary of Israel? Can we openly articulate that as American Jews we can no longer ask American foreign policy to support policies which contradict the ethical heart of what it means to be Jewish? Can we, in good conscience and faith, appeal to Christians, Palestinians, and people of good will around the world to help us end the occupation and if we do not heed the call, to force us to stop for our own sake?

For this is the place we have arrived, well beyond the pledge of loyalty and the private criticism that has abounded for so many years. The uprising challenges the power of the Israeli government and the heart of the Jewish people. But the power to inflict injury and death remains. And therefore the power to change our history, to redefine our inheritance, to alter what it means to be Jewish remains in the hands of those who would see the occupation continue. And with the occupation come a myriad of policies around the world which bring only shame to those who invoke the victims of the Holocaust to legitimate terror.

With the uprising we have lost our innocence; a Jewish theology of liberation must begin with this loss. A weak and helpless people has arisen with a power that surprises and now saddens us. A people set apart returns to the history of nations less as a beacon than as a fellow warrior, living at the expense of others, almost forfeiting its sense of purpose. The commanding voice of Sinai and of Auschwitz beckons us to struggle to reclaim the ethical witness of the Jewish people.

24

"Letter to a Political Prisoner" (excerpt)

JANICE HILL

(In honor of Karl Gaspar, a former political prisoner in the Philippines, and the forty-five people who resisted the nuclear-war-making of General Electric on April 5, 1983)

It will take a great act of imagination
to save the world
I want to begin.

We will travel the way of love
and leave behind us a trail of seeds
to root between the rocks.
They will arrest us
for littering their battlefield
with life.
But no matter.

A Theology of Peace

DOROTHEE SÖLLE

REFLECTIONS

One thing I learned from my sisters in the feminist movement is that in order to understand someone you have to know him or her. You have to have a deeper knowledge than just what books a person has read or written—that is not so important. Therefore, I would like to introduce myself to you. That's my first point. Because I am a Christian theologian, my second point goes back to the New Testament. I will share with you my views about the Pax Romana and the Pax Christi. Then, because I am a political activist, too, I will make a point about bilateralism and unilateralism, and a last one about resistance.

I grew up in the 1930s in Germany. I was fifteen when the war—what some people call "the German catastrophe"—ended. And I spent the next ten years of my young adulthood as a pupil and student reflecting on the most important question my generation had to ask. There was only one question in our minds and that was: How could this have happened? How was it that all these nice people we knew, all these educated Germans, gassed six million people in the heart of cultured Europe?

We, my generation, went around and around with this question. We went to our fathers and mothers and uncles and aunts and professors and teachers. We asked the question in many ways. We asked them, "Where were you when it happened? What did you do? Didn't you hear anything? Didn't you smell something? What of the gas? And what did *you* do in those years? What was your life like? Did you know what was going on?" We also asked about our traditions, our philosophical, theological, and cultural traditions. Martin Luther, for example. Wasn't there something of anti-Semitism already there? To what did that lead? What were the effects of the thinking of Nietzsche and others? We asked these questions of those who lived in the midst of the German catastrophe, that most perfect murder in our history—the Holocaust.

We got the most terrifying answer. The people told us: "We didn't really know what was going on. You know, we lived in a remote place, a small town. We didn't have Jewish relatives. And we had no contact with Communists whatsoever. So we really didn't know what it was, we really didn't know how bad it was. We had heard something about concentration camps but we just thought these were for criminals."

This was the terrifying response we got to this most important question of my generation. As I think about these years of my youth I realize that I do not want my children at some future time to ask me: "Mom, what did you do when Ronald Reagan and George Bush were preparing for the nuclear holocaust? What did you do when this all happened to Europe? When the preparation for World War III was underway what did you do?" I don't want to say, and I cannot say, "I didn't know." I do know. And all of you know too. There is no way not to know what the U.S. government prepares for. You know what is going on. You have the obligation to know. You have to clarify in your minds where you stand right now with that certain knowledge of the plans of those who rule the world. With that said, I am going to try to share with you my reflections on where I stand on this matter.

But first, let me make a second remark about where I came from. I came from a Protestant theology which, through these German political events, became highly politicized. I asked myself: "Out of what did Hitler and National Socialism grow? Was this part of a certain culture there before, the culture of capitalism? Is there an interrelatedness between a certain form of capitalism and this form of theology that at particular points in history necessarily leads into fascism?"

It took me quite a while to figure out all of this, to become aware of what was going on and what the right answer was. I think I learned the most from the Vietnam War. It was that war that helped me to make a final break with capitalism. I found my way from liberal bourgeois thinking to democratic socialism slowly, slowly, step by step. It took me quite a while. And then I had to develop my theology in constant dialogue with my politics for there was no way for me to do theology in the abstract, focused on the life afterwards or somewhere other than where I lived. Only very much later did I come to understand that what was happening to my theology was feminist in the sense that I was taking my context (my being, my class background, my theology, my very existence) seriously.

I had always read and written abstractly; I was someone who learned theology as you may study other fields of inquiry. But I no longer wanted to make theology into what one might call a science. It was more than that. It had to do with praxis. And with a changing world. I was grateful therefore when, after quite a while of my struggling and moving and thinking in the direction I called political theology, the people in Latin America developed the theology of liberation, and gave me a name for this thing I had in mind already. They gave it a name and taught me how to think along their lines. They also taught me that liberation theology has many dimensions—for instance black theology, the theology of the poor, the theology of the indigenous people, the theology of feminists, and, adding one more dimension (that is the goal of my discussion), the theology of peace.

The theology of liberation presupposes that we have an understanding of oppression; otherwise, we do not need a new theology. There are those people who talk about freedom, claiming that we have it. They speak of this so-called freedom of the market. They have no understanding of oppression, their own or anyone else's. They do not need to do liberation theology. We who do liberation theology have to have a need for it. That means we have to understand our own oppression. After December 1979, after that momentous decision to nuclearize Europe and make it into a target, to make it a first-strike position from which the Americans could devastate the Soviet Union and wipe out Soviet cities in four or five minutes—after that decision, many of us Christians thought about our own oppression that is caused by militarism.

The name of the oppression is sexism, classism, rich against the poor, racism; and it is also militarism. Oppression is militarism because militarism keeps the system together and makes all these other forms of oppression work. It protects these other forms and gives the system the security to go on with exploitation, to go on with sexism, racism, classism. For all of this you need strong military force, and this is what the president of the United States today quite well understands. But the following poem, called "Saturday before Easter '81," speaks to the ultimate price for this militarism:

> Oh when
> will the graves finally be empty
> the exhuming of victims unnecessary
> the pictures gone
> of children sprayed with a new poison
> that turns the skin black and peeling
> and makes the eyes sink to their sockets
> oh when will the graves finally be empty
> of mutilated bodies
> in el salvador
>
> When I first became a christian
> I wanted to see christ
> striking me down on the road to damascus
> I pictured the place something like gottingen
> the empty tomb was no more than a fairy tale
> for the unenlightened
>
> Now I have been becoming a christian
> for a long time
> and I have occasionally seen jesus
> the last time as an old woman in nicaragua
> who was learning to read she was beaming

not just her eyes also her hair thinned by age
and her twisted feet
she was beaming all over

But I've also grown poorer
depressed I scurry through the city
I even go to demonstrations
half expecting courage to be passed out there
and I'd give anything to see
the other half of the story
the empty tomb on easter morning
and empty graves in el salvador.

I spend half of my time and work in the United States teaching at Union Theological Seminary in New York City. The rest of the year I am back home in West Germany, in Hamburg, where I live as a writer and an activist for the peace movement. This little poem, "In reagan's country," comes out of this divided life.

What on earth are you doing in reagan's country
my friends in Germany ask me
you have no business there
but it isn't true
that history belongs to the victors

what on earth are you doing in a marble palace
built with rockefeller billions
that they call a church
but it isn't true
that the bible belongs to the militarists

what on earth are you doing in the middle of the war
that the rich wage against the poor
on the side of those with power
but it isn't true
that the occupied countries belong to the occupiers

the truth is my friends
that the foxes have holes
and the birds have nests
but he hath nowhere to lay his head
only a few friends
for whose sake he stayed

THE NEW TESTAMENT

A grounding in scripture is very important. It helps us to understand our own situation and to understand liberation theology not just as a fad or something which Marxists use to undermine Christianity or the West. Something important grows out of biblical reading and understanding of the Jewish and Christian traditions in the light of the struggles in which we are now engaged. But to understand what I am saying you have to go back to the Bible and read it in a different way.

Let's reconsider the second chapter of Luke, the story of when Jesus was born. You all know this beautiful story of when Mary and Joseph travel from their home town of Nazareth to this other place called Bethlehem. I think there are two different kinds of peace that show up in this story of the birth of Jesus according to Luke's gospel. The first verse mentions Caesar Augustus's decree: "All the world should be enrolled for purposes of taxation." Joseph and Mary had to travel from Nazareth to Bethlehem because of the enrollment. This was a legal measure the Roman emperor used to exploit and keep under control the subjected inhabitants of the Roman provinces.

The Roman administration had to get hold of the people in these provinces. This measure of registering them was a part of a system which was called the Peace of Rome, or the Pax Romana. The system consisted of a center, which was Rome, and a periphery, which was the conquered provinces. Now in the geopolitical center of this world there was material abundance, greed for new commodities and pleasures, moral corruption, psychic emptiness, and lack of feeling. Whoever has read any of the old Roman authors knows what I am talking about. On the edges of this order in the center, which was overwhelmed with material abundance, there were the provinces, dominated provinces, where there was unbelievable misery—lack of food, shelter, work, and education. There existed, psychically speaking, an apathetic hopelessness of the masses, of the impoverished. They didn't think that anything could change for them and some of them were very sick.

Now if you think for a second about the New Testament as a whole surely it comes to your mind how many sick people there were around. There is almost no page in the little book that does not mention the blind, the lame, the crippled, and those with other diseases. Picture the scene in your mind. There is no medicine around, no decent food, no shelter. Nothing but misery and disease. And that is the world into which Jesus Christ was born. It is a world of exploitation; the socio-economic reality was misery and oppression. The hired workers in the vineyard in Jesus' parable who wait all day long for a job are a good mirror of what was going on. There was no work, there were no wages, and there was misery everywhere.

Many other texts of the New Testament talk about the landless, the hungry, the diseased, and the possessionless masses. The historical situation of all these stories is the Pax Romana. And the strange thing about this is that when I learned history as a little girl in quite a good school in Germany my teachers told me the Pax Romana was a wonderful thing. These were the fantastic Romans! They had an excellent legal system; they built all these roads all over Europe and to other places; they had running water and all of that. But no one told me about the reality of misery in these provinces. And what was happening in the New Testament is happening the same way in North America today. It was all over wheat prices! The Romans wanted to get these cheap imports for themselves. And that was why they had to have so many wars. The system was designed to serve the interest of the center. And the poor countries around Rome were exploited by the center. The periphery was poor and the system was set up so that the rich became richer and the poor became poorer. That is the reality in which Jesus Christ was born.

Now, to have such forms of extreme exploitation, you need violence because the system would not work without it. People would not choose to exploit themselves. If you want to dictate through the laws of economy and exchange, then you need military force to keep the exploited people down. You need an extremely sophisticated army, as the Romans had, to keep all these provinces down in misery so that the rich could become richer and the poor become poorer. For that, Roman militarism was developed and built up. And that is the greatest achievement of Roman culture—Roman militarism. This is what we call the Pax Romana, peace built upon militarism.

Remember that when Jesus was born the angel came to the poor, landless proletarians who were called shepherds. The angel spoke to them and said: "Peace for all people of good will in the world. Peace on earth." He didn't say "peace afterwards" or "pie in the sky" or something like that—but "peace on earth." The peace the angel was talking about and the peace for which Jesus Christ lived and finally died was a different peace than the Roman peace. It is what we call the Pax Christi. Peace of Christ. And the fundament on which this peace is built is justice, because you cannot have an authentic peace without justice.

What sort of peace do we really want? The New Testament gives us two responses: either Caesar's peace, which is the peace built on militarism, or Christ's peace, which is the peace built on justice. If we choose Christ's peace we must begin by working for justice in order to get to peace. We won't have any peace in El Salvador under the ruling government. There is no possibility of having Christ's peace if you have this type of exploitation. Therefore, we have to think of the fundament on which we build peace, asking, What sort of peace do we really want?

The root cause of war is exploitation: that is, economic and political injustice. If you feed the people, if you provide them with jobs, they will live in peace and then there won't be any wars. You need justice as the fundament of peace. That is what the Bible tells us. It is full of that theme. One of the Psalms says that justice and peace kiss each other. I think it is a beautiful image—because justice and peace belong together.

I am critical of the role of the churches. In my own country, in Germany, and in the United States, what the church is saying is that you can have it both ways. In a way the church preaches that you can have the Pax Christi, the peace of your soul, a relation with God up there for you as an individual. You can have that—that's the peace of Christ. But for the outward world you need something else. You need something like the Pax Romana. You need the military. You need so-called security. You need bombs. You need napalm. You need gas. You need all of that which we have and more. The churches try to compromise between the Pax Christi and the Pax Romana and try to find a way to have both.

But I think the New Testament is very clear. You can't have both. Jesus was killed under the Pax Romana as a criminal. They called all people like Jesus subversives or terrorists. The whole Roman Empire developed a language which is very familiar to us today. They called those who called for justice, worked for justice, lived for justice terrorists or subversives. They had to be crucified. It happened not only to Jesus. It happened to other people.

The New Testament has to be understood as a document of, a struggle for, a kind of peace different from the one we have right now. When Jesus said "Blessed are the peacemakers," he named ordinary people, including women, because around Jesus there were always many women who went with him, women without any hope in a worldly sense of the word. He named the poorest of the poor, and they went with this prophet from Galilee, following him.

And to these people, fisher folk and others, Jesus said: "Blessed are the peacemakers." *Peacemaker* is a wonderful word which was also used by Roman officials, and by conformist intellectuals, for their Caesars. They flattered Caesar Augustus by calling him a peacemaker. They even put this on the coins of the Roman Empire. The word *peacemaker* was always related to those on top—to the Caesar, to the Emperor. He was called, by those who believed in his system, "peacemaker." But Jesus took this word from the top and brought it down to the bottom, to the poorest. He said they were going to be the peacemakers, and he said the peacemakers are blessed. He had a peace different from the Pax Romana in mind.

So if we want to ground ourselves on sound biblical theology we have to think about peace in a way that is different from the way our culture thinks about peace. We have to found our peace on justice, as we have to found liberation on justice, and not on a balanced system of exploitation as did the Romans.

You all know the military expression "the window of vulnerability." The MX was built supposedly in order to close the window of vulnerability which some general in the Pentagon had theoretically discovered. Then the experts found out that the MX wouldn't close the window of vulnerability, but Reagan said that he had to have it anyhow, whether or not it closed the window of vulnerability. He had to have it because it would teach the world a lesson. So we needed it for strategic reasons, for political reasons. When I first heard this expression it hurt me so much because I have a certain understanding of the human being which is based on the Bible: people are vulnerable as long as they are alive. It is not, therefore, an ideal for me to become invulnerable. And the ideal for a nation to have no vulnerability is to me a strange patriarchal and capitalist ideal.

The following little poem about vulnerability is called "The Religious Dimension in the So-Called Peace Movement." It is "so-called" because one of the leading newspapers in my country, the Frankfurt *Zeitung*, always referred to the peace movement for many years as the "so-called peace movement." And what the writers meant was that the real peace movement was the army and NATO because they think that it is they who keep the peace. Here is the poem:

> A window of vulnerability says ronald reagan
> to justify the arms build-up
> must be closed
> A window of vulnerability is my skin
> Without moisture and without touch
> I must die
>
> A window of vulnerability is being wrought
> as answer by Peacemakers to closing the window
> my country cannot live
> we need light to be able to think
> we need air to be able to breathe
> we need a window to heaven

POLITICS

On this question of how to achieve liberation, peace, and justice I am what we call in Europe today a nuclear pacifist. I would like to make you acquainted with this whole idea. After the above-mentioned 1979 decision of NATO, I was what I would call now an unconscious bilateralist. In other words, I had this idea that these people were simply crazy. Why didn't these men sit down together, go for a conference, talk, and find ways to contract with each other? I thought that as they had been able to escalate the arms race up and up and up during the last years, so they should surely be able to de-escalate it. Once the West had the capacity to kill every Russian eleven times; now it was up to fourteen times. I wondered: What is the need for that? Who wants that? And I thought with negotiations, contracts, people going to Geneva or Stockholm, things could change.

But then, after I studied a great deal of neutral peace research like that coming out of the Stockholm Institute for Peace Research, I began to focus on the meaning of "the balance of power." Who is ahead and who is behind? Who has more and who has less? I think it is not honest if we talk about the arms race as if two runners had started at the same point. They didn't. One had the atomic bomb and threw it. And one of the two was ahead between three to five years with any new kill weapon. That was true for the atomic bomb (what they call today a baby bomb), the neutron bomb, and napalm.

So, I had to ask: Is it really my hope that the big powers get together and negotiate until they find a way to de-escalate? I realized that that wasn't hope enough for me because it hadn't worked for thirty years. Actually, what had been done had been counterproductive. I studied some of the Salt 1 treaties. It is an interesting thing to understand how the system works. They had allowed the permitted number of weapons to be so high that both superpowers had nothing better to do than fill up the stockpiles, to have more weapons! That I discovered was the first consequence of Salt 1.

The second point — any one in law knows this — is that if you make a nice good law against, for example, economic criminals, you will always have the smartest criminals who circumvent it. They will commit the crime in a different way so the law cannot catch them. And that happens with any form of arms build-up too. As soon as some forms of weapons were forbidden, the industrial-military-scientific complex became very busy inventing other better weapons. There was no real will to change, to become a more peaceful world. The will was really to escalate and build up and make money on it. And that is what happened to Salt 1.

And now Salt 2 has never been signed by the government of the United States, any real negotiations so far have failed. I do believe now, and this was a slow learning process for me, that it doesn't make sense to wait until the two superpowers get together and make some agreements. Let me go a little deeper into this. Think of a conflict, say a marriage conflict. It is a rationalistic illusion to think that someone like a marriage counselor could come in and say: "Now let's reason and you do the dishes twice a week and you don't complain every evening when he comes home." I don't think it really works like that. For change and reconciliation there is a certain point where one of the two has to move a tiny speck forward. Quite alone. You can't wait for the other side to do it. You can't wait until the two agree. That is too rationalistic; it is a bourgeois illusion to think this way. Real reconciliation starts when one side takes one step forward quite alone and at its own risk.

That is one of the insights of the new European Peace Movement, and that is what has moved us from bilateralism to unilateralism. The Dutch, who were really leading in this movement, had a wonderful phrase, "Free the world from nuclear weapons and begin it in the Netherlands." Now the Netherlands is surely not the most dangerous country in the world for the nuclear holocaust. But the Dutch are aware that they have nuclear weapons as well and they want to get rid of them alone. Behind this philosophy of unilateralism is a certain existential understanding of peace. You have to love peace, not as a business person tries to make a deal with peace, not as these negotiators who go to Geneva. That is, peace has to start somewhere and there is no other place than your own country or group. A Jewish thinker said: "When if not now, where if not here, and who if not we?"

I was in a worship service on peace in Washington several years ago and the thing that moved and enlightened me more than anything was a black spiritual, "It's me, oh Lord, standing in the need of prayer. It's not my brother, it's not my sister. It's me, oh Lord, standing in the need of prayer." We added a few verses: one was "It's me, oh Lord, standing in the need of prayer. It's not the Russians, not the Cubans. It's me, oh Lord, standing in the need of prayer." That is the spirit we need. Exactly that spirit — where we understand it is we, it is not they. It doesn't make any sense to wait for them, or wait for the world. I do not believe in that. I believe that the peoples of the world have to compel their governments to stop this madness. Just to stop it as it is and slowly come down. The only hope is in these unilateral steps.

More and more people, at least in Europe, understand this. But not enough people in the United States do. Several years ago I talked with a peace researcher who agreed with me completely but said, "You can't sell this to the American audience. They won't buy it. If we are to start with something here we have first of all to convince people that we do not need superiority." You know, this has been one of my deep disillusions. There have been so many people in this country who signed the documents for the freeze — congressmen and legislators — and who later, when Reagan asked them for more money for the toys for the boys, offered no resistance. Yet, they signed the freeze. I can't understand that. It's absolutely irrational to me. They cheated the people who worked for the freeze by saying that they wanted the freeze and then they gave Reagan whatever he asked for.

This skyrocketing arms build-up you have now in this country has to do with a lack of understanding by the people who may not yet be ready for peace. There is a need to understand what war is and how militarism oppresses people. And you cannot understand if you reduce your political analysis of the whole world to the East-West conflict. You really miss the point. To tell the people of El Salvador or Nicaragua fighting for their freedom that they are agents of Soviet Marxism is crazy, a reflection of an ideology aimed at dividing the world between the East and the West when the real dynamics are to be found in the North-South conflict. The East-West conflict is used as a front to build up the arms race for all these coming wars we will have because the poor don't want to get poorer. If the poor get poorer, those wars will come. This is why those committed to antimilitarism must also be concerned with the Third World and starving people everywhere. You don't need guns for war. Hunger does it. Disease does it. Lack of schooling does it. But we don't feed the people—we build more bombs. This is the greatest crime in which the First and the Second Worlds are involved. Those who understand the relationship between the North-South conflict and the East-West conflict know they must work in solidarity with the poor. We will have justice and peace or exploitation and this build-up of the arms race.

The point of entry for liberation theology is an understanding of the poor. Their voice is God's voice. And they tell us: "Stop this, stop this! We don't need more bombs. We really don't. We need justice." Peace is more than a business where you make a deal with someone else. It is often a matter of a first step, made quite alone. I reflected on this in a poem called "Unilateralism or god's vulnerability":

> Why are you so one-sided
> people often ask me
> so blind and so unilateral
> I sometimes ask in return
> are you a Christian
> if you don't mind my asking
>
> And depending on the answer I remind them
> how one-sidedly and without guarantees
> god became vulnerable in christ
> where would we end up
> I offer for consideration
> if god insisted on bilateral agreements
> with you and me
> who welch on treaties
> by resorting to various tricks
> where would we end up
> if god insisted on bilateral agreements
> before acting
>
> Then I remind them
> that god didn't come in an armored car
> and wasn't born in a bank
> and gave up the old miracle weapons
> thunder and lightning and heavenly hosts
> one-sidedly
> palaces and kings and soldiers
> were not his way when he
> decided unilaterally
> to become a human being
> which means to live without weapons

RESISTANCE

My last point is resistance. I think what we in the First and Second Worlds have to do is educate ourselves and others to the need to form a resistance movement. We need to resist those forces of oppression in our own midst. And one way to do this is to work with the peace movement. There are other forms of solidarity movements for Third World peoples, but we who live in this country have to build a strong political movement. For me, it has been through the Democratic Socialists of America that I found I could work together with like-minded people. The church is very good, too, but one old rule we had in the Christians for Socialism movement in Germany was that you have to have two legs, so to speak—one in the political organization, be it a union or a party or something like that, and one in the religious institution. You have to work on both sides of the street.

And the way to work on both sides is through resistance—resistance to evil. The word *resistance* in my country, Germany, has become more and more important in the last years, going back to the tradition of the anti-fascist resistance in Europe. There are some people in my country, like some church leaders, who would say to us, "What do you need a resistance for? We don't need any resistance. We are not living under Hitler. We live under a democratically elected government. So why do you talk about resistance?" But we in the movement know why we have to talk about resistance. And many of the people I meet in the United States know as well why they have to become resisters.

I want to share with you a poem which is about some of my resisting friends, Daniel Berrigan and his friends, who are more pacifist than I. The poem is called "When I was asked for the 572nd time what I thought about violence."[1]

> My pacifist friends
> proceeded with extreme violence
> at an innocent general electric plant
> located in a peaceloving town
> named king of prussia
> when they used an instrument of violence
> the old-fashioned hammer
> to render some harmless instruments of security
> namely, atomic missiles useless
>
> To justify their irresponsible action
> they quoted a man
> from the eighth century bc
> whose followers they appeared to be

and who was apparently possessed by the crazy idea
of beating swords into plowshares
on behalf of a higher being

And in the interest of lower beings
people too lazy to work and fringe groups
this violent coalition
of the very high and the very low
for what they call god and what they call the poor
represents for us in the neutral middle
a genuine threat to security[2]

I do believe that we need to organize resistance and that the insight of liberation theology is of primary importance for us. That is what I am standing for: not just to learn from other historical situations but to understand what liberation theology's call is for us who are inside the rich First World. Where is our battlefield? What and where is our oppression? What are we going to do? We have to develop new forms of resistance against this military, capitalist machine which rules us.

The following poem is entitled "Fear not."[3]

Those in power can no longer overlook the hand-
     writing on the wall
their subjects think twice about nodding in agree-
     ment
the weapons dealers no longer dare to walk all over
     the weak
bishops stop equivocating and say no
the friends of jesus block the roads of overkill
school children learn the truth

How are we to recognize an angel
except that he brings courage where fear was
joy where even sadness refused to grow
objections where hard facts used to rule the day
disarmament where terror was a credible deterrence

Fear not resistance is growing

I think resistance grows in the world right before our eyes. And I wish that the whole Christian church would slowly move into the community of resisters. We have some hopeful signs. I am thinking of the World Council of Churches. I participated in their international conference in 1983 and the final statement was very clear in its language. The council used the phrase *a crime* for the arms race, a crime against humanity. It stated that a crime against the poor is being committed when money is used not to feed the poor but to build on earth nuclear weapons. It is a crime and anyone who is involved in such an activity is what we would call a criminal.

When the preparation for war was judged to be a crime at Nuremberg, many German industrialists and generals were incensed to be judged criminals. What about now? The Green Party in my country has created another Nuremberg Tribunal. They dare to talk about the crimes of those who are preparing World War III.

I want to close with one more poem, a prayer of intercession for peace written for a special peace service. It is called "Blessed are the peacemakers: Prayer of intercession in the Lubeck cathedral, September 6, 1980."

> Jesus our brother
> you break the rifle in two
> and make your followers
> fearless and militant
> > those who rule over us say catch up
> > and mean buildup
> > they say defense
> > and mean intervention and first strike
> > they say peace
> > and mean oil
> Jesus let us become like you and not put up with the
> > lie
> we will not put up with militarism
> not over us not next to us not in us
>
> Lord have mercy . . .
>
> Jesus our brother
> you disrupt weapons deals
> you butted in
> you organized resistance
> > we have hidden from the misery of the poor
> > we live in an opulent palace bristling with weapons
> > we build up our defenses and let others starve
> Jesus let us become like you and not put up with
> > their dying
> we will not serve militarism
> not with words not with money not with our life's
> > time
>
> Lord have mercy . . .
>
> Jesus our brother
> you bring the death industry to a halt

you drive the desire for absolute security out of our
hearts
you free us to defend ourselves
the generals in our country want to wear medals
again[4]
it will cost only a hundred and fifty thousand marks
you were betrayed for only thirty pieces of silver
Jesus teach us to understand what life is
that those who do not fight back are on the wrong
track
let us become your brothers and sisters who make
peace

Lord have mercy . . .

25

Conclusion: Vision

ROBERT FREDERICK HUNTER, JR.

"For I was hungry and you gave me something to eat, I was thirsty and you gave me something to drink, I was a stranger and you invited me in, I needed clothes and you clothed me, I was sick and you looked after me, I was in prison and you came to visit me."

Then the righteous will answer, "Lord when did we see you hungry and feed you, or thirsty and give you something to drink? When did we see you a stranger and invite you in, or needing clothes and clothe you? When did we see you sick or in prison and go to visit you?" . . . [Jesus replied], "whatever you did for one of the least of these brothers of mine, you did for me" [Matt. 25:35–40].[1]

In this passage from Matthew, Jesus associates himself with the poor and oppressed of the world—so much so that he states that to feed them, to clothe them or to visit them in prison is to do it to him. That is why when Jesus entered the Temple as recorded in the twenty-first chapter of Matthew, he became angry because of the dishonest dealings that he found there. Merchants had set up booths for selling the needed articles for sacrifice in a way that took advantage of the poor travelers who came too far to bring their sacrifice with them. Jesus' wrath was kindled because the very place that was supposed to be a comfort and support to the poor had become a "den of thieves" (Matt. 21:13).

North American religion has often been such a den of thieves. Much of our theology has become a justification for the rich and powerful. Our understanding of true worship too often does not reflect the words "if you would be my disciples you must take up your cross and follow me" (Mark 8:34). Instead the message has been associated with a false pietism that supports an individualism and other-worldly religionism that at best ignore, and more often support or cause injustice.

It is ironic that the Bible, which was the sacred literature of an oppressed people, has so often become the justification for oppression and greed. This temptation is already seen in the New Testament church as related in the book of James. James warns the church of his day about the favoritism that was growing up among them.

> If you show special attention to the man wearing fine clothes and say, "Here's a good seat for you," but say to the poor man, "You stand there" or "Sit on the floor by my feet," have you not discriminated among yourselves? . . . You have insulted the poor. Is it not the rich who are exploiting you? Are they not the ones who are dragging you into court? [James 2:3–6]

There is no doubt that the prophetic stance of both the Old and New Testaments presents religion as a challenge to the wealthy who have gained that wealth by exploitation of the poor. As Kosuke Koyama reminds us, true worship is defined in Micah as doing justice, loving mercy, and walking humbly with God. And in the time of Isaiah it is recorded that the people began to ask God why they were fasting and God did not answer. The prophetic word was that while they were fasting they were exploiting their workers. This was not the kind of fast that God wanted. Rather God wanted a fast that was to "loose the chains of injustice and untie the cords of the yoke, to set the oppressed free and to break every yoke." It was to "share your bread with the hungry and to provide the poor wanderer with shelter" (Isa. 58:6–7).

The writers in the present volume have seen the injustice as it has affected their communities and they are compassionately but passionately challenging society to become that haven for the poor and oppressed in the United States. They see the coffers of the rich being fed at the expense of their communities. They also see a church in North America that remains comfortable and even supposes that God is behind the enormous accumulation of wealth. Revelation 18 presents a city that resembles the imperialistic inclinations of our own society. The city is a very rich city that (1) "gave herself excessive luxuries," (2) provided wealth for all the business people (merchants) of the earth, and (3) enticed the other governments to join in its illegitimate (adulterous) activities. The chapter presents the destruction of the city because of its violent excesses.

In the list of cargo items exported from the city are mentioned the bodies and the souls of people. This is a stark way of implying the effects of the idolatrous pursuit of wealth. It reveals the results of the exploitation of people for the sake of money.

We see this exploitation today in a number of tragic situations. One example is the closing of plants around the United States. In recent years it has become even more acceptable than in the past for companies to assure their profit margins by laying off workers — workers who have worked for years at a company and even have seen the company in terms of family. This has created massive unemployment and hardship for lower- and pre- viously middle-income people. The hardship has been even greater because of drastic cutbacks in job training, legal services, and federal support for low-cost housing. In cities such as Detroit, medical care is so lacking that the infant mortality rate approximates that of impoverished Third World countries.

Our foreign policy also demonstrates a lack of care for the well-being of people. We are the world's biggest supplier of arms. Many times we sell arms and give support to countries, only to have those same weapons used against us. The weapons sold to the Shah of Iran become weapons in the hands of our "enemy." Support for Iraq and the failure to condemn the use of chemical weapons against Iran come back to haunt us. And what will become of the weapons given to the dictator king of Saudi Arabia to "defend" it against Iraq? While we have allegiances with exploitive regimes throughout the world we have also involved ourselves in helping to over- throw duly elected leaders in such places as Guatemala, Dominican Repub- lic and Chile. We continue to invest in South Africa in the face of its anti- democratic and vicious policies with respect to the majority of its popula- tion. Such exploitation and resulting deaths signal the reality of a society engulfed in an atmosphere of destruction for the sake of its wealth.

While the reality of death surrounds us, much of the popular religious fervor is anemic in the face of these realities. Instead of a prophetic denouncement of false values, much of popular religion has attached itself to values of wealth without coming to terms with the true exploitative nature of wealth in this country and its effect on the masses of people, including the devoted Christians among poor Hispanics in New York and the Southwest, Native Americans, blacks in Harlem or the South Bronx, and unemployed women and children throughout the country.

A theology that remains oblivious to these realities is a theology that is a reversal of the biblical exhortation to feed the hungry and clothe the naked. It is a counterfeit of the conversion called for by the prophets — to *do* justly and love one's neighbor as oneself. Conversion in biblical terms was not just an emotional response, but a fundamental challenge to turn to God and do things differently. Such is the challenge that we are faced with in the United States.

Transformation must occur at a number of levels. (1) There must be a transformation of the self-identity of the communities that have been crushed by oppression and an affirmation of those communities. (2) There must be a vision of solidarity among the particular communities. (3) And the empowerment coming from an enhanced self-image and commitment to solidarity must be translated into goals for political and corporate action.

The first level of transformation must be a restoration of the self-images of the oppressed communities — a psychological and spiritual healing. A landmark study done in the 1940s and repeated in 1987 showed that a majority of black children chose white dolls over black ones. These children were also more likely to attribute positive traits to the white dolls than to the black dolls.[2] Such a study shows the low self-esteem that is inherent in a racist society and the need for oppressed communities to challenge the negative images of themselves. We find black-on-black crime, Hispanics turning on Hispanics, Native Americans turning on one another, and women struggling among themselves — all have stories to tell of communities fighting among themselves with such hostility and viciousness that it reveals the deep-seated damage done to the image of the community.

As Mar Peter-Raoul shows in her essay in this book, liberation theology ia a theology that is concerned for the whole person. It is both a call to a spirituality of prayer, praxis, song, and a challenge to social change — a socio-political, liberating theology. In this context James Cone asserts that the vision of a new black community must begin with an emphasis on black unity and self-love. Orlando Costas, as a part of his four goals, states that Hispanic stereotypes must be challenged and overcome, and a new Hispanic identity must be awakened. In their pastoral letter the Catholic bishops of Appalachia make it clear that healing can come to Appalachia only if the people are freed in spirit as well as in terms of economic and political reality. Elisabeth Schüssler Fiorenza sees the need for a feminist theology that has "found God in our soul." And Ada María Isasi-Díaz tells us that the beginning of *mujerista* theology is the powerful act of naming oneself — the act of self-identification.

At the second level, transformation must not only affirm the identity within the communities but ignite solidarity among communities. The writers see the ultimate vision as unity among the communities standing in solidarity against oppression. Costas suggests that the Hispanic, black, and Latin American communities have mutually beneficial perspectives which compliment and challenge each other. Cone and Vine Deloria challenge the black and Native-American communities to view their struggles in the context of the international struggle against monopoly capitalism. Koyama and Marc Ellis challenge their communities — which have achieved a certain degree of relief from oppression — to identify with others "for the sake of others" and not let their relative positions of strength allow them to oppress those who are in the bowels of the struggle to end oppression.

The third level of transformation is the translation of the first two levels into social and political realities. This third level is a call for fundamental change — not "moderate solutions." Bayard Rustin, the long-time political and civil rights activist, has written that moderates

apparently see nothing strange in the fact that in the last twenty-five years we have spent nearly a trillion dollars fighting or preparing for wars, yet throw up our hands before the need for overhauling our schools, clearing the slums, and really abolishing poverty. My quarrel with these moderates is that they do not even envision radical change;

their admonitions of moderation are, for all practical purposes, admonition to the Negro to adjust to the status quo, and therefore immoral.[3]

Fundamental change requires understanding social, political, and economic life from the perspective of the poor. Liberation theologians in Latin America argue that political life is not neutral. One either sees life from the perspective of the rich or from the perspective of the poor. We cannot avoid taking sides. Michael Harrington has said that "You must stand somewhere to see social reality and where you stand will determine much of what you see and how you see it."[4] The deterrent to seeing social reality from the perspective of the poor is that in most countries of the world (East and West) the control of social analysis and policy is in the hands of the elite. This is true of everything from biblical interpretation that ignores the fact and content of scripture written from the perspective of the poor, to the actual running of the governments of the world. In the East, as Harrington sees it, the governments have been controlled by a "bureaucratic, dictatorial elite; in the West they are under the guidance of a partnership between governments and corporate leaders. Nowhere in the world are they subject to the will of the vast majority whose labor and ingenuity are the source of the socialization process."[5]

While this is true in general, the potential for democracy has been demonstrated in several incidents where people have shown a determination and solidarity to prevent injustice. One case was the outcry against the Reagan nomination of Robert Bork to the Supreme Court. Another was the outcry against an order to deduct all charitable handouts (including blankets and soup given at soup kitchens) from monthly allotments from Social Security insurance. The outcry caused the order to be rescinded in one day.[6] In Mobile, Alabama, the Ku Klux Klan was sued for seven million dollars and one of its members convicted of murder because of the efforts of a determined mother (whose son was murdered) and the Southern Poverty Law Center.[7] All of these incidents give hope for the potential for political change given an awareness of class issues and a determination and solidarity. As people in the United States become aware of class issues and the potential for power in solidarity, the vision will advance to the levels of national and international politics. This is important because only rarely in U.S. politics is there a candidate from the major parties who even purports to run with a nonelite perspective. Exceptions might be George McGovern in 1972 and Jesse Jackson in 1984 and 1988. We need to see the importance of these coalition candidates. We need to support their efforts to pull together different groups (which often act independently). We should understand that politics in this country must include the perspective of the "underside of history" so that history is no longer merely the story of the elite.

Coalitions of course do not often begin with a national perspective. Much is being done by unsung heroes in communities across the country. The examples in Part 3, though not exhaustive, demonstrate that from the fields of California to the cells of Sing Sing and on to the inner-cities of New York and Detroit, people are involved in acts of courage, commitment, and determination to bring change.

Structural change will mean that economic, political, and social decisions are made democratically; not left to the so-called forces of the market, which really are the forces of the elite acting in their own self-interest. There is nothing in the scriptures or human experience to suggest that justice comes from an economic power struggle in which everyone tries to make as much as he or she can. Instead, the scriptures and human experience suggest that justice is best served when the neediest in society are considered human and capable and are afforded a voice in solidarity with others.

The theologies of liberation presented in this volume are the cries coming from communities that have not been afforded such justice. They are the challenges to realize this oppression as a spiritual problem needing structural change. May the God of justice give us the ears to hear and the heart to act.

Notes

INTRODUCTION

1. Gustavo Gutiérrez, "Liberation, Praxis, and Christian Faith," in *Frontiers of Theology in Latin America*, ed. Rosino Gibellini, (Maryknoll, N.Y.: Orbis Books, 1979), pp. 17, 18.

2. Robert McAfee Brown, *Theology in a New Key: Responding to Liberation Themes* (Philadelphia: Westminster Press, 1978), pp. 136–37.

1. SOUTH BRONX TO SOUTH AFRICA: PRAYER, PRAXIS, SONG

1. Daniel Berrigan, "Foreword," in Ched Myers, *Binding the Strong Man: A Political Reading of Mark's Story of Jesus* (Maryknoll, N.Y.: Orbis Books, 1988), p. xxiii.

2. Phillip Berryman, "Basic Christian Communities and the Future of Latin America," *Monthly Review* 36, no. 3 (July–August 1984), p. 27.

3. Otto Maduro, *Religion and Social Conflict* (Maryknoll, N.Y.: Orbis Books, 1982), p. xxv.

4. Gustavo Gutiérrez, "A Theology of Liberation," *Monthly Review* 36, no. 3 (July–August 1984), p. 96.

5. Ibid.

6. Cited in Theo Witvliet, *A Place in the Sun: Liberation Theology in the Third World* (Maryknoll, N.Y.: Orbis Books, 1985), p. 133.

7. Gutiérrez, "A Theology of Liberation," p. 102.

8. Ibid., p. 97.

9. Witvliet, *A Place in the Sun*, p. 92.

10. Ibid., p. 91.

11. Ibid., p. 92.

12. Allan Boesak, "Black Theology and the Struggle for Liberation in South Africa," *Monthly Review* 36, no. 3 (July–August 1984), p. 134.

13. Cited in David Hein, "Bishop Tutu's Christology," *Cross Currents* 34, no. 4 (Winter 1984), p. 496.

14. Witvliet, *A Place in the Sun*, p. 82.

15. *The Kairos Document* in *From South Africa—A Challenge to the Church!* (Closter, N.J.: Theology in Global Context Program).

16. Virginia Fabella, ed., *Asia's Struggle for Full Humanity* (Maryknoll, N.Y.: Orbis Books, 1980), p. 5.

17. Marianne Katoppo, *Compassionate and Free: An Asian Woman's Theology* (Maryknoll, N.Y.: Orbis Books, 1981), p. 75.

18. Letty Russell, *Human Liberation in a Feminist Perspective: A Theology* (Philadelphia: Westminster Press, 1974).

19. Robert McAfee Brown, *Making Peace in the Global Village* (Philadelphia: Westminster Press, 1981), p. 96.

20. Myers, *Binding the Strong Man*, p. 452.

21. Ibid., p. 8.

22. Robert Maynard, "No Middle Class in New York City," *Press and Sun-Bulletin*, April 8, 1989.

23. Josh Barbanel, "How Despair Is Engulfing a Generation in New York," *New York Times*, April 2, 1989.

24. "America's Third World," in *New World Outlook* (July–August 1988).

25. Richard Shaull, *Heralds of a New Reformation: The Poor of North and South America* (Maryknoll, N.Y.: Orbis Books, 1984), p. 87.

26. Brown, *Making Peace*, p. 26.

27. Myers, *Binding the Strong Man*, p. 451.

28. Ibid., p. 28.

29. Ibid., p. 451.

30. Ibid., p. 455.

31. Ibid., p. 453.

32. Virgilio Elizondo, "Mestizaje as a Locus of Theological Reflection," in *The Future of Liberation Theology: Essays in Honor of Gustavo Gutiérrez*, ed. Marc Ellis and Otto Maduro (Maryknoll, N.Y.: Orbis Books, 1989).

2. LIBERATION THEOLOGIES IN THE AMERICAS: COMMON JOURNEYS AND MUTUAL CHALLENGES

1. *Time,* February 4, 1985, p. 56.

2. Virgilio Elizondo, *Galilean Journey: The Mexican-American Promise* (Maryknoll, N.Y.: Orbis Books, 1984), p. 18.

3. From Milton Nascimiento, Pedro Casaldáliga, Pedro Tierra, and Dom Helder Camara, *Mass of the Quilombos*, trans. Ruy and Marta Costa.

4. See *Prophets Denied Honor: An Anthology on the Hispanic Church in the United States*, ed. Antonio M. Stevens Arroyo (Maryknoll, N.Y.: Orbis Books, 1980), pp. 113–140.

5. *Jíbaro*: the Puerto Rican peasant or person from the mountains.

6. *Flamboyán*: the flame tree, noted for its bright red-orange flowers; it is very common in Puerto Rico.

7. *Coquí*: a small frog native to Puerto Rico; it is noted for its high-pitched call.

8. *Batey*: an Indian word for the unpaved central plaza of a village; it has come to mean the area immediately surrounding a house where people gather to talk or socialize.

9. *La peleíta monga*: an idiomatic Puerto Rican expression for a way of "beating around the bush" in order to gain something.

10. *¡Ay Bendito!*: a traditional Puerto Rican expression that has been weighted with connotations of fatalism by contemporary commentators.

3. BLACK THEOLOGY: WHERE WE HAVE BEEN AND A VISION FOR WHERE WE ARE GOING

1. Joseph Washington, *Black Religion* (Boston: Beacon Press, 1964).

2. See James H. Cone, *God of the Oppressed* (New York: Seabury Press, 1975),

and *My Soul Looks Back* (Maryknoll, N.Y.: Orbis Books, 1986), chap. 1.

3. Washington, *Black Religion*, p. 143.

4. James H. Cone, *Black Theology and Black Power* (New York: Seabury Press, 1969).

5. James H. Cone, *A Black Theology of Liberation*, 2d ed. (Maryknoll, N.Y.: Orbis Books, 1986).

6. J. Deotis Roberts, *Liberation and Reconciliation* (Philadelphia: Westminster Press, 1971).

7. Major Jones, *Black Awareness: A Theology of Hope* (Nashville: Abingdon Press, 1971).

8. Cecil Cone, *Identity Crises in Black Theology* (Nashville: AMEC, 1975).

9. Gayraud Wilmore, *Black Religion and Black Radicalism: An Interpretation of the History of Afro-American People* (Maryknoll, N.Y.: Orbis Books, 1983). Originally published by Anchor Press/Doubleday, 1973.

10. Malcolm X, *By Any Means Necessary*, ed. George Breitman (New York: Pathfinder, 1970), p. 155.

11. Malcolm X, *The Speeches of Malcolm X at Harvard*, ed. Archie Epps (New York: Morrow, 1968), p. 133.

7. UNION OF ETHICAL WALKING AND THEOLOGICAL BEHOLDING: REFLECTIONS FROM AN ASIAN AMERICAN

1. Jerry Falwell, *Listen, America!* (New York: Bantam Books, 1980), p. 85.

2. *New Republic* (July 15, 1985), p. 28.

3. Ibid.

4. The paper was delivered at a conference entitled "Ecumenical Consultation on Racially Motivated Violence Toward Asians and Pacific Islanders in the United States" (held December 14–15, 1984, at Christ United Presbyterian Church, San Francisco), p. 15.

5. Ibid., p. 17.

8. *MUJERISTAS:* A NAME OF OUR OWN

1. Ada María Isasi-Díaz, "Toward an Understanding of *Feminismo Hispano* in the U.S.A." in *Women's Consciousness, Women's Conscience*, ed. Barbara H. Andolsen, Christine E. Gudorf, and Mary D. Pellauer (New York: Winston, 1985), pp. 51–61.

2. "I am a woman searching for equality,
   I will not put up with abuse and wickedness.
   I am a woman and I have dignity,
   and justice will soon be a reality."
      Words by María del Valle and Mildred Bonilla.

3. "Women, you are women,
   because you have known how to recognize,
   the fact that you are powerful."

4. "Today I sing to the God of my people with my guitar,
   I sing a song of a woman who liberates herself.
   God listened to the cry of our people,
   made an alliance with the poor and the exploited,

　　　and freed woman from the chains
　　　imposed on her with cruelty for centuries."

5. I am much indebted to the work of black feminists who have preceded us in this struggle to name ourselves. Their use of the term "womanist" has influenced me immensely. I am particularly grateful to Katie Cannon, Joan Martin, and Delores Williams, with whom I have had the privilege of sharing much. See especially Delores S. Williams, "Womanist Theology: Black Women's Voices," chap. 4, above.

6. Cantico de Mujer
Rosa Marta Zárate Macís

1. Hoy Canto al Dios del Pueblo en guitarra [Luc. 1:46–55]
　　un canto de mujer que se libera,
　　Dios se solidariza con mi causa,
　　me consagra portavoz de la esperanza.
　　Dios escuchó el clamor de nuestro pueblo [Jud. 8:21–28]
　　se alió al empobrecido y explotado
　　y a la mujer libera de cadenas
　　impuestas con crueldad por tantos siglos.
　　¡DICHOSA MUJER LA QUE SABE SER FIEL [Jud. 13:30, 14:9–10]
　　AL QUEHACER DE IMPLANTAR
　　LA JUSTICIA Y LA PAZ!
　　¡BENDITA SERA LA MUJER QUE HACE OPCION [Luc. 8:1–3]
　　POR LA CAUSA DE DIOS [Nican Mopohua],
　　POR LA LEY DEL AMOR!

2. Harás justicia a todas las mujeres
　　que firmes no cayeron ante el yugo
　　nos das la libertad y reivindicas [Gen. 1:27].
　　¡Oh, Dios, tu semejanza originaria!
　　Al mal pastor que causa tanto daño
　　al gobernante infiel que vende al pueblo,
　　a todo quien oprime tú destruyes
　　sin piedad del poder tú derrumbas.

3. Nos llamas a gestar en nuestro vientre
　　mujeres y hombres nuevos, pueblo fuerte
　　Nos unges servidoras, profetisas [Matt. 27:55–56],
　　testigos de tu amor que nos redime
　　Has puesto en mi cantar una esperanza [Marcos 16:1–8]
　　Seré eco de tu amor que reconcilia
　　Espada de dos filos sea mi canto [Jud. 9:10–14]
　　pregón de un Evangelio libertarios.

7. Ada María Isasi-Díaz and Yolando Tarango, *Hispanic Women: Prophetic Voice in the Church* (San Francisco: Harper & Row, 1988).

8. José Míguez Bonino, "Nuevas Tendencias en Teología," *Pasos* (1985), p. 22.

9. Isasi-Díaz and Tarango, *Hispanic Women*, pp. 105–6.

10. I want to thank María Antonietta Berriozabal and Yolanda Tarango with whom I discussed at length using *mujeristas* as our "name." I also want to thank many Hispanic sisters who never allowed me to rest comfortably under the name "feminist."

11. Charles Curran, *Catholic Moral Theology in Dialogue* (Notre Dame, Ind.: Fides, 1972), p. 53.

12. Juan Luis Segundo, *The Liberation of Theology* (Maryknoll, N.Y.: Orbis Books, 1982), p. 118.

13. Norman K. Gottwald, "Socio-Historical Precision in the Biblical Grounding of Liberation Theologies" (unpublished address to the Catholic Biblical Association of America, San Francisco, August 1985), p. 11.

14. Virgilio Elizondo, *Galilean Journey* (Maryknoll, N.Y.: Orbis Books, 1984).

15. The best-known examples of this are the four volumes of *The Gospel of Solentiname* (Maryknoll, N.Y.: Orbis Books, 1982).

16. Segundo, *Liberation*, p. 121.

17. Ibid., p. 119.

18. Curran, *Moral Theology*, p. 64.

19. Stanley Hauerwas, "The Moral Authority of Scripture: The Politics and Ethics of Remembering," in *The Use of Scripture in Moral Theology*, ed. Charles E. Curran and Richard A. McCormick (New York: Paulist Press, 1984), p. 245.

20. Dianne Bergant, "Exodus as a Paradigm in Feminist Theology," in *Exodus — A Lasting Paradigm*, vol. 189 of *Concilium*, ed. Bas van Iersel and Anton Weiler (Edinburgh: T & T Clark, 1987), pp. 100–106.

21. Much of the material in Exodus comes from the J source. P provides a framework for the J material, while E has been used to supplement J. The core of the material of the pericopes here examined comes from the supplementary source, E. Supplemental material has to have some significance, whether literary, historical, or theological, for it to be considered worth adding. That the compilers/editors of the present text added this pericope would indicate that in some way it is intrinsic to the history, the theme, the theological understanding of the exodus.

22. "The two midwives have apparently Semitic names. Puah may mean 'splendid one' or perhaps 'girl.' ... Shiphrah appears ... on a list of Egyptian slaves and means 'fair one' " (Brevard S. Childs, *The Book of Exodus* [Philadelphia: Westminster Press, 1974], pp. 8–12).

23. J. Cheryl Exum, " 'You Shall Let Every Daughter Live': A Study of Exodus 1:8–2:10," *Semeia* 28 (1983), pp. 3–82.

24. "The attribute *Hebrew* applied here to the midwives represents the first use in Exodus of this term, which is due to recur a number of times in the continuation of the Book. ... The word in question signifies in general people who were aliens in their environment, and were mostly employed as servants or slaves. In Egyptian texts, the aforementioned Egyptian term refers to enslaved people, who were compelled to do forced labour in the service of the pharaoh. In the Bible the children of Israel, or their ancestors, are called *Hebrews* particularly when the writer has in mind the relationship to the foreign environment in which they find themselves. ... Here, in Exodus, whilst the children of Israel are still free men, they are called by their honoured designation, *children of Israel*, even when pharaoh speaks of them (v. 9). But after the commencement of their servitude, they are usually referred to as *Hebrews*" (U. Cassuto, *A Commentary on the Book of Exodus* [Jerusalem: The Magnum Press, The Hebrew University, 1967], p. 13).

25. "Depatriarchalizing in Biblical Interpretation," *JAAR* 41 (1973), p. 34.

26. Childs, *Exodus*, p. 16.

27. Exum, "You Shall Let," p. 72.

28. Ibid.

29. Samuel Terrien, "Fear," in *The Interpreter's Dictionary of the Bible*, vol. 2, ed. Emory Stevens Bucke (New York: Abingdon, 1962), p. 257.

30. Ibid., pp. 258–59.

31. Verses 18–19 relate the confrontation between the pharaoh and the midwives. Pharaoh had ordered them directly and, therefore, he is the one to whom they have to report. Because they have defied his direct order, their defiance is a direct action against him. But their defiance in the form of noncompliance is so clever that the best the pharaoh can do is to reword his order and impose it in general upon everyone. Therefore, from now on the pharaoh will find it all the more impossible to hold anyone accountable for not following his orders.

32. Exum, "You Shall Let," p. 74.

33. Ibid.

34. Isabel Allende, *The House of the Spirits* (New York: Knopf, 1985), pp. 358–68; Charlotte Bunch, *Passionate Politics* (New York: St. Martin's Press, 1987); Nancy Hartsoch, *Money, Sex and Power* (Boston: Northeastern University Press, 1985); and Carter Heyward, *The Redemption of God* (Washington, D.C.: University of America Press, 1984).

15. JUSTICE HOUSE

1. Larry Rasmussen, "New Dynamics in Theology," *Christianity and Crisis* (May 16, 1988).

22. FOR WOMEN IN MEN'S WORLDS: A CRITICAL FEMINIST THEOLOGY OF LIBERATION

1. From Sandra Maria Esteves, "For Tulani," in *Ordinary Women: An Anthology of Poetry by New York City Women* (New York, 1978), p. 44.

2. Carol P. Christ, *Diving Deep and Surfacing: Women Writers on Spiritual Quest* (Boston: Beacon Press, 1980).

3. Beverly Ann Schlack, "The 'Poetess of Poets': Alice Meynell Rediscovered," *Women's Studies* 7 (1980), pp. 111–126, 113f.

4. Ntozake Shange, *for colored girls who have considered suicide, when the rainbow is enuf* (New York: Macmillan, 1977), p. 63. See also Christ, *Diving Deep*, pp. 97–117.

5. See the articles in *Frauen in der Männerkirche*, ed. B. Brooten and N. Greinacher (Münich-Mainz, 1982).

6. Hildegunde Woller, "Im Schatten des Vaters," in *Frau und Religion: Gottesefahrungen im Patriarchat*, ed. Elisabeth Moltmann-Wendel (Frankfurt, 1983), pp. 174–177 — my translation.

7. Virginia Woolf, *Three Guineas* (New York: Harcourt Brace Jovanovich, 1963), pp. 60–63.

8. See Thomas S. Kuhn, *The Structure of Scientific Revolutions* (Chicago: University of Chicago Press, 1962); Elizabeth Janeway, "Who Is Sylvia? On the Loss of Sexual Paradigms," *Signs* 5 (1980), pp. 573–89.

9. See, e.g., Sandra Harding and Merrill B. Hintikka, *Discovering Reality: Feminist Perspectives on Epistemology, Metaphysics, Methodology, and Philosophy of Science*, Studies in Epistemology, vol. 161 (Boston: D. Reidel, 1983); L. F. Pusch, *Feminismus: Inspektion der Herrenkultur* (Frankfurt, 1983).

10. See Haig Bosmajian, *The Language of Oppression* (Washington: University Press of America, 1974); S. Tromel-Plotz, *Frauensprache — Sprache der Veranderung* (Frankfurt, 1982).

11. See D. Griffin Crowder, "Amazons and Mothers? Monique Wittig, Helene Cixous, and Theories of Women's Writing," *Contemporary Literature* 24/2 (1983), pp. 117–44; Griffin Crowder underlines these differences in her discussion of French and American feminism.

12. See, e.g., S. A. Bonzales, "La Chicana: Guadalupe or Malinche?", in *Comparative Perspective of Third World Women: The Impact of Race, Sex, and Class*, ed. Beverly Linsay (New York: Praeger, 1980), pp. 229–50.

13. See A. Barstow Driver, "Review Essay: Religion," *Signs* 2 (1976), pp. 434–42; Carol P. Christ, "The New Feminist Theology: A Review of the Literature," *Religious Studies Review* 3 (1977), pp. 203–12; *Womanspirit Rising: A Feminist Reader in Religion*, ed. Carol P. Christ and Judith Plaskow (San Francisco: Harper & Row, 1979), pp. 1–17.

14. See C. Halkes, *Gott hat nicht nur starke Sohne: Grundzuge einer feministischen Theologie* (Gutersloh, 1980); E. Gossmann, *Die steitbaren Schwestern: Was Will die feministische Theologie?* (Freiburg, 1981).

15. See my articles "Feminist Theology as a Critical Theology of Liberation," *Theological Studies* 36 (1975), pp. 605–26; "Towards a Liberating and Liberated Theology," *Concilium* 15 (1979), pp. 22–32; "To Comfort or To Challenge?", in *New Woman, New Church, New Priestly Ministry*, ed. M. Dwyer (Rochester, 1980), pp. 43–60; and "Claiming the Center," in *Womanspirit Bonding*.

16. See Zillah R. Eisenstein, *The Radical Future of Liberal Feminism* (Boston: Northeastern University Press, 1981) for an analysis of "capitalist patriarchy."

17. For a review of the literature see my "Discipleship and Patriarchy: Early Christian Ethos and Christian Ethics in a Feminist Perspective," in *The American Society of Christian Ethics: Selected Papers: 1982*, ed. Larry Rasmussen (Waterloo, 1982), pp. 131–72.

18. See my "We Are Still Invisible: Theological Analysis of 'Women and Ministry,'" in *Women and Ministry: Present Experience and Future Hopes*, ed. D. Gottemoeller and R. Hofbauer (Washington, 1981), pp. 29–43, and "Emanzipation aus der Bibel," *Evangelische Kommentare* 16 (1983), pp. 195–98.

19. Mercy Amba Oduyoye, "Reflections from a Third World Woman's Perspective: Women's Experience and Liberation Theologies," in *Irruption of the Third World*, ed. Virginia Fabella and Sergio Torres (Maryknoll, N.Y.: Orbis Books, 1983), pp. 246–55, and 250.

20. See especially Marianne Katoppo, *Compassionate and Free: An Asian Woman's Theology* (Maryknoll, N.Y.: Orbis Books, 1981); Elsa Tamez, *The Bible of the Oppressed* (Maryknoll, N.Y.: Orbis Books, 1982).

21. See especially also Jacquelyn Grant, "Black Theology and the Black Woman," in *Black Theology: A Documentary History, 1966-1979*, ed. Gayraud Wilmore and James Cone (Maryknoll, N.Y.: Orbis Books, 1979), pp. 418–33.

22. See especially Nelle Morton, "Towards Whole Theology," in *Sexism in the 1970s* (Geneva, 1975), pp. 56–65.

23. See *Frau und Religion*, pp. 31ff.

24. For a fuller development of such a feminist hermeneutics see my book *In Memory of Her: A Feminist Theological Reconstruction of Christian Origins* (New York: Crossroad, 1983), especially pp. 3–95, 343–51.

25. For such an approach see C. J. M. Halkes, "Feministische Theologie: Eine Zwischenbilanz," in *Frauen in der Mannerkirche*, pp. 158–74, and the excellent work of Rosemary Radford Ruether, *Sexism and God-Talk: Toward a Feminist Theology* (Boston: Beacon Press, 1983).

26. From Renny Golden, "Women Behind Walls: For the Women in Cook County Jail and Dwight Prison," in Renny Golden and Sheila Collins, *Struggle Is a Name for Hope* (Minneapolis: West End Press, 1982).

23. THE PALESTINIAN UPRISING AND THE FUTURE OF THE JEWISH PEOPLE

1. Michael Lerner, "The Occupation: Immoral and Stupid," *Tikkun* 3 (March/April 1988), p. 8. Lerner continues: "The crisis in Israel is a moment of truth for all of us. It should be responded to with the deepest seriousness and with the full understanding that the choices we make now may have consequences that reverberate for centuries to come" (p. 12).

2. Johann Baptist Metz, *The Emergent Church: The Future of Christianity in a Postbourgeois World*, trans. Peter Mann (New York: Crossroad, 1981), p. 19. This is *not* an attempt to compare the Nazi period with the Israeli-Palestinian conflict or to create a scenario of evil Israelis and innocent Palestinians. Neither do I want to suggest that Palestinians have been victimized only by Israelis. It is to suggest that Israel, at this point in history, is powerful and thus the reponsibility is clear. Further, it is to suggest that even justice is not enough. We can move forward only *with* the Palestinian people.

3. For a discussion of dissent and Israel's nuclear capability see Rudolf Peierls, "The Case of Mordechai Vanunu," *New York Review of Books* 35 (June 16, 1988), p. 56. Also see Jane Hunter, "Vanunu and Israel's Nuclear Crimes," *Israeli Foreign Affairs* 4 (February 1988), p. 3. For the fate of the young during the uprising see *Palestinians Killed by Israeli Occupation Forces, Settlers, and Civilians During Uprising, December 9, 1987, through April 18, 1988* (Chicago: Database Project on Palestinian Human Rights, 1988), and *Children of the Stones* (Jerusalem: Palestinian Center for the Study of Nonviolence, 1988). For the response of Irving Greenberg to the uprising see his "The Ethics of Jewish Power," *Perspectives* (New York: National Jewish Center for Learning and Leadership, 1988). For the response of Elie Wiesel see his "A Mideast Peace — Is It Impossible?" *New York Times*, June 23, 1988, p. 22.

4. A major task of theology is to nurture the questions a people need to ask about the future they are creating. In its time Holocaust theology did this and thus reoriented most of Jewish theology and Jewish secular thought. But today Holocaust theology is distant from the history we are creating and therefore applies past categories to present realities. Our behavior is filtered through this framework: that which cannot happen within this framework thus by definition is not happening. Two options appear. Either we lose touch with the history we are creating, producing dissonance, a sense of isolation, paralysis, or even cynicism; or if we understand the history we are creating, we do so uncritically. Hence the neoconservative drift in Jewish theology. When theology ceases to nurture the questions a people need to ask about the history they are creating, critical thought atrophies. In the case of the Jewish people more than thought is at stake: We are in danger of becoming everything we loathed about our oppressors.

5. For an important historical understanding of the interaction of Israel and

Palestine see Simha Flapan, *The Birth of Israel: Myths and Realities* (New York: Pantheon, 1987). Flapan, a life-long Zionist and resident of Israel/Palestine from 1930 until his death in 1987, writes that Israel's myths, "forged during the formation of the state have hardened into this impenetrable, and dangerous, ideological shield" (p. 8). To understand the contemporary scene, Flapan reassesses the birth of Israel and in a sense his own birth as a Zionist. On the subject of the Israel-South Africa relationship after its announced termination in 1987, see Jane Hunter, "South Africa Hurls Israeli Technology Against Angola, May Build Lavi Aircraft," *Israeli Foreign Affairs* 3 (December 1987), pp. 1, 5; and idem, "Israelis Help South African Air Force," *Israeli Foreign Affairs* 4 (April 1988), pp. 1, 8.

6. One such attempt to break through the silence is found in David Grossman's *The Yellow Wind*, trans. Haim Watzman (New York: Farrar, Straus and Giroux, 1988). In the wake of the uprising it became a bestseller in Israel and the United States.

7. For the first publication of the Committee Confronting the Iron Fist, see *We Will Be Free in Our Own Homeland: A Collection of Readings for International Day of Fast and Solidarity with Palestinian Prisoners* (Jerusalem, 1986). A report on *Yesh Gvul* can be found in "Israeli Doves Arousing Little Response," *New York Times*, March 1, 1988. See also "A Captain's Ideals Lead Him to Jail," *New York Times*, March 20, 1988, and Gideon Spiro, "The Israeli Soldiers Who Say 'There Is a Limit,'" *Middle East International* 333 (September 9, 1988), pp. 18–20.

8. For New Jewish Agenda's response to the uprising see Ezra Goldstein and Deena Hurwitz, "No Status Quo Ante," *New Jewish Agenda* 24 (Spring 1988), pp. 1–3. Arthur Hertzberg is probably the most articulate and widely read Jewish intellectual on the uprising. See his "The Uprising," *New York Review of Books* 35 (February 4, 1988), pp. 30–32, and "The Illusion of Jewish Unity," *New York Review of Books* 35 (June 16, 1988), pp. 6, 8, 10–12. Also see the cable sent to the President of Israel by Rabbi Alexander M. Schindler, President of the Union of American Hebrew Congregations, found in *AS Briefings: Commission on Social Action of Reform Judaism*, March, 1988, Appendix A. He begins the cable, "I am deeply troubled and pained in sending you this message, but I cannot be silent. The indiscriminate beating of Arabs enunciated and implemented as Israel's new policy to quell the riots in Judea, Samaria and Gaza, is an offense to the Jewish spirit. It violates every principle of human decency. And it betrays the Zionist dream." Also see Albert Vorspan, "Soul Searching," *New York Times Magazine*, May 8, 1988, pp. 40–41, 51, 54.

9. Shamir's response is a prime lesson in Holocaust theology. At a news conference in Jerusalem, Shamir said: "It is the height of temerity and hypocrisy that members of the terrorist organization speak of returning. This boat which loads its decks with murderers, terrorists who sought to murder us—all of us, each of us. They wish to bring them to the land of Israel, and demonstrate that they are returning to the same place in which they wished to slay us. We will and do view this as a hostile act, an act which endangers the state of Israel." Quoted in "Israel's Furious Over a Palestinian Plan to 'Return' to Haifa by Sail," *New York Times*, February 11, 1988, p. 15.

10. See Rosemary Radford Ruether and Herman J. Ruether, *The Wrath of Jonah: The Crisis of Religious Nationalism in the Israeli-Palestinain Conflict* (San Francisco: Harper & Row, 1988). For a fascinating Jewish response to Christian critical soli-

darity with the Jewish people see *Interreligious Currents*, ed. Annette Daum, 7 (Winter/Spring 1988), pp. 1–8.

11. The strains of this highly problematic and emotional relationship have increasingly come to the surface in recent years. Witness the upheavals in North American Jewish life relating to the Lebanese War, the massacres at Sabra and Shatila, the Pollard spy case, and now the uprising. My point is simply that the relationship between Jews in Israel and Jews outside of Israel cannot remain as it is without ultimately dividing the community at its very roots.

12. For Hannah Arendt's prophetic understanding of the choices facing the Jewish settlers in Palestine, see a collection of her essays *Hannah Arendt; the Jew as Pariah: Jewish Identity and Politics in the Modern Age*, ed. Ron H. Feldman (New York: Grove Press, 1978).

24. A THEOLOGY OF PEACE

1. The number 572 in the title of this poem has an ironic meaning for Europeans. Five hundred and seventy-two is the number of cruise missiles the United States wants us to place in our countries. This number comes up again and again. Some Dutch people, for example, tried to work on tax resistance and did not pay 5 gilden and 72 cents, a ridiculously small sum which messed up the whole system.

2. I must explain one more thing about this poem. When I am talking about peace there is always someone in the audience who stands up and asks me, "Now what do you say about violence?" Sometimes I say I really don't understand. Which violence do you mean? Do you mean the Pershing 2, which is very violent? What is violence? What do you mean? What is violence? Is it the propaganda put forth against any movement that wants to change things? Is that what you call violence?

In West Germany we have had huge demonstrations in recent years—150,000, 300,000, 400,000, half a million people participating. After a demonstration the anchorperson on the evening news would always say: "To our surprise this time no violence happened." That is what they thought news was—that a nonviolent movement caused no violence! If you think about such a crowd and if you think about sports, where often violence occurs, it is really a miracle how few violent occurrences there are at these demonstrations. This expectation of violence is the propaganda of the state and part of the ideology of the class struggle. The ruling class defends its own violence day by day by calling those who want to change things violent and subversive.

3. In this poem there is an allusion that needs explanation; it is an allusion to some acts of resistance. In Hanover we have something called a weapons fair where weapons merchants place, praise, and sell their beautiful weapons. A group of nonviolent pacifists went to Hanover and laid themselves on the ground so the weapons dealers had to step over them before they could enter. Now, we have a saying in German, "Someone goes over corpses," which means someone is so brutal that he or she will step over dead people lying on the ground. Literally the weapons dealers had to go over these people. And on the last day there was a little escalation of this symbolic nonviolent action. The resisters were naked, some were smeared with blood. So these trades people, these fine business people with their three-piece suits and little attaché cases, had to step over these naked, bloody people in order to go into the place where they wanted to make their deals. Finally the officials of the city of Hanover said they did not want this anymore and the weapons mer-

chants should look for another place for their fair — a tiny little victory for resistance.

4. One little controversy which occurred after the escalation of the whole arms buildup in the last years centered around the fact that the army in West Germany had no medals. After Hitler, when the rearmament came, the military were a little ashamed to wear them publicly. They didn't run around in their uniforms and they didn't wear their medals because they had a certain decent sense that there was still some blood on the medals. But then — I think it was in April 1980 or maybe 1981 — they decided they needed medals once again.

25. CONCLUSION: VISION

1. The passage is from the *New International Version*. This version uses noninclusive terms. Hence I have exchanged *kindred* for *brothers*.

2. *New York Times*, Monday, August 31, 1987.

3. Bayard Rustin, "From Protest to Politics: The Future of the Civil Rights Movement," in *Urban Planning and Social Policy*, ed. B. J. Frieden and Robert Morris (New York: Basic Books, 1968), pp. 339–40.

4. Michael Harrington, *Taking Sides* (New York: Holt, Rinehart and Winston, 1985), p. 1.

5. Ibid., p. 197.

6. *New York Times*, October 17, 1987, p. 1.

7. *New York Times*, November 1, 1987, p. 26.

Selected References

Balasuriya, Tissa, *Planetary Theology*. Maryknoll, N.Y.: Orbis Books, 1984.

Berryman, Phillip. *Liberation Theology*. New York: Pantheon Books, 1987.

Boston Theological Institute. *One Faith, Many Cultures: Inculturation, Indigenization, and Contextualization*. Maryknoll, N.Y.: Orbis Books, 1988.

Brown, Robert McAfee. *Making Peace in the Global Village*. Philadelphia: Westminster Press, 1981.

Collins, Sheila D. *From Melting Pot to Rainbow Coalition: The Future of Race in American Politics*. New York: Monthly Review Press, 1986.

Cone, James H. *A Black Theology of Liberation*. 2nd ed. Maryknoll, N.Y.: Orbis Books, 1986.

———. *Black Theology and Black Power*. New York: Seabury Press, 1969.

———. *For My People: Black Theology and the Black Church*. Maryknoll, N.Y.: Orbis Books, 1984.

———. *God of the Oppressed*. New York: Seabury Press, 1975.

———. *My Soul Looks Back*. Maryknoll, N.Y.: Orbis Books, 1986.

———. *The Spirituals and the Blues*. Maryknoll, N.Y.: Orbis Books, 1991.

Cooney, Robert, and Helen Michalowski, eds. *The Power of the People: Active Nonviolence in the United States*. Rev. ed. Philadelphia: New Society, 1986.

Corson-Finnerty, Adam Daniel. *World Citizen: Action for Global Justice*. Maryknoll, N.Y.: Orbis Books, 1982.

Costas, Orlando. *Christ Outside the Gate*. Maryknoll, N.Y.: Orbis Books, 1982.

Deloria, Vine, Jr. *God Is Red*. New York: Grosset & Dunlap, 1973.

Drinan, Robert F. *Cry of the Oppressed: The History & Hope of the Human Rights Revolution*. San Francisco: Harper & Row, 1987.

Elizondo, Virgilio. *Galilean Journey: The Mexican-American Promise*. Maryknoll, N.Y.: Orbis Books, 1984.

———. *"Mestizaje* as a Locus of Theological Reflection," in *The Future of Liberation Theology*, Marc H. Ellis and Otto Maduro, eds. Maryknoll, N.Y.: Orbis Books, 1988.

Ellis, Marc H. *Peter Maurin: Prophet in the Twentieth Century*. New York: Paulist Press, 1981.

———. *Toward a Jewish Theology of Liberation*. Rev. ed. Maryknoll, N.Y.: Orbis Books, 1989.

———. *A Year at the Catholic Worker*. New York: Paulist Press, 1978.

Ellis, Marc H. and Otto Maduro. *The Future of Liberation Theology: Essays in Honor of Gustavo Gutiérrez*. Maryknoll, N.Y.: Orbis Books, 1989.

Ellsberg, Robert, ed. *By Little and By Little: The Selected Writings of Dorothy Day*. New York: Alfred A. Knopf, 1983.

Evans, Robert A. and Alice Frazer Evans. *Human Rights: A Dialogue between the*

First and Third Worlds. Maryknoll, N.Y.: Orbis Books, 1983.

Golden, Renny and Sheila Collins, *Struggle Is a Name for Hope*. Minneapolis: West End Press, 1982.

Golden, Renny, and Michael McConnell. *Sanctuary: The New Underground Railroad*. Maryknoll, N.Y.: Orbis Books, 1986.

Guerrero, Andrés G. *A Chicano Theology*. Maryknoll, N.Y.: Orbis Books, 1987.

Guinan, Ed, ed. *Redemption Denied: An Appalachian Reader*. Washington, D.C.: LADOC, 1976.

Harding, Vincent, and Rosemarie Harding. *Martin Luther King, Jr., and the Company of the Faithful*. Washington, D.C.: Sojourner Book Service.

Harrison, Beverly Wildung. *Making the Connections: Essays in Feminist Social Ethics*. Ed. Carol S. Robb. Boston: Beacon Press, 1986.

Herzog, Frederick. *Justice Church: The New Function of the Church in North American Christianity*. Maryknoll, N.Y.: Orbis Books, 1980.

Holland, Joseph, and Peter Henriot. *Social Analysis: Linking Faith and Justice*. Maryknoll, N.Y.: Orbis Books; Washington, D.C.: Center of Concern, 1983.

Hurley, Neil P. *The Reel Revolution: A Film Primer on Liberation*. Maryknoll, N.Y.: Orbis Books, 1978.

Is Liberation Theology for North America? The Response of First World Churches to Third World Theologies. New York: Theology in the Americas (475 Riverside Dr., New York, N.Y.), 1978.

Isasi-Díaz, Ada María, and Yolanda Tarango. *Hispanic Women: Prophetic Voice in the Church*. San Francisco: Harper & Row, 1988.

Kavanaugh, John Francis. *Following Christ in a Consumer Society: The Spirituality of Cultural Resistance*. Maryknoll, N.Y.: Orbis Books, 1983.

King, Martin Luther, Jr. *Strength To Love*. Philadelphia: Fortress Press, 1963.

———. *Where Do We Go from Here: Chaos or Community?*. Boston: Beacon Press, 1967.

Lernoux, Penny. *Cry of the People: The Struggle for Human Rights in Latin America — The Catholic Church in Conflict with U.S. Policy*. New York: Penguin Books, 1982.

———. *People of God: The Struggle for World Catholicism*. New York: Viking, 1989.

McGovern, Arthur F. *Marxism: An American Christian Perspective*. Maryknoll, N.Y.: Orbis Books, 1980.

Maguire, Daniel C. *A New American Justice: A Moral Proposal for the Reconciliation of Personal Freedom & Social Justice*. San Francisco: Harper & Row, 1982.

Mahan, Brian, and L. Dale Richesin, eds. *The Challenge of Liberation Theology: A First World Response*. Maryknoll, N.Y.: Orbis Books, 1981.

Mische, Gerald and Patricia Mische. *Toward a Human World Order: Beyond the National Straight Jacket*. New York: Paulist Press, 1977.

Myers, Ched. *Binding the Strong Man: A Political Reading of Mark's Story of Jesus*. Maryknoll, N.Y.: Orbis Books, 1988.

Neal, Marie Augusta. *The Just Demands of the Poor: Essays in Socio-Theology*. New York: Paulist Press, 1987.

———. *A Socio-Theology of Letting Go*. New York: Paulist Press, 1977.

Nelson-Pallmeyer, Jack. *The Politics of Compassion: A Biblical Perspective on Hunger, the Arms Race, and U.S. Policy in Central America*. Maryknoll, N.Y.: Orbis Books, 1986.

O'Brien, Mark and Craig Little. *Reimaging America: The Arts of Social Change*. Philadelphia: New Society, 1990.

O'Gorman, Angie. *The Universe Bends Towards Justice: A Reader on Christian Non-violence in the U.S.* Philadelphia: New Society, 1990.

Ruether, Rosemary Radford. *Sexism and God-Talk: Toward a Feminist Theology.* Boston: Beacon Press, 1983.

Russell, Letty M. *Human Liberation in a Feminist Perspective — A Theology.* Philadelphia: Westminster Press, 1974.

Russell, Letty M., ed. *The Liberating Word: A Guide to Non-Sexist Interpretation of the Bible.* Philadelphia: Westminster Press, 1976.

Schüssler Fiorenza, Elisabeth. *Bread Not Stone: The Challenge of Feminist Biblical Interpretation.* Boston: Beacon Press, 1984.

———. *Claiming the Center: A Feminist Critical Theology of Liberation.* San Francisco: Winston Press, 1985.

———. *In Memory of Her: A Feminist Theological Reconstruction of Christian Origins.* New York: Crossroad, 1983.

Scott, Waldron. *Bring Forth Justice.* Grand Rapids, Mich.: William B. Eerdmans, 1980.

Shaull, Richard. *Heralds of a New Reformation: The Poor of North and South America.* Maryknoll, N.Y.: Orbis Books, 1984.

Sölle, Dorothee. *Of War and Love.* Maryknoll, N.Y.: Orbis Books, 1983.

Stevens-Arroyo, Antonio M. *Prophets Denied Honor: An Anthology on the Hispanic Church in the United States.* Maryknoll, N.Y.: Orbis Books, 1980.

Tabb, William, ed. *Churches in Struggle: Liberation Theology and Social Change in North America.* New York: Monthly Review, 1985.

Toton, Suzanne C. *World Hunger: The Responsibility of Christian Education.* Maryknoll, N.Y.: Orbis Books, 1982.

Wachtel, Paul L. *The Poverty of Affluence: A Psychological Portrait of the American Way of Life.* Philadelphia: New Society, 1983.

West, Cornel. *Prophesy Deliverance!: An Afro-American Revolutionary Christianity.* Philadelphia: Westminster Press, 1982.

West, Cornel, Caridad Guidote, and Margaret Coakley, eds. *Theology in the Americas: Detroit II Conference Papers.* Maryknoll, N.Y.: Orbis Books/Probe Edition, 1982.

Williams, Juan. *Eyes on the Prize: The Civil Rights Movement in America, 1954–1965.* New York: Viking, 1987.

Wilmore, Gayraud S. *Black Religion and Black Radicalism: An Interpretation of the History of Afro-American People.* Maryknoll, N.Y.: Orbis Books, 1983. Originally published by Anchor Press/Doubleday, 1973.

Wilmore, Gayraud S. and James H. Cone, eds. *Black Theology: A Documentary History, 1966–1979.* Maryknoll, N.Y.: Orbis Books, 1979.

Wilson-Kastner, Patricia. *Faith, Feminism, and the Christ.* Philadelphia: Fortress Press, 1983.

Yoder, John Howard. *The Politics of Jesus.* Grand Rapids, Mich.: William B. Eerdmans, 1973.

———. *The Priestly Kingdom: Social Ethics as Gospel.* Notre Dame, Ind.: University of Notre Dame Press, 1984.

———. *When War Is Unjust: Being Honest Is Just War Thinking.* Minneapolis: Augsburg Press, 1984.

Young, James, and Marjorie Hope Young. *The Struggle for Humanity: Agents of Nonviolent Change in a Violent World.* Maryknoll, N.Y.: Orbis Books, 1977.

Annotated References

Brown, Robert McAfee. *Gustavo Gutiérrez: An Introduction to Liberation Theology.* Maryknoll, N.Y.: Orbis Books, 1990. An overview of liberation theology, explaining its basic issues.

Cone, James H. *A Black Theology of Liberation: Twentieth Anniversary Edition.* Maryknoll, N.Y.: Orbis Books, 1990. A radical reappraisal of Christianity from the pained perspective of an oppressed black North American community, with critical responses by prominent theologians.

Elizondo, Virgil. *The Future Is Mestizo.* Bloomington, IN: Meyer Stone Books, 1988. The richness of Hispanic experience as a source for theological reflection and as a challenge to North Americans.

Fabella, Virginia and Oduyoye, Mercy Amba. *With Passion and Compassion: Third World Women Doing Theology.* Maryknoll, N.Y.: Orbis Books, 1988. The common struggle of Third World women—Protestant and Catholic, from Asia, Africa, and Latin America— to forge their own liberative theology.

Fanelli, Vincent. *The Human Face of Poverty: A Chronicle of Urban America.* New York: The Bookstrap Press, 1990. Presents the human costs of poverty as painstakingly documented by Fourth World Movement volunteers.

Felder, Cain Hope. *Troubling Biblical Waters: Race, Class, and Family.* Maryknoll, N.Y.: Orbis Books, 1989. A comprehensive and challenging look at the significance of the Bible for blacks, and the importance of blacks in the Bible.

Forcey, Linda Rennie, ed. *Peace: Meanings, Politics, Strategies.* New York: Praeger, 1989. An interdisciplinary text exploring the meanings of peace, both personal and systemic; suggests political approaches for change and poses philosophical, ideological, and pedagogical questions.

Harding, Vincent. *Hope and History: Why We Must Share the Story of the Movement.* Maryknoll, N.Y.: Orbis Books, 1990. The story of the black-led freedom movement shows us what that history teaches us today and how we can pass the lessons to a new generation.

Greene, Maxine. *The Dialectic of Freedom.* New York: The Teacher's College Press, 1988. A foundational text for transformative teaching and the achieving of freedom; urges the necessity for finding a praxis of educational consequence for the making of community.

Hultkrantz, Ake. *Native American Religions of North America.* San Francisco: Harper & Row, 1989. The world view of Native American religions, including the cosmic harmony, the powers and visions, the cycles of life and death.

Isasi-Díaz, Ada María and Tarango, Yolanda. *Hispanic Women: Prophetic Voice in the Church.* San Francisco: Harper & Row, 1989. A vehicle for Hispanic women to articulate their experience and the personal and communal theology that comes out of it.

Kismaric, Carole. *Forced Out: The Agony of the Refugee in Our Time*. New York: Random House, 1989. An essay in text and photographs of the plight of refugees in the world.

Laqueur Walter & Barry Rubin, eds. *The Human Rights Reader* (revised edition). New York: New American Library, 1989. A comprehensive sourcebook of historical human rights documents including those of more recent activist movements.

McGovern, Arthur. *Liberation Theology and Its Critics: Toward an Assessment*. Maryknoll, N.Y.: Orbis Books, 1989. A comprehensive analysis of the full range of criticism — theological, methodological, political, and ecclesial — made against liberation theology.

O'Halloran, James. *Signs of Hope: Developing Small Christian Communities*. Maryknoll, N.Y.: Orbis Books, 1991. The theory, theology, and practices of small Christian communities.

Plaskow, Judith and Christ, Carol P. *Weaving the Visions: New Patterns in Feminist Spirituality*. San Francisco: Harper & Row, 1989. A compendium of key writings in feminist spirituality.

Raphael, Pierre. *Inside Rikers Island: A Chaplain's Search for God*. Maryknoll, N.Y.: Orbis Books, 1990. The story of Fr. Raphael's effort to build a Christian community in the midst of Rikers Island.

Sandoval, Moises. *On the Move: A History of the Hispanic Church in North America*. Maryknoll, N.Y.: Orbis Books, 1990. Beginning with the arrival of the Spanish conquistadors and missionaries almost 500 years ago to the appointment of the first Hispanic bishop in 1970 and the continuing struggle for recognition today.

Thistlethwaite, Susan. *Sex, Race, and God: Christian Feminism in Black and White*. New York: Crossroad/Continuum, 1989. A feminist's exploration of the difference race makes in experiencing God.

Walsh, John J. *Integral Justice: Changing People Changing Structures*. Maryknoll, N.Y.: Orbis Books, 1990. How pastoral ministers can motivate people to commitment and action for social justice.

List of Contributors

Marya Barr is a member of Ground Zero's core community working in the Trident campaign, and a member of the Los Angeles-based Immaculate Heart Community.

Gregory Boyle, S.J. is pastor of Dolores Mission in Boyle Heights, Los Angeles.

César Chávez is president of the United Farm Workers of America.

James H. Cone is Charles A. Briggs Distinguished Professor of Systematic Theology at Union Theological Seminary, New York City.

Orlando E. Costas, who died in November 1987, was academic dean and Judson Professor of Missiology at the Andover Newton Theological School.

Vine Deloria, Jr., a practicing attorney, is also a professor at the Center for the Study of Race and Ethnicity at the University of Colorado at Boulder.

John Eagleson is an editor at Crossroad.

Marc H. Ellis is a professor of religion, culture, and society at the Maryknoll School of Theology.

Edward J. Farrell is pastor of St. Agnes parish in Detroit.

Linda Rennie Forcey, an associate professor of interdisciplinary studies and coordinator of the peace studies concentration at the State University of New York at Binghamton, is the author of *Mothers of Sons* and *Peace: Meanings, Politics, Strategies*.

Renny Golden is an activist poet and educator, and co-author of *The Sanctuary Movement: The New Underground Railroad*.

Jospeh G. Healey, M.M. is with the Maryknoll Language School in Tanzania, and author of *A Fifth Gospel: The Experience of Black Christian Values*.

Robert Hirschfield writes on issues of homelessness, death and dying, and the hospice movement.

Robert Frederick Hunter, Jr., is an InterVarsity chaplain presently serving at the University of Dayton and Wayne State University, and a visiting lecturer in religion at Earlham College. He writes and lectures on social justice issues.

Ada María Isasi-Díaz is the author of *Hispanic Women: Prophetic Voices in the Church*.

Arthur Jones is an editor-at-large for the *National Catholic Reporter*.

Vicki Kemper belongs to The Sojourner Community in Washington, D.C., and writes for *Soujourners* magazine.

Michael Kennedy, S.J. is pastor of Our Lady Queen of Angels Church in downtown Los Angeles.

Kosuke Koyama is a professor of ecumenics and world Christianity at Union Theological Seminary in New York City.

Art Laffin is a member of the Isaiah Peace Ministry in New Haven, Connecticut, and co-editor of *Swords Into Plowshares*.

Michael McConnell is co-editor of *The Sanctuary Movement: The New Underground Railroad*.

Chuck Matthei is with the Institute for Community Economics, Inc. in Greenfield, Massachusetts.

Luis Olivares, C.M.F. is associate pastor of Our Lady Queen of Angels Church in downtown Los Angeles.

Mar Peter-Raoul teaches praxis-centered courses in humanities, human services, and social justice (including liberation theology) at the State University of New York at Binghamton. She is active in prison ministry and in community building.

Elisabeth Schüssler Fiorenza is Krister Stendahl Professor of New Testament Studies at Harvard Divinity School.

Dorothee Sölle divides her time between New York City, where she is a professor at Union Theological Seminary, and Hamburg, Germany.

Steve Vanderstaay teaches English and Spanish in rural Iowa, and is writing a book based on oral histories of homeless Americans.

Delores S. Williams teaches theology and culture at Drew University. Her writings have appeared in a number of books, including *Weaving the Visions*.

Source Notes and Permissions

Aroniawenrate/Peter Blue Cloud's "A Totem Dance as Seen by Raven" is from *Akwesasne Notes* (Mohawk Nation, via Rooseveltown, NY 13683) 17, no. 15 (Fall 1985).

Marya Barr's "I Was Thirsty: Recalling August 6 and 9, 1945" first appeared in *Ground Zero* (Fall 1986).

Gregory Boyle, S.J., Luis Olivares, C.M.F., and Michael Kennedy, S.J.'s "Refugee Rights: The Cry of the Refugee" first appeared in *Catholic Agitator*, October 6, 1988.

César Chávez's "From the Fields of California" is an excerpt from an address given before the Comstock Club in Sacramento. The address was edited for the *Bakersfield, Californian*, June 24, 1984.

Catholic Bishops of the Appalachian Region, "This Land Is Home to Me," 1975 (edited version). The full text is available from the Catholic Committee of Appalachia, P. O. Box 953, Whitesburg, KY 41858.

Sheila Collins's "On the Death of Archbishop Oscar Romero and the First Anniversary of Three Mile Island" is from Renny Golden and Sheila Collins, *Struggle Is a Name for Hope* (Minneapolis: West End Press, 1982).

Marc H. Ellis's "The Palestine Uprising and the Future of the Jewish People" was first published as the afterword to the revised edition of *Toward a Jewish Theology of Liberation* (Maryknoll, N.Y.: Orbis Books, 1989).

Mari Evans' "I Am a Black Woman" is the title poem excerpted from *I Am a Black Woman* published by Wm. Morrow & Company, 1970. Reprinted by permission of the author.

Renny Golden and Michael McConnell's "Sanctuary in Chicago" is from their *Sanctuary: The New Underground Railroad* (Maryknoll, N.Y.: Orbis Books, 1986).

Gustavo Gutiérrez's poem is from Gustavo Gutiérrez and Richard Shaull, *Liberation and Change* (Atlanta: John Knox Press, 1977).

Joseph G. Healey's "Case Study of a Black Parish in Detroit" is reprinted from *World Parish* 21, no. 187 (Maryknoll, NY, February 1981).

Ines Hernández's "Para Un Viejito Desconocido Que Aun Conozco" is from *The Third Woman: Minority Women Writers of the United States*, ed. Dexter Fisher (Boston: Houghton Mifflin Co., 1980).

Janice Hill's "Letter to a Political Prisoner" is from *Of the Heart and the Bread: An Anthology of Poems for Peacemakers*, ed. Vernon Lee Schmid (New Jersey: Plowshares Press/Brandywine Peace Community, Box 8, Swathmore, PA 1985).

Robert Hirschfield's "The Feeding of a Multitude: Loaves and Fishes at Grand Central" first appeared in *Christianity and Crisis* (537 West 121st Street, New York, NY 10027), October 28, 1985. Used by permission.

Arthur Jones's "Liberation Theology Comes to the South Bronx" first appeared in *National Catholic Reporter*, February 13, 1987.

Vicki Kemper's "Sanctuary Community: 'We Will Continue' " is an edited version of her article "We Will Continue," which first appeared in *Sojourners* (July 1986).

Michael Kennedy, S.J.'s "Refugee Rights: To Walk in the Shoes of Another" first appeared in *Catholic Agitator*, October 6, 1988.

Chuck Matthei's "Empowering the Poor with Housing" from the Institute for Community Economics, Inc. Newsletter, November 24, 1988. Used with permission.

Art Laffin's "Hammers and Blood: Hope and Plowshares-Disarmament Actions" first appeared in *Catholic Agitator*, May 2, 1989.

Ruth Pelham's lines are from her song "Turning of the World" from her cassette tape "Look to the People" by Flying Fish Records.

"Prison Statement from Sing Sing" is an edited version of the statement, which was originally composed in the winter of 1987.

Steve Vanderstaay's "Justice House" first appeared in *Christianity and Crisis* (537 West 121st Street, New York, NY 10027), February 20, 1989. Used with permission.

Margaret Walker's "At the Lincoln Monument in Washington, August 28, 1963" is from her *Prophets for a New Day* (Detroit, MI: Broadsides Press).

Delores S. Williams' "Womanist Theology: Black Women's Voices" first appeared in *Christianity and Crisis* (537 West 121st Street, New York, NY 10027), March 2, 1987, pp. 66–67.

Nellie Wong's "From a Heart of Rice Straw" is from her *Dreams of Harrison Railroad Park* (Berkeley: Kelsey Street Press).

Rosa Marta Zárate Macías's "Cantico de Mujer" is used with permission.

DATE DUE